MISSION
UNACCOMPLISHED

MISSION UNACCOMPLISHED

AMERICAN WAR FILMS IN THE TWENTY-FIRST CENTURY

ALAN NADEL

University of Texas Press   Austin

Requests for permission to reproduce material from this work should be sent to
permissions@utpress.utexas.edu.

♾ The paper used in this book meets the minimum requirements of ANSI/NISO
Z39.48–1992 (R1997) (Permanence of Paper).

Library of Congress Cataloging-in-Publication Data

Names: Nadel, Alan, 1947– author.
Title: Mission unaccomplished : American war films in the twenty-first century / Alan
    Nadel.
Description: First edition. | Austin : University of Texas Press, 2025. | Includes
    bibliographical references and index.
Identifiers: LCCN 2024054306 (print) | LCCN 2024054307 (ebook)
    ISBN 978-1-4773-3261-0 (hardcover)
    ISBN 978-1-4773-3262-7 (pdf)
    ISBN 978-1-4773-3263-4 (epub)
Subjects: LCSH: War films—United States—History and criticism. | Motion
    pictures—United States—History—21st century.
Classification: LCC PN1995.9.W3 N33 2025 (print) | LCC PN1995.9.W3 (ebook) |
    DDC 791.43/658—dc23/eng/20250214
LC record available at https://lccn.loc.gov/2024054306
LC ebook record available at https://lccn.loc.gov/2024054307

doi:10.7560/332610

The University of Texas Press gratefully acknowledges the William and Bettye Nowlin Endowment in Art, History, and Culture of the Western Hemisphere for its support of this publication.

To my grandson, Oscar Adrian Nadel

*May you accomplish all the missions you have
yet to discover and to invent!*

CONTENTS

ILLUSTRATIONS

PREFACE

Wikipedia is an interesting resource. Neither definitive nor discredited, inaccurate nor reliably stable, it presents not facts, exactly, but facts-subject-to-amendment. If it is an imperfect medium, therefore, for describing the Iraq War, it may nevertheless be the war's structural twin, compiling information neither egregiously incorrect nor reassuringly coherent. On the unmade bed of its cumulative assembly, reality's slippage reclines. "The Iraq War," the Wikipedia entry begins,

> . . . was a protracted armed conflict in Iraq from 2003 to 2011. It began with the invasion of Iraq by the United States-led coalition that overthrew the Ba'athist government of Saddam Hussein. The conflict continued for much of the next decade as an insurgency emerged to oppose the coalition forces and the post-invasion Iraqi government. US troops were officially withdrawn in 2011.
>
> The United States became reinvolved in 2014 at the head of a new coalition. The insurgency and many dimensions of the armed conflict are ongoing. The invasion occurred as part of the George W. Bush administration's war on terror following the September 11 attacks in 2001 in the United States.

Without a solid definition of "war," the Wikipedia entry lists the war's multifarious facts, events, and strategies, comprising a war in which the warring parties shift, multiply, and fragment; in which outcome is discrete from victory, withdrawal discrete from termination, termination the precursor to escalation. Although the war could not have occurred without the US invasion, it had no trouble continuing after the United States withdrew most of its combat troops or failing to abate after they returned.

Although Wikipedia vaguely implies the war had a narrative arc and seems to delineate clear partisan sides, a sidebar lists ten separate belligerent groups that, between 2003 and 2011, were in opposition to the US force and its allies. The list of US allies, however, includes "Iraq," the nation that the United States had invaded to start the war. Even more curious than listing Iraq as a US ally is the compilation of forces that Wikipedia lists as the opposition. A cursory acquaintance with those groups reveals that the list does not constitute a side in the war but instead a brutal spectrum of rival factions, responsible for thousands of one another's deaths. At the same time, calling the conflict, even in part, a civil war oversimplifies the confluence of assaults—on battlefields, in cities and villages, and along the countryside—coming from all directions, and going in all directions. "Statistical estimates" of Iraqi "deaths from violence" (also listed in a Wikipedia sidebar) have discrete entries ranging from 151,000 to 1,033,000, making the margin of error in this list larger than all but one of its individual entries. The dimensions of the conflicts in Iraq in this century could consume more space than this entire book and still fail to forge a definition of "war" satisfactorily incorporating under that rubric all relevant elements, including, for example, "enemy combatants," "extreme rendition," "Blackwater contractors," or "Abu Ghraib."

Despite the pervasive mayhem pursuant to the US invasion, Senator John McCain, while running for president in 2008, vowed to keep American troops in Iraq for one hundred years if necessary. But necessary for *what*? While virtually no American leader would say the war was a total waste of lives and tax dollars, none have credibly indicated what the costly American and Iraqi flesh had purchased. After the missions that instigated the war were exposed as erroneous, justifications for the sacrifices on which the war fed from 2004 to 2011, from 2014 to 2017, and in between, alternated between flimsier and fuzzier.

That deadly vagueness troubled me, as it did many Americans who became befuddled and perturbed by the absence of a narrative giving credible purpose to the war. Since film too requires informing narratives, I was struck by how many films about the war seemed devoid of a coherent narrative structure. As the number of these films reached a critical mass, I began to realize how much their absence of a governing mission mirrored the war's. In addition to reflecting the Iraq War's peculiar composition, the films also seemed to interpret the war in productive ways, ways that merited the explication and historicizing to which this book is devoted.

I am grateful to Stacy Takacs, who encouraged me at the early stages of this project, and to my graduate and undergraduate students who helped me engage with the book's core themes in a number of classes. My research assistants during the period of my writing, Emily Naser-Hall, Daria Goncharova, and Mike Derevianko, were invaluable in freeing up my time and helping me organize my life so as to make my writing and research productive. Throughout, Jim Burr has been a helpful, supportive, and enthusiastic editor. My colleague at the University of Kentucky, Jordan Brower, provided excellent, detailed feedback on the early chapters, and Donald Pease, as always, raised provocative questions that made clear where my argument needed to be clarified or strengthened; I am grateful for his insight and guidance here, and throughout my career. I am also extremely grateful to Tim Melley, whose comments, in part adapted in the first chapter, articulated with insight and focus some of my central points. Jordan, Don, and Tim were meaningful assets in the making of this book; I was fortunate to have had their generous assistance. Finally, my wife, Sharon Kopyc, as always, with love and understanding, helped me navigate the psychological demands of a profession under siege, along with the agonizing glitches of a computer desktop often in as much disarray as the physical desktop on which it resides, and as the world, quotidian and global, in which we all reside.

Portions of the introduction and chapter 4 were delivered as papers at the Society for Cinema and Media Studies conference in Seattle and at the 2021 Virtual Conference.

A portion of chapter 2 was delivered as a paper at the 2022 International Society for the Study of Narrative Conference in Chichester, United Kingdom.

A shorter version of the discussion of *Lost* in chapter 4 was a plenary presentation at the annual Futures of American Studies Institute at Dartmouth College and subsequently published: Duvall, John N., and Robert P. Marzec, eds. *Narrating 9/11: Fantasies of State, Security, and Terrorism.* "Lost in Iraq" pp. 118-141. © 2015 Johns Hopkins University Press. Reprinted with permission of Johns Hopkins University Press.

MISSION UNACCOMPLISHED

A BANNER DAY FOR A WAR THAT OUGHTA' BE IN PICTURES

On May 1, 2003, referring to the Iraq War, President George W. Bush declared, "Mission Accomplished." But the mission had *not* been accomplished. How could it have been, given that it was never fully formulated, its tasks never completely defined, its long-term goals never concretely established? Bush's triumphant declaration, therefore, reflected no crucial turn in events but rather a mind-set established before the invasion of Iraq, which not only precluded formulating a complete mission but also promoted deep psychological denial of the truth that an unformulated mission is no mission at all. Thus, most significantly, the "Mission Accomplished" banner flying from the bridge of the aircraft carrier USS *Abraham Lincoln* changed nothing because, given how the war was conceived, its situation could not be changed, as best illustrated by several of the Bush-Cheney-Rumsfeld[1] administration's failed attempts to manufacture a mission ex post facto.

The events surrounding 9/11 and the invasion that followed, however, created conditions that invalidated the trajectory of the traditional war narrative, the kind of narrative most effectively epitomized a few years earlier by the film *Saving Private Ryan* (1998). Instead, the neocon Bush-Cheney-Rumsfeld administration projected the invasion as liberation rather than conquest. Hence, the administration reasoned, the war required no more than free-market economics to establish a democratic, independent Iraq. Since, prior to the invasion, Secretary of Defense Donald Rumsfeld said he would fire anyone on his staff who mentioned an Occupation plan, the war's mission could be accomplished without a surrender. I capitalize "Occupation," as I will throughout the book, when using that word to designate the official stage concluding wartime, distinguishing it from (in lower case) a job, profession, or career. Asserting victory independent of surrender, however, conflated the stages of warfare and Occupation, so that, after the president's declaration of victory, the war became an occupation that lacked a temporal limit or a mission that could accomplish one.

This conceptual reformulation, which ascribes to war a timeless dimension, impels important questions about the occupation of the American soldier in the twenty-first century, when national policy substitutes liberation for conquest, and libertarian economics for pragmatic governance. These substitutions raise important questions about how American warfare and the nation's ability to contain wartime have changed with the construction of the all-volunteer army, composed largely of people fighting for mercenary reasons, and the privatization of military tasks, creating a cadre of mercenary personnel working for military reasons. The resulting conversion to warfare as a job has profound effects not only on the "employees" who work at perpetuating it but also on the sense of nation and community traditionally accustomed to believing that peacetime differs radically from wartime.

A working premise of this book, therefore, is that these issues are grounded in cultural narratives that a nation iterates about its historical identity, a concept that I explain more fully in chapter 1. Working from that premise, careful analysis of motion pictures can help make the culture's most instrumental narratives legible. Because *Saving Private Ryan* is based on cultural narratives reflecting the dominant paradigm for the American understanding of war in the second half of the twentieth century, chapter 2 examines it at length to consolidate the tenets of the war films in the pre–Mission Accomplished era. A careful reading of the film helps make clear, by contrast, the unique qualities of the post–Mission Accomplished war films, which implicitly deny the distinction between wartime and peacetime, a distinction in *Saving Private Ryan* underscoring the narrative that aberrant wartime disrupts normative peace. War's traditional mission had been to restore peace, to return to normal. Although the nation always had professional soldiers, for most Americans the military was not an occupation but a form of national service. After that service had been performed, those temporarily serving—at the end of World War II, sixteen million men—could resume normal life. For that reason, in *Saving Private Ryan*, the euphemism for successful service is "earning the right to go home."

Thus, prior to "Mission Accomplished," combat films do not take place after surrender is obtained and victory declared. There are no pre-2003 films in which the soldiers do not know why they are supposed to be fighting, and none in which they do not know what they were supposed to accomplish to achieve peace. In Korea, for example, they fought to restore the security of the 38th parallel and the Demilitarized Zone separating North and South Korea. In Vietnam, the goal was to stop North Vietnamese aggression into South Vietnam. As chapter 2 explains, these goals were clearly articulated and consistent with a generally bipartisan American foreign policy, even when the strategies in Korea, and, additionally in Vietnam, the merit of the war's objectives, were vigorously questioned.

It is not surprising, therefore, given the cultural conditions of the Cold War, that the plot structures of war films set in Korea and Vietnam generally conformed to those of World War II films. Even if many Vietnam war films openly critiqued the values of the political leaders who had conceived the war and the judgment of the military leaders who planned its missions, all the films recognized a relationship between achieving the mission and returning to peacetime. Consider that even though *Apocalypse Now* (1979) portrays Vietnam as a hellscape designed by Hieronymus Bosch and navigated by Dante, its narrative is governed by Willard's (played by Martin Sheen) determination to fulfill his mission. No matter how secret, psychotic, or psychosis-inducing the mission is, no matter how much the audience is encouraged to realize how irrelevant it was to achieving America's objectives in Southeast Asia, the mission nevertheless provided the plot's unremitting rationale. *Platoon* (1986), too, is organized around a series of jungle missions, and even though the platoon is replete with violent enmity, all the men know that they are fighting the North Vietnamese Army and Viet Cong, and that if that army is defeated the war will end, and they will go home. *The Deer Hunter* (1978) is a more confusing representation of the Vietnam War, in that almost half of the film takes place in Pennsylvania, and many of the scenes in Vietnam present fantasies about the war—e.g., compelled and later competitive Russian Roulette, presented as a sporting event—so far-fetched as to almost morph the film from the combat war genre into dystopian science fiction. Even so, the North Vietnamese and Viet Cong are clearly presented as the enemy and as unambiguously evil. The central characters enlist to defeat them, not simply to toil at a military job in Vietnam, for no reason. They are there, like the soldiers in *Platoon* or *Apocalypse Now* (or *Full Metal Jacket* [1987]), to fight an identified enemy, with a clear objective in mind.[2] The soldiers in post–Mission Accomplished films have no such raison d'etre. In numerous post–Mission Accomplished films, wartime and peacetime provide concurrent, alternative occupations, neither of which delimits the other. As Robert Burgoyne astutely notes about twenty-first-century war films, "there is no teleological resolution" (xxii).

The political and historical conditions that created the irresolvable dilemma of the Iraq War are, as chapter 3 shows, uncannily well glossed by the television series *Lost* (2004–2010), a series that manifests the same confused and conflicting cultural narratives that made the US execution of the Iraq War and its concurrent Occupation/occupation a "fiasco," the label given to it by the title of

Thomas Ricks's acclaimed book on the gaps, gaffes, and factional disarray that characterized the US incursion.

The films I discuss, therefore, represent the post–Mission Accomplished troops as engaged in an occupation rather than overseeing the entrance into peacetime that a formal Occupation initiates. For that reason, accomplishing a war's mission without obtaining a surrender necessarily alters the war film genre by reconfiguring the traditional war narrative in reportage, in cultural artifacts, and in the public imaginary. What most concerns me is that an Occupation's efficacy depends on an unconditional surrender. In the absence of that surrender, soldiers often struggle to distinguish between "us" and "them." As the Iraq War and the films about it illustrate, it is hard for the soldiers to understand whom they are supposed to be protecting from other Iraqis, and against whom they are supposed to be protecting themselves. Beyond what these narratives reflect about the public imaginary (or imaginaries) and how they impact the acceptance of new narratives, I am interested in how they contribute to redefinitions of the (formerly) interdependent concepts of "peacetime" and "wartime."

The salient traits of this war film genre, therefore, include the professionalizing of soldiers and the representing of the war as a series of quotidian tasks. The films' episodes present discrete examples of a day's work rather than the chronicle of people on a mission, so that the soldier's job is not determined by a target or military objective but by contractual time spans, such as workdays or tours of duty. The war itself, as an arbitrary and endless activity, becomes a normalized alternative to the life of peaceful domesticity rather than a temporary aberration from it, necessary to restore that domestic life.

This crumbling distinction, as chapter 4 explains, informs in complementary ways both *Jarhead* (2005) and *The Hurt Locker* (2008). In the two films, soldiers toil at grueling, often hazardous, jobs, without a clear objective or any sense of how their labor contributes to fostering one. In *Jarhead*, they work in anticipation of a war that is relentlessly threatening to arrive, but never does, combined with periodic reminders that their workday nevertheless can be lethal. In *The Hurt Locker*, conversely, the men have an occupation that threatens their lives on a daily basis, without any understanding of how it affects the warfare that envelopes them.

This pervasive confusion about US objectives operated at macro and micro levels, a problem investigated in chapter 5 through close attention to *Green Zone* (2010), a film about the fruitless search for weapons of mass destruction (WMDs) in 2003, which exposes the competing forces in the US government and the Department of Defense, mirroring the sectarian divisions within dismembered Iraq. These films reflect the way that US actions in Iraq were as indifferent to the best interests of America as the Iraqi actions were to the welfare of Iraqis. Acute awareness of their own pointlessness is as apparent to a small GI unit overseeing a checkpoint in Samarra as to those coordinating things in the Green Zone. Some of the GIs in that unit, the focus of *Redacted* (2007), understand that the United States has violated and murdered Iraqis for no reason, and consequently they conclude that violation and murder are, in effect, job perks, the spoils of war. As a result, they rape and murder a fifteen-year-old Iraqi girl, then kill her family. Taken together, these films foreground how a war without a mission seriously impairs the ability to distinguish between ally and adversary, even though that distinction is war's precondition. This situation is well glossed by the film *Us* (2019), which is not about the Iraq War but rather about the long-standing American cultural narrative of "us" and "them" that both enabled and discredits the US invasion.

The "lingering mood . . . of fraught emotional suspension" (xxii) that Burgoyne finds in many films about the war leads, by the second decade of the twenty-first century, to films that explicitly question service in Iraq, given that without a mission the rewards of the war are difficult to imagine and, in any case, greatly exceeded by the risk. Chapter 6, therefore, looks closely at *Eye in the Sky* (2015), *American Sniper*, and *Billy Lynn's Long Halftime Walk*, films that in various ways directly explore the ostensible purposes for military occupation in the War on Terror.

Yet another genre of American war film, explained in chapter 7, emerged at the end of the Obama presidency. Based on a cultural narrative that represented war as neither fulfilling a mission nor providing a viable occupation, these films concentrate on a scene of danger so acute that the only practical option is getting out. The 2017 film *Get Out*, although not about the Iraq War, underscores the need to escape the life-threatening implications of the film genres Hollywood has promoted and white America has tacitly accepted. In this way, it too announces the urgency of getting out of a life-threatening generic complacency. *Dunkirk* (2017) and *Hacksaw Ridge* (2016), in the same spirit, emphasize the imperative to evacuate the scene of combat.

If the reason for military service is debated implicitly in *American Sniper* (2014) and extensively in *Billy Lynn's Long Halftime Walk* (2016), *13 Hours* (2016), set in Libya, confronts the theme most directly. The film, which chronicles the assault by Libyan insurgents on the American diplomatic outpost and the CIA compound in Benghazi that resulted in four American deaths, abandonment of both sites, and Libya's designation as a failed state, concludes with the five surviving contractors all deciding to change their occupations. More recent war films such as *Dunkirk* and *Hacksaw Ridge* replace advancing a mission with saving lives by enabling soldiers to escape, in *Hacksaw Ridge* because they are seriously wounded, and in *Dunkirk* because, overwhelmed and defeated, they must flee the advancing Nazi troops.

The fact that this "get out alive" genre—most commonly reserved for disaster movies—articulates its historical moment of production is reinforced by several contemporaneous get-out-alive films not explicitly about war, including *Captain Phillips* (2013), *Deepwater Horizon* (2016), and *Sully* (2016). Using imagery uncannily similar to that of the get-out-alive war films, these films also feature men who find the dangerous potential of their occupations suddenly realized, with simple and immediate escape the only solution.

SINS OF COMMISSION AND NO MISSION

At the most pragmatic level, post–Mission Accomplished Iraq quickly turned into a site of anarchic violence in a civilian charnel house. To make matters worse, Rumsfeld diverted large portions of the Pentagon budget from bolstering the US military to hiring private contractors—suppliers and mercenaries—paid five to ten times as much as their enlisted counterparts while exempted from military discipline and permitted to shirk such basic obligations as supplying food and water to the troops. At the same time, Bush-Cheney-Rumsfeld touted the business opportunities that oil-rich Iraq offered, but only, they made clear, for those nations that had supported the invasion. Instead of undergoing an Occupation, Iraq would provide lucrative occupations for opportunistic entrepreneurs who would flourish in the new Iraqi economy, absent of the marketplace inhibitors found in Saddam Hussein's authoritarian state or stifled in a US economy overly regulated by American liberals. From this perspective, showing that Occupation was unnecessary would, moreover, demonstrate how well the marketplace solves all problems.

Under these circumstances, what does it mean to fight a war that has no mission? First of all, it makes it hard, if not impossible, to justify taking lives or jeopardizing the lives of soldiers tasked with doing so. And that absence of justification confounds narrative coherence, as reflected by Bush-Cheney-Rumsfeld's floundering strategies and rationales. Not surprisingly, films attempting to narrativize portions or aspects of the war expressed the same frustration in ways that distinguished the genre from twentieth-century war films underscoring the exceptionality of war. Many war films since 2003, instead, have represented war as an ill-conceived and ineptly run occupation in another country, and, for the soldier, a very unexceptional extension of ordinary labor in newly militaristic forms.

In contrast with post–Mission Accomplished films, the traditional combat films of the World War II and post–World War II era regarded wars as special events of limited duration, requiring noble sacrifice to return the nation and the world to peace. This cultural narrative underscored an American exceptionalism grounded in the assumption that Americans considered war abnormal. Refusing to be corrupted by conflict, they did not fight to prosecute war but to end it, sustained by the belief that doing so would let them resume their peaceful lives in the United States. Even the Vietnam War retained its clear, albeit not clearly attainable, mission despite a steadily increasing portion of the population that found its justification dubious. Although this situation accounts for the relative paucity of Vietnam combat films, it did not significantly alter their narrative structure in the way that fighting a war without a mission has.

After 2003, years of fighting a war that was officially over but nonetheless unending could not generate cultural narratives structured on the premise that fulfilling a mission would achieve a justified end. Having been victorious and simultaneously deprived of any path to victory, the soldiers in Iraq operated in a strange purgatory of occupational tasks, terrorizing and terrorized, in an indefinite War on Terror. It is somewhat clear that the cultural narratives this condition generated could not easily be represented by the narrative structure of a film such as *Saving Private Ryan,* which relied upon and extolled cohesion.

Much contributed to that cohesion beyond the patriotic energy galvanized by what FDR called "a day of infamy." But the unity that the initial shock of Japan's sneak attack on Pearl Harbor inspired was consolidated through the efforts of governmental and private agencies. In addition to the commercially mandated genre conventions, these included rigid oversight by studio executives and even more rigid censorship. The Motion Picture Production Code, adopted in 1930 and enforced from 1934 to 1967, standardized representation across genres, with strict controls over the treatment of religion, crime, bona fide authority figures, and all forms of "immoral" behavior.[3] While the Production Code did not have a specific category for war films (as it did, for example, for crime films), the general prohibition against graphic gore and vulgar language and gestures made war films, and especially scenes of the dying and the wounded, very subdued relative to their subject matter. The most common way, for example, to indicate a soldier had incurred a fatal wound was to show a small trickle of blood at the corner of the dying soldier's mouth.

On top of that, during World War II, more than fifteen hundred film scripts were reviewed by the Office of War Information (OWI), established in June 1942, to guarantee the proposed films would support the war effort. Thus, even within the formal structure of American motion pictures, with all their possible ideological implications, and the explicitly ideological agenda of the Production Code, the war film was narrowly and rigidly crafted, especially during World War II. The consequent homogeneity of war films, and of the general body of domestic dramas and comedies, underwrote uniform cultural narratives reinforced with great ubiquity.

Many factors contributed to the contrast between this uniformity and the diffuse focus of twenty-first century war films, including the absence of the Office of War Information, the demise of the Production Code Administration, and the slow deterioration of a narrative asserting that "In the end, we're all Americans." Since a history of the civil rights movement alone would belie that narrative, the question is not whether it ever accurately reflected the conditions in the country or on the battlefield. Rather than worrying about the veracity of the dominant cultural narratives, therefore, I want to focus on the work that they did to suppress the many other histories incompatible with a kind of soft patriotism. In the growing fragmentation of American culture, exacerbated by the multiplication of new media outlets, instead of unifying national narratives (or national myths), we more commonly find competing cultural narratives unifying subcultures in tribal antipathy to one another.[4]

Just as wars require narratives, so do war films. If this is obvious, less so is how to gauge the correlation between these interdependent narrative phenomena. The story of the war—the stuff of historiography—serves as the referent for the stories about it. At the same time, as Hayden White has shown, the cultural narratives surrounding historical events structure historical construction.[5] Historical narratives, in other words, are constative, in that they identify the characteristics of a specific war and describe the events that exemplify those characteristics. But they are also performative, in that historiography supplies a culture with its accepted truths, the body of cogent narratives that are crucial to its mediation of reality.

The specific example of that phenomenon that this book examines is its relationship to war films made about American soldiers engaged in a seemingly unending war, after that war's mission had been officially "accomplished." The reason this topic seems important is that popular films narrativize culture; that is, they supply stories with narrative forms that make those stories legible for an intended audience. In Hollywoodese, this practice is expressed in clichés such as: "We have to tell the story in ways that people can relate to it." In other words, we have to create a matrix between the story we want to tell and the narrative forms that strike audiences as "natural." At the same time, the iteration, broad circulation, and broadcasting of specific narratives—e.g., the Communist threat—encourage people to accept them naturally. As Daniel Binns, looking at films as producing discursive formations, succinctly puts it, "genre thus becomes dynamic and iterative" (10).

CHAPTER I

NARRATIVE, CULTURE, AND CINEMA

Before I directly engage the post–Mission Accomplished films, it will be helpful to explain the approach to culture and cultural criticism in which my analyses are grounded. Key is the term "cultural narrative," which is based on the presumption that the stories a society tells itself about itself are crucial to distinguishing between *self* and *other*. Idioms such as "that's not something *I* would do," "*they* don't understand *me*," or "*they* make *me* feel like I don't belong" caption identity narratives endemic to interpersonal relations. Comparable narratives provide the connective tissue for family cohesion, ethnicity, "identity politics," or patriotism, to name a few cultural formations.

When these formations reach a critical mass, we call them cultures or subcultures. In professional athletics, for example, analysts often refer to a "team culture," that is, the narratives shared by team members and leadership that create a common attitude and identity. The same process creates the culture of a team's fan base. (An old joke about Philadelphia fans, whose culture combines ultra-enthusiasm with commensurate anger and dissatisfaction, is that when there are no professional games in town, the Philly fans go down to the airport and boo landings.) Many political organizations or leaders create similar subcultures, sometimes called cults, sometimes called movements. Regardless of the size or configuration of these cultural units—as small as a family or book club, as large as a nation or an organized religion—I hold as axiomatic that their mediating mechanism is narrative formulation.

To be clear, let me stipulate that I am using "narrative" to designate the operating system of the mind that employs temporal frameworks to create databases that catalogue, prioritize, and instrumentalize phenomena. As with all databases, this cataloging is requisite for recognition, recall, and retrieval. From this perspective, advanced Alzheimer's disease can be viewed as the breakdown of the mind's narrativizing capacities, which are the prerequisite for classification and retrieval. Conversely, the construction of a culture and its sustaining verities requires frequent iteration of its privileged narratives, in sundry, variegated forms and venues. Put simply, ubiquity gives narratives the aura and, consequently, the authority of nature. In the 1950s, as I explained in *Television in Black-and-White America*, primetime broadcast television sustained the narrative, dating back to the colonial period, that in America, public space is white, and, therefore, Black bodies moving unchecked in public space constitute a public menace. Similarly, after the Bush-Cheney-and-surrogates' barrage of speeches and talking points associating Saddam Hussein with "evil," Al Qaeda, and Hitler, a cultural narrative connecting Iraq both to 9/11 and to Nazi aggression achieved substantial cogency.[1]

CULTURAL NARRATIVES

Because, clearly, culturally shared narratives of this sort must undergird any commitment to war, it would be useful to explain more fully the concept of cultural narratives before examining the Iraq War and several films made during its long tenure.

In his 1957 preface to *Mythologies*, Roland Barthes writes that the starting point for the essays in that collection was "usually a feeling of impatience with the 'naturalness' which common sense, the press, and the arts continually invoke to dress up a reality which, though the one we live in, is nonetheless quite historical: in a word, I resented seeing Nature and History repeatedly confused in the description of reality, and I wanted to expose in the decorative display of that-goes-without-saying the ideological abuse I believe was hidden there" (8). The fifty-four essays that follow in *Mythologies* illustrate that nothing is more artificial than "nature." In the post–World War II era alone, Western culture has engaged in numerous debates about "unnatural" behaviors and practices, as illustrated, for example, by the divergence and revision of sodomy laws and marriage laws.

In 1993, the Texas legislature passed a law banning homosexual and heterosexual sodomy. When two conservative legislators celebrated the successful vote by shaking hands, journalist Molly Ivins wrote that the Speaker had to send the sergeant-at-arms over to reprimand them both because under the new law, "it's illegal for a prick to touch an asshole in the state."[2] Her pithy comment not only concisely identifies an instance of Nature being confused with History but also questions the logic of a "nature" that needs legislative enforcement: so much for the idea that natural law is . . . natural. To the contrary, Nature functions as a free-floating signifier that consolidates narratives into ideological categories with rubrics such as "women are naturally passive, and men are naturally aggressive"; "people naturally gravitate toward authoritarian leaders"; or "war is just part of human nature." At various historical moments, for various cultures, the natural world was considered hostile or heathen, at other times benign or Edenic. These positions employ the authority of Nature, at specific moments, to ascribe referential cogency to some cultural narratives and to invalidate others.

Disguising these historical conditions as natural is accomplished through the mechanism of *second nature*, the mental process of invoking ideas learned so thoroughly their manifestations can bypass conscious thought.[3] Accomplished musicians play instruments as though doing so were second nature; experienced drivers handle automobiles in the same way. When first behind the wheel of a car, moving at the slowest speed demands concentration to minimize errors and achieve erratic competence. After a few years of experience, however, people deftly cruise down a highway, carrying on a conversation while searching for a radio station, and yet they still can usually react swiftly to an unexpected event. None of this mastery comes naturally. Ordinary driving, moreover, entails so many narratives, with so many variables, that even a short, simple trip cannot be rehearsed. Instead, competent drivers, like accomplished musicians or facile typists/keyboardists, handle their tasks as though they were second nature.

Watching motion pictures is another example of this phenomenon. Viewers confronting a relentlessly counterintuitive assemblage of shots—on the average, one every three to seven seconds—taken from different angles and perspectives, photographed in sundry spaces, often integrating discrete actions and time frames, consolidate those shots into a coherent reality, one that seems to follow a set of natural laws as clear as those governing everyday life. This is because American moviegoers have been drilled in the codes of cinematic representation for more hours than they have practiced playing music or preparing for a road test.

In the same way that the codes constructing cinematic reality have, for the average viewer, become second nature, so too have the narrative codes constructing cultural reality. The iteration of historically specific narratives, therefore, accumulates a critical mass, just as the repetition of musical scales does, becoming second nature in the same way, for example, that learning to read does. It is a process where codes (of phonetics, grammar, syntax, usage) are internalized so that they disappear into a production of general legibility. In the same way, the narratives that become commonplace—"that-goes-without-saying," as Barthes puts it—provide a template for a specific group, at a specific time, to incorporate variant narratives. For that group, those narratives, therefore, achieve legibility and thereby provide the mediating process through which that group can incorporate new narratives into its repertoire of reality.

A "cultural narrative," in this context, is a story that delimits the reality shared by any cultural unit, one as particular as a family or as vast as a nation. Hence, for some American subcultures, *evolution* is a "theory," in the sense that the word *theory* designates a scientifically valid explanation, an understanding for which factual data provide explanatory heft. For other subcultures, *evolution* is a "theory," in the sense that the word designates a speculation, an untested hypothesis, in the case of evolution, one born of demonic inspiration.

Every cultural unit, I am arguing, can therefore be defined by the particular configuration of the narratives it aggregates into one of three groups: foundational truth, transactional truth, and patent absurdity. Most twenty-first-century Americans accept as a foundational truth, for example, that people jumping out of tenth-floor windows will fall, not fly; that the Earth is a globe, not a platform; that germs, not evil vapors or magic curses, cause disease. Similarly, most contemporary Americans believe it patently absurd to claim that Martians (or Venezuelan Communists, or Jewish space lasers) control American election outcomes. In the transactional category, most Americans, even when not agreeing on the actual cause of a forest fire, will accept several narratives as plausible (e.g., arson, careless campers, lightning, downed electric power lines) while ruling out the possibility that the fires resulted from the community's failure to make appropriate ritual sacrifices to a Greek (or Pagan or Norse) god or that their region of the nation is being punished by God for tolerating (promoting?) homosexuality.[4] According to Megachurch pastor John Hagee, "God caused Hurricane Katrina to wipe out New Orleans because it had a gay pride parade the week before and was filled with sexual sin"[5] (but he failed to explain why, under those circumstances, the French Quarter was spared).

In this context, it is possible to define a culture or subculture as a diagram of the narratives they assign to these three categories: the certain, the plausible, and the absurd. Because legibility is constantly mediated, however, these categories are fluid, so that the classification of narrative categories not only achieves legibility but also helps determine it. The array of narratives deemed plausible, at any moment, by any group inflects their assimilation of new phenomena. While it is unlikely that I would explain any disagreement I had with a neighbor or colleague on the basis that an evil demon had inhabited his body and possessed his soul, I knew an anthropologist who worked in urban Brazil in the 1980s, where such an explanation, while not a certainty, was considered plausible rather than absurd.

CULTURAL WORK

Understanding a "culture" as defined by the diagram of these three categories of narrative means that "cultural work" is any activity or practice that, for a specific group, reinforces or discredits the cogency of a specific narrative. With this in mind, we could say that Jeanine Basinger insightfully identifies the cultural work of the World War II combat film as supporting a cluster of cultural narratives by providing answers to fundamental questions about American identity:

What makes a good life and what makes a good person? What should we be willing to kill or die for? —and how do you die right? If you had to die young, what would make you a noble sacrifice, and what would make it all a waste? . . . What about when the war was over, and you returned home having killed? Would it change you forever? It was one thing to agree cheerfully to work in a group, and to accept the group over the individual for the war effort, but how did you do this? . . . How could you be a good American, and furthermore was it really a good thing to be? (73–74)

As the last question here implies, the cultural work of answering these questions invokes a form of American exceptionalism. Moving from "good life" and "good person" to "good American," World War II combat films iterate the narrative, Basinger demonstrates, that enables Americans to go to war. In other words, the combat films help create the ideological space that allows American soldiers to abandon what they see as the American way of life, while still remaining "American," that is, good, peace-loving souls. This narrative of good people going to war, however, requires a notion of war as finite. "The idea that wars are bound in time," Mary Dudziak reminds us, "continued to animate American culture in popular accounts of the 'good war'" (40).

All these generically mandated details contribute to the narrative that there are consequences when soldiers do what comes naturally because, it is presumed, war is not second nature for Americans. This narrative promotes the idea that forces of nature collaborate in the interest of "Manifest Destiny," a phrase popularized in the 1840s to encourage the annexation of Texas on the basis that the "Anglo-Saxon race," by virtue of its genetic (and moral?) superiority, was destined to control the continent of North America.[6] In other words, natural forces instrumentalized through the unique American character mandated Anglo-Saxon dominion.

That same American character was destined to emerge victorious in World

War II, such that when some soldiers' nonmilitary acts prove fatal, they do not reveal the soldiers' flaws so much as evidence the superior American character. They show that Americans do not allow themselves to be corrupted by warfare; it is not, this narrative asserts, in an American's nature to abandon core values. At the same time, errors in military judgment also show that those unable to subordinate their peaceful inclinations to the temporary demands of wartime must fall victim to forces of natural selection, which in the long run only makes the American character more fit for survival. Those who prevail in preserving the American way are those who resist remaining preoccupied with peace-time practices in the face of war and who, equally, resist making warfare their occupation.

WARTIME, PEACETIME, AND MOVIE-TIME

If narrative, as I am using the term, is a temporal concept, that is, a mechanism that catalogues phenomena across matrices of time, then it is important for this discussion to acknowledge that wartime and movie-time both depend on the acceptance of exceptional temporalities. While not synonymous, these two unique imaginings of time disrupt the rhythms upon which the patterns of ordinary life rely. Watching a movie requires diverting the acts of imagination from their role in quotidian realities—crossing a street, writing a report, making and keeping a medical appointment—to navigating (temporarily) an imaginary elsewhere, in the same way that people at war, whether in the battlefield or on the home front, must suspend the way they normally imagine their lives in order to accommodate some form of the heretofore unimaginable.

On the home front, these temporary alterations can include reorganizing economic priorities, at the national level affecting specific production goals and the allocation of the materials employed in meeting those goals, and at the individual level impacting the rationing of goods and the commitment of per-sonal service. They can involve taking temporary or unconventional jobs and going without the proximity of companions and loved ones. They also involve psychological economies, such as trying to imagine the extraordinary condi-tions that have become the norm for some of those companions and loved ones. Or they may entail attempting to block out images of that wartime site, the military front or combat zone, where that population of absent loved ones, through a process of extreme conditioning, mobilizes for perilous conditions; where they don new uniforms in the interest of uniformly confronting peril; where they are enveloped in a world of actual or imminent death, death which they must inflict, or avoid, or suffer.

No doubt, different parties in wartime imagine different tasks and dangers, just as moviegoers imagine activities in which they do not partake and dangers that they do not undergo. In any case, movie-going imposes demands of a much shorter duration than wartime, be it the Six-Day War (1967) or the Hundred Years' War (1337–1453). The demands of wartime and movie-time, however, share the common anticipation of returning to normal, so that both temporalities entail narratives of their own termination. Like most experiences, they are bracketed, but within the parameters of wartime and movie-time, the unimaginable is endured by virtue of its presumed bracket. In this way, wartime resembles movie-time, albeit without the insulation from peril.

Thus, as Dudziak has pointed out, "once war has begun, time is thought to proceed on a different plane" (22). "There are two important consequences of this shift [into wartime]," Dudziak explains, "first we have entered a time that calls for extraordinary action, and second, we share a belief that this moment will end decisively, so that this shift is temporary" (22). Dudziak's compelling examination of what constitutes wartime juxtaposes juridical, cultural, and mythological understandings of the temporal frame that delimits and is delimited by states of war. In vast and vastly contradictory contexts, she shows, the time of war becomes visible through the ostensible transparency with which the "postwar period" provides a knowable demarcation, a posterior complement to the anterior "prewar period." She also explains how endless war, or an endless array of warlike activities, makes anachronistic the terminology framing "wartime." Thus, the treatment of war as though it constituted a finite period exemplifies another Barthian myth.

Like the myths Barthes analyzes, wartime and peacetime are in no way natural, however much they both may employ linguistic tropes analogous to those describing seasons. If time itself is not a natural phenomenon,[7] neither is the arbitrary separation of war and peace: "Just as clock time is based on a set of ideas produced not by clocks but by the people who use them, wartime is also a set of ideas derived from social life, not from anything inevitable about war itself" (Dudziak, 21).

Many conflicts in American history exemplify this. The conflicts in Korea and in Vietnam occupied the entire span of what has been called the *post*war period; Vietnam, in fact, occupied the postwar period while also ending that period without exactly starting its own wartime period. Before the Vietnam War, the United States was at war in Vietnam, and after that war-that-had-no-beginning officially ended, the United States was still at war in Vietnam. Throughout that time, despite the absence of active hostilities in Korea, the United States was (and is?) at war there too. No surrender, no treaty, no resolution, or formal terminus officially separates the postwar period, when combat raged on the Korean peninsula and prisoner-of-war camps overflowed, from the second decade of the twenty-first century, when neither is the case. More recently, the United States engaged in the nation's "longest war" *in* Afghanistan, but not *with* Afghanistan.

Some wars, in other words, can seem horrifyingly endless, just as some films can be so tedious that they seem to go on forever. To the extent that this book may touch on the kinship between the way the American audience regards war and movies, however, it does so only to highlight how the paradigms that forged that kinship have proved inadequate for accommodating some informing narratives of twenty-first-century life. In addition, "since the Iraq War," David LaRocca points out, "we have added a new model for investigation: the preventative or preemptive war, which shifts the prosecution of war to a wider network of agents—not just commanders and soldiers, but also to politicians and policymakers, diplomats and lobbyists, the intelligence and clandestine services, and even journalists and image-makers" (16). Further compounding our comprehension of wartime is the fact that contemporary war films, as LaRocca notes, are "not strictly about distant lands and peoples but also about our everyday experience of war—the way we live with it on the terms of the so-called twenty-four-hour news cycle, which is in turn a series of instantaneous updates aiming for 'breaking news'" (26). It is one thing, moreover, to *represent* the world cinematically and another to *understand* it cinematically. Unfortunately, for over a century American mass culture has so extensively proliferated cinematic representation that much of the population—perhaps all of the population to varying degrees—understands many aspects of their personal life and national history in cinematic terms, or, more specifically, in terms of the Hollywood style.

Dudziak's argument is further complicated by the War on Terror, which commenced in 2001, because that war actively rent the connection between "war" and "hostilities," the latter of which seems, in the past decade, to have evaporated without having been terminated, without some enemy combatants having been tried or released from captivity, without the legal status of those combatants having been clearly articulated, any more than the status of the war in which they allegedly participated.

These are just some of the vagaries entailed in combating an adversary bearing the name "Terror." "Terror" can neither surrender nor be annihilated. It cannot be brought to the negotiating table or surrounded and contained, not only because it has no constitutive body—a faction, militia, government, or army—but more importantly because "Terror" is not territorial, not external to its adversary. If terrorists exist out there, the only way we know they do is that they have done something that profoundly and uncannily disturbs us. Terror is a form of debilitating fear that we cannot extinguish completely, no matter how hard we struggle with the feeling. While it can never surrender to us, periodically we surrender to it, to the fear we experience about events we imagine.

In this state of terror—or, at least, in this age of terror—Dudziak confronts us with our myth: If this war is declared without an object and allows no method for victory, should we not admit we will never find peace because peace is only a myth, sustaining the idea that war has a purpose? Because the ontological as well as the sociological implications of this recognition are too vast for this study, I will engage the issue of war's purpose only in regard to the performative implications of believing that war's generic purpose is to restore peace. If peacetime provides wartime with its mythological limits, the idea of peace has traditionally given war its purpose and, with that purpose, permitted its exceptional temporality.

In its implicit temporal parameters, moreover, wartime echoes Hollywood cinema and its well-honed conventions of cinematic representation. Hollywood, as a commercial vending machine, learned very early how to adapt its product to the commercial demands of weekly consumers, that genre-driven audience at the foundation of Hollywood's mode of production and distribution. Studios relied on repeat buyers who understood the content of their sight-unseen purchases. And genre labels enabled large audiences to purchase nonrefundable tickets for westerns, romances, horror films, or gangster films because they knew what to expect.

The structural vehicle for these genres was movie-time, the seamless intersection of a history (factual, fictive, or both), the events that unfold against those historical backgrounds, and the actual time during which a viewer consolidates those elements. Movie-time is thus a composite of three durations—the time of the screening, the time of the events represented during the screening, and the timespan of the story that these events represent metonymically. As such, movie-time is the temporal instrument that organizes the story being told into a specific sequence of shown events, covering a specific duration of time, such that the story could be concluded with nothing apparently unresolved in a standardized screen time (roughly 80 to 140 minutes). Within the parameters of movie-time, during which the spectator exempted herself from the demands of the quotidian world, all the necessary story elements were established, complicated, and wrapped up, allowing the spectator to return, satisfied, to everyday normality.

Thus, movie-time, like wartime, followed—or laid out, while appearing to follow—a trajectory in which the impediments put into place at the outset dissolved before the screen-time ran out. In crime stories, the criminals were brought to justice; in romances, the lovers united; in musicals, the show went on (so that the lovers could unite); in horror, the menace was subdued or destroyed (which allowed the lovers to unite); in westerns, the human or physical elements were tamed (which allowed the lovers to unite [unless the hero rode off in search of new elements to tame]). The exhibition demands vital to industrial cash flow mandated that all plot objectives, from settling the West to opening a show on Broadway, take roughly the same amount of screen-time. On screen, Bonnie and Clyde's entire lawless spree took roughly as long as it took Marilyn Monroe to learn how to marry a millionaire, the investigative reporters in *Spotlight* to expose Catholic Church pederasts, or Dorothy to travel to and from Oz. Some things—Moses freeing the Hebrews and delivering the Ten Commandments, the Civil War and Scarlett O'Hara's three marriages, or Phineas Fogg's trip around the world in eighty days—took up to one hundred minutes more. These temporal constraints mandated, in the classical Hollywood style, that all actions and details be motivated, that is, that they contribute to the efficiency by which Hollywood films negotiated compacts between story-time and screen-time to produce, in movie-time, an event with a clear beginning and no loose ends.

This is the same consolidation that Dudziak finds in the construction of wartime. In defining wartime, in other words, she is also describing what we do when we proceed through the doors of a movie theater or stream a movie by summoning it into the viewing space of our homes. From the perspective of Hollywood's overdetermined narratives, therefore, wartime was well suited for genre production in that its conflict was easy to establish and its resolution, be it of a specific battle, a larger initiative, or the entire war, was clear and completely consistent with the cultural narratives that most members of the audience shared. "In American wartime thinking," Dudziak points out, "there is . . . a powerful sense of determinism" (23).

While Dudziak is not arguing that wartime is derived from movie-time, or vice versa, it is clear that these two imaginary time frames share common assumptions about the relationship between normality and plot that can be found in Aristotle's *Poetics* when he defines drama in terms of disruption. At that moment when the time is ready for action, a conflict emerges; then complications, revelations, and reversals occur, all of which find resolution and produce denouement. In wartime, the resolution is the surrender, and the denouement is the (often implicit) Occupation of the defeated belligerent's territory and governance. Hollywood plotting and editing, moreover, contributes to naturalizing notions of time and resolution that, like the concept of wartime, are counter-historical and counterintuitive. Continuity editing, for example, is a formal system for relating discrete shots in such a way as to encourage viewers to feel as though they are seeing a story instead of watching a movie. This is done by sequencing shots to provide a perspective inaccessible to any single human consciousness.

For example, in a matter of a few seconds, we may see a human figure approach a house by turning into a walkway from the sidewalk. Not only is the figure visible from head to foot but also the walkway, the lawn, and part of the second story of the house fit into the fixed framing of our field of vision. In an instant this shot is replaced by a finger on a doorbell. On the screen the doorbell occupies more space than the entire door in the preceding shot; the finger on it, according to constant proportionality, would have to be at least five feet long. In one second, the image of the doorbell disappears, but not the sound. We see a woman in a chair look up to the right of the frame, in the direction of the "EXIT" door at the front of the movie theater. She stands and walks toward it, but before she reaches the border of the screen, she is replaced by a hand on a doorknob. Again, if we adhere to the proportionality of the screen, the doorknob is smaller than the doorbell we saw earlier, but larger than the back of the chair in which the woman sat. As the door opens, the camera tilts up and pulls back to show a man wearing the same coat as the one we saw from behind in the first shot, but he's much larger. To make sense of this sequence, we must allow ourselves a degree of omniscience that enables us to occupy a viewing position that, without moving, has access to the front and back of things and people. We must also have a calculator in our brain that allows us to translate size into distance, even though our distance from the screen remains unchanged. And importantly, we need to fill in temporal gaps of varying duration. It took a few seconds for the man to walk up the walkway, while the woman got from her chair to the door almost instantaneously. But the pushing of the doorbell was almost simultaneous to the woman's looking up.

This very simple shot sequence, taking no more than six seconds, illustrates the thousands of times continuity editing calls upon us to recalibrate time and space to accommodate the demands of the narrative in which we have situated our imagination. Such recalibration, I am arguing, is a form of cognitive training that encourages us to relate to many aspects of our lives as structured cinematically. Planning for expected events—a wedding, an exam, going to the Super Bowl—or coping with unexpected events, we can draw on the techniques we have rehearsed ad nauseam watching films to help condense or expand, as necessary, our sense of time and our role in navigating it.

This is not the only way in which wartime and war films reconfigure time. In the traditional war film, time is divided into periods when men see action and periods between action. If these divisions are sometimes predictable and, at other times, sudden and random, they nevertheless share a chronic apprehension, either the immediate apprehension of combat or the suspended apprehension of its imminence. This tension between suspended and active conflict is particular to war and precluded from peace. Although potential violence is present in many aspects of life, as it is in the film genres that represent them, in war and in war films the condition of active or suspended combat circumscribes all other circumstances. In the police drama, for example, specific events—an undercover sting, a police raid, the investigating of crime scenes where the perpetrator may still be present—entail tension, often extreme tension, as in, for example, *The Silence of the Lambs* (1991), between suspended violence and its sudden realization. The war film, however, uniquely subordinates all other life and livelihood to that tension. So long as the war goes on, the tension between action and its imminence is omnipresent. Only after the ultimate mission— enforced surrender and ensuing Occupation—is accomplished does time reacquire its normative peacefulness. One could argue, in fact, that the references to home that punctuate most war films provide the contrast necessary to remind the audience of war's unique periodizing.

Paul Virilio sees additional ways that war and cinema have been conflated. He argues convincingly that war is not only an encounter between hostile forces but a way of visualizing that encounter: "There had been no war without representation" (6). Virilio thus traces the logistics of perception to illustrate how the technology of cinematic representation existed in a symbiotic relationship with the logistics of warfare:

> Already evident in the flash-back and then in feed-back, the miniaturization of chronological meaning was a direct result of a military technology in which *events always unfolded in theoretical time*. As in cinema, what happens is governed not by a single space-time principle but by its relative and contingent distortion, the capacity for repressive response depending upon the power of anticipation. (60, italics in the original)

For Virilio, the technologies of visualization impact the production of warfare and also of cinema, such that their condensation of time and distance becomes a synergistic way of knowing in a multifarious environment that cannot be comprehended sequentially. This very insightful understanding of the construction of warfare as knowledge omits, however, perhaps because it has no mechanical features, the role of narrative that disciplines problems inherent in the logistics of perception. The complexity of the codes of cinematic representation can thus be employed to simplify the process of comprehension.

MISSION ACCOMPLISHED: ROLL THE CREDITS

Perhaps this particularly strong conflation of war films with warfare encouraged the Bush-Cheney-Rumsfeld regime to conceptualize the invasion of Iraq cinematically, or perhaps they were seduced by cinema's capacity to simplify, to make a phenomenon as multifarious as war easily consumable. What remains confounding, however, is how they remained so magnificently obtuse. Given their abundant archive of government documentation and their access to extensive expertise regarding issues and logistics, how did they organize a war according to a genre that elides the arduous, boring work entailed in taking charge of a country of more than twenty-five million people, reconciling its violent factions so as to govern it in a peaceful and prosperous manner at the same time as reformulating its entire system of governance in such a way as to sustain its safe sovereignty as a functioning member of an economic, political, and social community of peaceful nations? At stake here is the difference between the military/political end to a war and the cinematic end.

In that regard, I argue here, as I have in several papers, articles, and books, that we have been conditioned to understand the world cinematically.[8] In *Flatlining on the Field of Dreams*, for example, I discuss the films of the 1980s to show how, in formal as well as thematic ways, they made the policies of Reaganism—what G. H. W. Bush, for example, called "voodoo economics"—seem natural. They gained, I argued, a significant portion of their credibility because they "manifested the cinematic notion of reality with which the American public had been indoctrinated since the baby boom" (xi). When we combine this proclivity with the narrow parameters of the traditional war film, a huge disparity emerges between the strength of the cinematic conclusion and the state of the war. Thus, the commander-in-chief stood aboard an aircraft carrier, just as General Douglas MacArthur stood on the USS *Missouri* on September 2, 1945, declaring the war over, while troops were still dying in Iraq, while sectarian violence and civilian bloodshed characterized daily life in the country that had not surrendered.

Although some form of military response to 9/11 was inevitable, the specific choice of Bush-Cheney-Rumsfeld to invade Iraq, the specific contortions employed to make that invasion seem the fitting—if not destined—response to the attack, the (lack of) planning that went into the response, and the war(s) that followed, all contributed to an understanding of warfare that significantly challenged the premises of the combat films of the second half of the twentieth century. Those premises were deeply steeped in the foundations of peacetime America, which construed the objective of war as eliminating the (evil) enemy so that peace-loving Americans could resume normal lives. To that general mission, all specific missions contributed, from capturing a machine-gun nest to piloting the *Enola Gay* over Hiroshima. In this way, all the missions in World War II participated in the narrative of forcing the Axis surrender.

Conceiving the war in cinematic rather than strategic, legal, and geopolitical terms had, as we now know, mortal consequences. It is now clear how misguided and shortsighted it was to devise a government advertising campaign using Saddam Hussein as the outlet for 9/11 animus. Putting aside the dubious wisdom of a public relations campaign turning Saddam into a movie villain, the reckless stupidity of staging a war as if one were making a movie entailed freeing the United States from the work involved in maintaining civil order or governmental stability by presuming that the safety of American troops and the civil life of a conquered country would take care of themselves. With horrifying complacency, the administration, after destroying Iraq's infrastructure, firing its police force, and crushing its economy, blamed the Iraqis for the resulting chaos. Staunchly, Bush-Cheney-Rumsfeld maintained that the United States had helped the Iraqis enough. The rest was up to them. In a Hollywood movie, these problems could quickly be resolved or ignored, following a principle of the classical Hollywood style, which structures plots to eliminate loose ends and divert our attention away from anything that is unresolved. But no matter how much Bush-Cheney-Rumsfeld implicitly imagined the war as a movie, and no matter how much they staged photo-ops to insist it could be resolved cinematically, American troops kept fighting. After May 1, 2003, however, they did so without a mission, that is, without anything they could do to return America and Iraq to peacetime.

Shortly after the declaration of "Mission Accomplished," moreover, the failure of accomplishment coupled with the continuation—in some ways, escalation—of American military action created a war unable to "accomplish" a discernable objective and thus one deprived of a "mission." If, as Binns contends, "no other genre depicts the passing of time—the turning points of civilization—more frequently than the war film genre" (6), then what is the consequence of a war film genre that depicts war as absent of turning points? Instead of *pursuing* the goal of an accomplished mission, the Iraqi action became a war *pursuant* to the declaration of one, turning American military activity into the occupation of operating a military activity. This construction of war as occupation is consistent, as well, with the "all-volunteer" military, the aggressive privatization of many military services, and the assignment of not only regular Army personnel but also Reservists and National Guardsmen on multiple war zone deployments. The prolonged effects of war as an occupation made it increasingly apparent that the occupation of occupying Iraq and Afghanistan was not just a dangerous job but a meaningless one. Since withdrawal of occupying forces follows the formal Occupation, the events that turned the Iraq War into an occupation precluded progress toward surrender and Occupation. The post–Mission Accomplished war, therefore, changed the theater of war from a place where lives were lost in the process of completing a mission to a place where losing lives was the sole military occupation, as nothing aside from the death count defined the vicissitudes of US-Iraq military involvement.

For that reason, Bush-Cheney-Rumsfeld's proclamation "Mission Accomplished" consolidated the failure of their war to validate the narratives invoked to sustain it: no surrender, no WMDs that focused the US invasion, no destruction of Al Qaeda, no proof connecting Al Qaeda to Iraq. Because the mission to compel a surrender had failed, moreover, the restoration of peacetime had been deferred, indefinitely, such that American troops, still fighting and dying, could accomplish nothing that could end their war and send them home.

WARS CHANGE BUT THE SENSE OF MISSION REMAINS

Although the histories of both the Korean and Vietnam Wars differ from World War II, in all three of those wars, the mission was clear and sustained. That is not the only way the wars differed from the Iraq invasion.

Although the United States led the United Nations forces in the Korean War (to which eighteen nations contributed), it was not an American war. The United States was never attacked, nor was war declared in 1950 when North Korean troops crossed the thirty-eighth parallel separating North Korea from South Korea. The UN police action's clear mission—restoring the established division between North and South—required no conquest, surrender, or Occupation. Despite General MacArthur's attempt to turn this international policing effort into the invasion of China, US/UN incursions were rebuffed, and MacArthur's career was terminated; so were active hostilities. For these reasons, the Iraq War was a complete inversion of the Korean conflict. The Korean mission was accomplished, and because accomplishing it entailed no border changes, no surrender or Occupation was necessary. Since the conflict did not conform to the World War II trajectory, which is much more amenable to cinematic rendition, fewer war films were set in Korea, and those that were tended to replicate the World War II formula, with a few wrinkles, chief among them the increase in "rescue" plots, not surprising in that half of the active war had far less to do with securing borders than exchanging prisoners.

The Vietnam War challenged the traditional war narrative in a different way. Ever since I can remember, a third rail of politics has been for any elected official or candidate to say that, in any instance, American soldiers "died in vain," as if doing so deprecated the soldiers' lives, when exactly the opposite is the case. Those sentiments extol the worth of soldiers' lives by condemning the politicians and officers who treated those lives as expendable by sacrificing them pointlessly.

If we say an American killed in Vietnam died in vain, that does not discount the numerous instances in which individual soldiers lost their lives saving others. We have thousands of citations for such heroic acts of self-sacrifice. But that does not negate the fact that heroism would not have been required were the soldiers not forced to fight a needless war. The "mission" of the Vietnam War was to contain the spread of Communism. That mission in Vietnam failed; nevertheless, so did the spread of Communism, in Europe as well as in Asia. The Vietnam War was unnecessary to contain Communism because even during the height of the Cold War, the United States had productive working relationships with some Communist countries, most notably Tito's Yugoslavia, and even before American troops withdrew from Vietnam, the United States had begun to establish relations with Communist China. Instead of fomenting a war, all the United States had to do was allow its puppet regime in South Vietnam to comply with 1954 Geneva Accords that mandated national elections in 1956, and, following Ho Chi Minh's almost certain victory, announce "Ho is another Tito." He had long indicated his interest in a working relationship with the United States by cooperating with the Office of Strategic Services during World War II and making repeated overtures to President Harry Truman after the war.

One result of such an alliance would have been a strong buffer against Chinese expansion (Vietnamese/Chinese border wars followed shortly after the US withdrawal), and another would have been a strong trade partner and economic base in Southeast Asia. Most important, that course of action would have averted the loss of fifty-eight thousand American and more than two million Vietnamese lives, as well as the profound domestic unrest of the late 1960s and the rapid expansion of the military-industrial complex, against which President Eisenhower cautioned. Perhaps the money saved could also have been employed in domestic programs that would have allowed America to discover whether the "Great Society" envisioned by Lyndon Johnson was feasible.

This list of the potential benefits of rapprochement with Vietnam in 1956 could go on at length; not so the benefits of the Vietnam War. The United States fought in vain. The war's mission was misguided, its execution ill-conceived, its goals unachievable. A recorded phone call as early as 1964 showed that President Johnson knew this, but he, his administration, a bipartisan majority of elected officials, and his successors continued to misinform the American public.[9] But even the often-audacious Lyndon Johnson never claimed the mission was accomplished at the same time as casualties and troop commitments were escalating, as George Bush did in 2003. Nor does any record show Ho Chi Minh was actually an Ayn Rand libertarian whom Johnson, using falsified intelligence reports, claimed was a Communist, in the way that Bush-Cheney-Rumsfeld represented Saddam as an Islamic terrorist to fabricate connections between him and Al Qaeda; nor did Johnson attempt to connect Ho with the Japanese attack on Pearl Harbor, in the way Bush-Cheney-Rumsfeld linked Saddam to 9/11.

Perhaps we can attribute these restraints to Johnson's surfeit of scruples, not a characteristic that tends, anecdotally, to be associated with him. Such disinformation campaigns were uncharacteristic, more likely, because they were unnecessary, given that the informing narratives endemic to American cultural citizenship in the 1950s and 1960s were more generally accepted and well-entrenched. This is why, throughout the bulk of the post–World War II period, US foreign policy, it is generally accepted, was bipartisan, as evidenced by such programs and initiatives as the Marshall Plan, the Berlin Airlift, NATO, SEATO, the Peace Corps, the Bay of Pigs invasion, to name a few. In the late 1950s, the residual effects of McCarthyism (long after McCarthy's personal influence, along with his liver, had irreparably deteriorated) included the purging of government workers and university faculty, the standardization of loyalty oaths, and ads on billboards, in subways, and on television featuring Soviet Premier Nikita Khrushchev saying "We will bury you!" Thus, in the early 1960s, it was not hard to marshal popular support for the policy of Communist containment, when the population, overwhelmingly, saw Communism as a universal threat.[10] Concerns about Communists in Southeast Asia, Eastern Europe, Latin America (consider the 1962 Cuban Missile Crisis) fit well into cultural narratives about American exceptionalism and threats to it that made the majority of Americans simultaneously proud and wary.

UNTENABLE, BUT A MISSION NONETHELESS

Since an actual war provides the "historical" time frame, the plots of war films have to conform, at least nominally, to public assumptions about historically specific war narratives. One reason for the genre's decline in the 1960s, therefore, is that as the Vietnam War continued to escalate, the domestic scene that represented the war's normative alternative made the traditional war film's narrative structure untenable. For many reasons, establishing a homology between World War II and Vietnam was impossible, in part because no event—no "day of infamy"—violently ruptured normal domestic practices. American soldiers, moreover, were not fighting in Vietnam to protect in any literal way the American way of life. It was never possible to represent the United States as under attack by Vietnam or in any danger of ever being so. Despite persistent demagoguery and evocations of the ominous "Domino Theory," the Vietnamese never threatened American safety. The 1968 Tet Offensive, in which the Viet Cong nearly captured the American embassy in Saigon, resembled Pearl Harbor neither strategically nor geopolitically, and attempts to substitute rhetorical threats for historical facts never galvanized public belief that Americans faced imminent Viet Cong assault.

There were those who argued, for example, that Communism was a monolith under which all countries were puppet states controlled by Moscow, and therefore that the only way to contain the spread of Communism worldwide was to defeat Communism everywhere. That universalist view, reflected in the "Domino Theory," imagined adjacent countries as akin to rows of dominoes, so that the toppling of one would precipitate the fall of the next, in a chain of events that would eventually encircle the globe. Thus, defeat in Vietnam would impel the Communist takeover of Cambodia, which would cause Laos to collapse, and then, in succession, Thailand and Indonesia, followed in order by Australia, New Zealand, Japan, and, in due time, Hawaii. In other words, the American population was asked to believe that Communist control of Vietnam would foment the inevitable takeover of Pearl Harbor. Combining aggression and subversion, the inscrutable Communists, if not immediately checked, would succeed where Tojo had failed, using seductive propaganda to turn thousands of Hawaiians, surfers by day, into guerrillas by night, the "Oahu Cong." Yet a third argument for the war was that the United States had made a commitment to South Vietnam, which it had to keep, lest its role as the "Leader of the Free World" come into question. Finally, there were those who simply said, "But we're there. Perhaps we should not have gone into Vietnam, *but we're there!*"

However much the grip of these rationales on the public imaginary increased or ebbed, none successfully unified a national effort or enlisted the nation in the cause of shared sacrifice. In the 1940s, citizen gardeners cultivated homegrown produce to facilitate rationing, but by the 1960s, weed-covered "victory gardens" had succumbed to home gardens growing weed. Whether the threats propagated by Vietnam War narratives were too abstract, or too absurd, or simply contradicted by the facts (e.g., the US "commitment" was to the government it had set up), they could not energize the nation's citizens, especially since the war did not "start" but grew gradually over a ten-year period of minor involvement, during which time the informing rationales continued to fluctuate. Thus, when US involvement finally became a major action (increasing from

FIGURE 1.01. *"The Domino Theory." Source Unknown.*

25,000 troops in 1964 to 250,000 troops in 1965, to half a million in 1966), no dramatic event spurred the escalation or impelled the country to declare war.[11]

The failure of any of the war's rationales to establish the requisite gravitas, therefore, resulted in a fracturing of national narratives. For many Americans, the fact that the war's scale greatly exceeded its motivation indicated that their own government ought not to be trusted and supported. Millions marched in protest; some went to jail rather than serve in the military; others opted for one of several loopholes to avoid the military draft; others just left the country. The Vietnam War, in fact, threatened normal life inversely, fomenting increasingly obtrusive and ostentatious rejections of the cultural norms that had preceded the war: as the war escalated, fewer and fewer Americans desired a return to the repressed and conformist social conventions of the 1950s, and the notion of sacrificing for a war effort never acquired an intensity comparable to the virulent anti-war effort. In consequence, during the Vietnam War, very few war films were made, and those, such as *The Green Berets* (1968), which drew on then-superannuated World War II narratives, failed to consolidate a war effort; instead they became symptoms of the nation's rifts.

The Vietnam War films also reconfigured the understanding of duration. Because of the Vietnam War's asymmetry, the United States faced no threat of being conquered, which allowed soldiers to rotate between a site of war and a home at peace. Whereas in World War II soldiers were enlisted for the duration, in Vietnam they were required to spend only one tour of duty (eleven months) in the war zone. There was no compelling need to fight until it was over, over there, and with draft calls at fifty thousand per month, no shortage of replacements. Soldiers rotated into the war, and once their rotation was complete, they rotated out, requiring them to make an official request—in some cases even to reenlist—before they could reenter the war. For those in the service, war was probable; for those facing the draft, it was likely. The rest rotated into and, if they were lucky, out of the time when conditions of adversarial violence structured their lives. Some volunteered, some made a career choice, but the majority were conscripted. The soldiers differed from those in World War II, all of whom were required to serve as combatants under the temporal arc that terminated when the mission of the war was accomplished, that is, when a mutual agreement between the victors and the vanquished—a surrender—initiated the Occupation.

Finally, just as the Vietnam War had no distinct beginning, it promised no foreseeable conclusion. North Vietnam would never surrender. Why should it, when twenty-five years of combating French and then American forces was a mere blip in Vietnam's two-thousand-year struggle for independence? Especially since it was winning? Especially since, even if the Hanoi government were overtaken by US forces, the guerrilla warfare could not be suppressed in every village? In Vietnam the United States was not fighting to coerce enemy capitulation, as it was in World War II, but rather to avoid withdrawing troops from the country, something that eventually became unavoidable.

But, as the war continued to demonstrate, without surrender, there could be no victory, just a perpetual campaign. Under the "pacification" program, the objective of US forces was to pacify specific villages in the South by ridding them of the Viet Cong and, at the same time, destroying the supply lines facilitating the flow of insurgents and contraband into the South. The purpose of this program was to win "the hearts and minds" of the villagers. Despite brutal population cleansing, the program never succeeded in sorting those favorable to the South from those unsympathetic to rule of the regime that had destroyed their villages, killed their neighbors and relatives, or abruptly divorced them from their land and their possessions. Nor did the massive American firepower that enabled these procedures win the hearts of a significant number of occupied or dispossessed villagers. By presuming that the conditions making surrender possible were imminent, in other words, the pacification program precluded the conditions that could make surrender possible. In the end, as we know, the failure to effect a surrender meant ceding the occupied areas, along with everything else, to the population that had refused to surrender. But this was all done by default, rather than by agreement.

Even so, the war retained a clear, albeit ethically dubious, mission: to destroy the Viet Cong and thereby halt guerrilla activity that threatened a series of US-backed regimes in South Vietnam. These circumstances did not so much alter the basic narrative of the war film genre as diminish its popularity to the point of near extinction. It was not so much that the Vietnam War's objectives were unclear as that the mission itself was not acceptable enough to provide commercial viability for a film genre about pursuing those objectives, or for such films to generate wide public enthusiasm. And it still remains unlikely that the Vietnam War effort will reemerge as catalyst for popular war films.[12]

Even though President Reagan called the Vietnam War America's finest hour, and, as Susan Jeffords has shown, his comments contributed to films participating in the "remasculinization of America," the Vietnam War failed to provide an apt focus for popular war films. Despite the success of *The Deer Hunter* (1978) and *Platoon* (1986), the history of the war and the history of the nation's response to that war have made it generally incompatible with the tenets of the war film genre, lodged in a national mission to make short-term sacrifices, on the battlefront and the home front, pursuing the mission to end the aberration of wartime so as to restore the norms of peacetime.

To put it simply, the traditional war film celebrates victory or celebrates sacrifices made in the pursuit of it by employing a shorthand that anticipates victory or implies its imminence. This anticipation allows a narrative arc condensing the energies that justify war as the path to peace, even when individual episodes involve soldiers who are confused about their duties or are justifiably questioning orders or plans. During World War II, the Office of War Information, in support of the war effort, kept this questioning to a minimum; in the 1950s, McCarthyism had a similar effect. The changes in American culture and government practices between the 1950s and the 1970s allowed for more open criticism of military practice and American foreign policy. In 1966, for example, Senator William Fulbright, chair of the Foreign Relations Committee, published *The Arrogance of Power*, an open critique of the policies surrounding the objectives and the execution of the Vietnam War. It is hard to imagine a comparable work published by the chair of the Senate Foreign Relations Committee during the Korean War. Although Fulbright's book indicated that American culture had shifted, such that it admitted cultural narratives expressing a broadening diversity of cogent perspectives on American identity and direction, the book still recognized that the Vietnam War had a clear mission; the formulation and execution of that mission, in fact, lay at the heart of the book's criticism.

The Iraq War differs from its predecessors in this regard, because any mission formulated to address a contrived rationale cannot be real, and therefore one cannot debate the right or wrong way to carry out such a mission. For the same reason, filmmakers were hard-pressed to construct narratives in which characters risk their lives to solve problems that do not exist.

CHAPTER 2

PRIVATE RYAN AND THE LAST GOOD WAR (NARRATIVE)

The resurrection of the war film genre, therefore, depended on *Saving Private Ryan*'s (1998) returning audiences to the "good war" in a film presented as the apotheosis of the traditional American war film narrative. Manifesting most of the conventions that, as Jeanine Basinger has shown, define the traditional war film, *Saving Private Ryan* devotes much energy to establishing the fact that the men in the unit have normal lives stateside, to which they wish to return, so much so that every aspect of their mission is framed by its role in ending the war, that is, in facilitating the normal transitions from combat to surrender, to formal "Occupation," to withdrawal of occupying troops and the resumption, for all former belligerents, of normal civilian life. Because the men in *Saving Private Ryan* are in for the duration, their military service will last as long, and only as long, as Hitler stays undefeated. The causal connection between their success and the duration of their military service, like the causal connection between the success of their specific mission and of the entire war effort, is axiomatic to the genre. Without the idea of a normal peacetime life, the role people play in wartime becomes incomprehensible, that is, unsuitable for classical Hollywood narratives that feed on the satisfaction derived from the union of desired goals with the people desiring them.

The impossibility of the Vietnam or Korean war narratives accommodating this merger of wartime and movie-time, coupled with the disjuncture between the cultural narratives of such films with those surrounding these non-Aristotelean wars, has proved an unsurmountable obstacle, despite a few lauded exceptions, to resurrecting the war film genre. *Saving Private Ryan*, made over twenty years after the last American troops withdrew from Vietnam, demonstrated that successfully reviving the war film genre required returning the audience to the "good war," that is, a war with trajectories and dicta that conformed to the conventions of cinematic representation, grounded in the unregulated chaos of wartime, the mythological normality of peacetime, and the arbitrary reality with which movie-time reconciles peacetime and wartime, causally and ethically. This is one of the reasons that "World War II became for Americans what war should be" (Dudziak, 61). As Charles Burnetts points out, it is "difficult to ignore the extent to which *Private Ryan*'s ideology has become something of a template in terms of its revival of the war/combat genre in mainstream cinema and television of the last fifteen years" (7).

Basinger has done an exemplary job of identifying the tropes and conventions that define the World War II combat film. According to her, a very large number of such films produced between 1941 and 1959 operate according to a narrow set of norms. The combat units in these films typically comprise a "democratic ethnic mix" from which the hero is "forced to separate himself because of the demands of leadership" (56). The groups have internal conflicts attributable to personalities and attitudes, while their combat enemy, in general, remains faceless. Although their world is absent of women, the domestic home front stays present in their conversation, as does war propaganda. Their limited range of activities, "writing and receiving letters, cooking and eating meals, exploring territory, talking and listening, hearing and discussing news, questioning values, fighting and resting, sleeping, joking" (57), sets the parameters of their restricted state, further underscoring their extraordinary locale already defined by "maps, military advisors, and official dedications" (57).

In this context, we can posit that affirming that implicit equivalence between "American" and "good" may constitute some of the combat films' most cogent cultural work. Given the vastness and the urgency of World War II, moreover, these films, unsurprisingly, feature variations of a basic American character, one who is generally provincial (Brooklyn rendered as much a provincial locale as Biloxi), religious, community-minded, and fundamentally peaceful. The fact that these typical Americans are thrust into a harrowingly unnatural struggle for survival supports the unambiguous premise that these largely nonprofessional soldiers must win. Victory in war ought not, as it should in sporting events, go to those who are most able, but to those who are most decent, and perhaps the surest proof of decency, in typical American World War II films, is that the profession of soldiering does not come naturally. Americans are not represented as aggressors, but rather as defenders protecting their decent, domestic, and, above all, peaceful way of life. They are presented less as the match for their German and Japanese enemies than as the surrogates for their American audience. The World War II combat films thus created a site of identification for the audience not by seducing it into the subject position of professional killers, but by reminding viewers how much our soldiers remain peace-loving Americans, imbued, even in jungles, deserts, submarines, and fox-holes, with that quintessence of domestic community first identified with the American character by de Tocqueville.

Referring to a dramatic moment in *Saving Private Ryan* when Captain Miller (Tom Hanks) decides to spare a Nazi soldier who was in the machine-gun nest that killed one of his men, Albert Auster points out how this moment "underscores the difference between the American GI and other armies and is another source of American triumph in [the film]. Although Americans fight with ferocity and sometimes do commit atrocities in the fog of war . . . this is the exception rather than the rule. In other instances, the American voice of conscience and commitment to the rules of war prevails" (210). Thus, as John Bodnar explains, "while the Spielberg film reveals the brutality of war, it pre-serves the World War II image of American soldiers as inherently averse to bloodshed and cruelty" (805).

One of the principal tasks of these combat films, therefore, is to construct a narrative that connects the imminence of American triumph with its sol-dier's lack of affinity for war. The Germans and the Japanese will fail because, as invaders, they are fighting *for* war; Americans will prevail because they are fighting to end it. Consistent with this theme, World War I, we should remem-ber, was dubbed "The war to end all wars." American death in these films, there-fore, is a sacrifice made in the interest of restoring peace, not an occupational hazard in the pursuit of normalizing conquest. That the professional soldier is both requisite for and inimical to peace is especially iterated, Basinger notes, by the motif of killing off the professional soldier upon whom survival and victory have depended throughout the film, never more radically and shock-ingly than in *Sands of Iwo Jima* (1949), where Sergeant Stryker (John Wayne) is shot after combat seems to be over and victory assured. As Basinger puts it, "like war, Wayne is a necessary evil" (153). "The suggestion is being made," she explains, "that men like Wayne's Sergeant Stryker are needed when they are needed, but that they are not needed for peacetime. . . . Furthermore, what we want to strive for is continual peace, which means rejection of the Strykers of the world" (153). Supportive of this narrative, typical World War II combat films establish a number of specific "don'ts." Expressions of triumphant joy are dangerous because "you can't feel pride and joy in the work of killing. When you take a moment to act as a prideful and selfish individual, they'll get you" (Basinger, 53) as surely as they will if you stand up in a foxhole, and, Basinger points out, anyone who climbs a tree in a war film will die. War also allows no time for nostalgia, so "sink into your past and you lose your life" (52).

Saving Private Ryan best identifies the narrative conventions of the traditional war film that most differentiate it from the twenty-first-century war film genres this book discusses. Most importantly, *Saving Private Ryan* emphasizes a characteristic of almost all World War II films made in the 1940s and 1950s: the tacit assumption that war is an aberration, the goal of which is to restore peace. Therefore, before 9/11, the premises of the films to which *Saving Private Ryan* is an homage fit a narrative trajectory wherein peace is the norm that war disrupts. In peacetime, people engage in sundry organizations and activities that sustain predictable social, political, and material economies. These practices of everyday life situate families in the flow of generational transition that secures, or attempts to, the regular acquisition of food, shelter, clothing, health, and welfare.[1] Recognizable because they assert the accepted narratives of a given culture, these practices organize the culture's loosely shared values, goals, and norms. To the extent that violent intrusions, such as earthquakes, epidemics, or wars, disrupt normal practices, ordinary life must be subordinated, temporarily, to the demands of critical immediacy, to a generic "war effort." Whether they take place on the home front or in some theater of operations, the war effort's extraordinary actions are aimed at creating the conditions for their own elimination. Returning to normal life, in which states of exception are no longer necessary, justifies such extraordinary activities as invasion, conscription, battles, rationing, redeployment of energies, and sedition laws. Because, in American war narratives, the theater of operations rarely overlapped with the home front, Americans have regarded war as particularly unnatural and figure themselves in the popular imaginary as anti-authoritarian, domestically focused, peace-loving subjects, occasionally forced by dire circumstances to abandon normal life: "We won't come back 'til it's over, over there!" or, as the fourth stanza of the national anthem proclaims,

> Oh! thus be it ever, when freemen shall stand
> Between their loved homes and the war's desolation!

THE "GOOD WAR" (FILMS)

Pearl Harbor, by creating the unnatural division between home front and war front, enabled the crystallization of these distinct sites by consolidating them into a coherent, interdependent cause. World War II was the "good war," therefore, because Americans were fighting to end the war and thereby restore the peace that would end the fissure. Prior to Pearl Harbor, the international goals and allegiances of the United States had been debatable. A strong contingent—

the Popular Front—emerged uniting moderates, liberals, progressives, and American Communists, all of whom saw national interests and moral imperatives as aligned with the defeat of fascism. At the same time, a strong America First movement, sympathetic to the racial nationalism of the Third Reich and hostile to the economic reforms of FDR's New Deal, saw the fascist regimes in Europe as the most appropriate allies for the United States. The German American Bund, formed in 1936 with the goal of enlisting Americans of German descent to the cause of Nazism, was successful enough to hold a public rally at Madison Square Garden in 1939 that attracted more than twenty thousand members and sympathizers.[2] At the outbreak of World War II in Europe, in 1939, these groups, which would have preferred that the United States join the conflict in support of the Axis countries, lobbied for rigid neutrality, so much so that, in September 1941, Republican Senator Gerald Nye of North Dakota initiated hearings to scrutinize Hollywood, an industry heavily controlled by Jews, based on the suspicion that the studios were making films that were too anti-Nazi. In fact, if anything, quite the contrary was true.[3] Although by 1939 the sympathies of a strong majority of those in the film industry were anti-Nazi, the studios continued to balance commercial interests against their domestic image and their growing humanitarian concerns.

Concerns about promoting anti-fascist sentiments, of course, evaporated a few months after the Congressional hearings concluded when, following the attack on Pearl Harbor, the United States declared war on Japan. The Axis powers, in turn, declared war on the United States, and the mobilization of a national war effort generally replaced fears about American interventionism. National unity was further promoted by the creation, in 1942, of the Office of War Information, a propaganda apparatus that, in the interest of the war effort, prevented the production of any films perceived to be anti-war or that portrayed America in a negative light. It requires no literary theorist to see how Hollywood film narratives were a perfect scaffold for such unifying efforts. Since antiquity, epics have been structured around singular overarching trajectories: Achilles must expiate his wrath; Odysseus needs to get home. At all costs, Oedipus must free Thebes of the plague, such that every part of his investigation contributes to this goal. As with classical Hollywood movie-time, World War II was intended to leave no loose ends.

In films about World War II, therefore, stories of the home front, like those of the battlefront, illustrate the need for managing the tribulations of wartime in the interest of restoring peacetime. The climactic moments of the 1944 musical film *Meet Me in St. Louis* make this point stunningly when Esther Smith, played by Judy Garland, sings "Have Yourself a Merry Little Christmas" to her sister, Tootie, played by eleven-year-old Margaret O'Brien. Although set in 1900 and ostensibly about a Midwestern family's relocation to New York City, the scene focuses on the fact that an unforeseen disruption threatens to alter permanently the life of every member of their middle-class family. Friendships, romances, prospects for starting a family, along with the details of familial normality and the ritual festivity of holidays and special events, have been tainted, put on hold, or, even worse, permanently thwarted. Christmas, as the quintessence of gaiety and hope—having parties, opening presents, gathering with loved ones—cannot produce its traditional haven of goodwill, its prospect for peace on Earth. Instead, the holiday invokes for Esther and Tootie reminders of everything the occasion cannot at this moment provide, all the traditions that threaten to be permanently rent.

Looking out the window, from a dark bedroom, Garland sings to O'Brien perhaps the saddest of all Christmas songs. The lyrics persistently elide the present moment by evoking thoughts of an unknowable future, wherein the prospect of restoring a lost past might reside. Acknowledging current woes, the song expresses the hope that "next year" those troubles "*will* be out of sight." Admitting heavy hearts, it expresses hope that the condition will change: "*make* the Yuletide gay." Implicitly understanding that troubles are close at hand, it imagines a future when these troubles "*will* be miles away." Because things have radically changed, life is not as it once was; those "happy golden days" seem profoundly distant ("days of yore"), as indicated by the absence of "faithful friends who are dear to us" coupled with the hope that the time may come when they "*will* be near to us, *once more*." At this moment, these loved ones are absent, and that desired future, when "someday soon, we all will be together," is by no means certain. It will only happen "*if* the fates allow." As the lyrics used in the film emphasize, "until then, we'll have to muddle through somehow."

O'Brien, who cries while Garland sings, is not inspired. Nor, no doubt, was the movie audience for whom O'Brien's tears, even more than the poignancy of Garland's voice, consolidated their emotional state. Like O'Brien, they were being reminded of what they would not have, being asked to remember those who would not be home for Christmas: those young men—sons, brothers, and lovers; spouses, cousins, and classmates—some of whom would never be together again. The song finally envelops the Christmas season of 1944 with the unifying narrative of the war effort, "to muddle through, somehow."[4]

Other films more explicitly incorporated narratives of the war effort's disruption of domestic life. *Mrs. Miniver* (1942), *Tender Comrade* (1943), and *Since You Went Away* (1944), among many others, detail the personal conflicts, crises, and sacrifices of women on the home front. "Directing female energy and keeping the lid on sexual equity," Thomas Doherty explains, "the [woman war film] genre functioned as a kind of cultural safety valve, albeit one that vented as much pent-up emotion as it shut off" (*Projections*, 155).

In *Tender Comrade*, four married women working at a defense plant share a house and a car to help make ends meet while their husbands are overseas. Doris's (Kim Hunter) husband returns, but Jo (Ginger Rogers), shortly after giving birth to her son, learns that her husband (Robert Ryan) has been killed in action. *Mrs. Miniver*, released the previous year, features Greer Garson playing a mother trying to sustain a family in wartime. Although *Mrs. Miniver* is an American film, it is set in England, where the war effort, already in its third year, includes not only dealing with the absence of men and coping with knowledge of the peril those men were confronting, but also finding shelter from Nazi bombs and burying those who do not. One of the victims is Mrs. Miniver's newlywed daughter-in-law, Carol (Teresa Wright), who is struck by errant machine-gun fire from planes in a dogfight over the countryside near their home. The most popular film of 1942, *Mrs. Miniver* consolidates the narratives of millions of American families adapting to wartime, as Mrs. Miniver's "doll house is shattered by the blitz" (Doherty, *Projections*, 167).

The United States had been at war as long as England had in *Mrs. Miniver* when *Since You Went Away* was released in July 1944. In that film, Anne Hilton (Claudette Colbert) is an American wife and mother who, like Mrs. Miniver, has to adjust her responsibilities to the demands of the war, in a film where, as Doherty puts it, "the absent patriarch leaves an aching emotional gulf in the lives of his wife and daughters" (*Projections*, 170). Because her husband is overseas, Anne must divide her energies between parenting (pre- and late-adolescent daughters), contributing to the war effort, and dealing with the social and economic problems into which the war has thrust her family. She does this while navigating fears of imminent tragedy and occasions of grief, not only her own but also those of her family and neighbors. The film defines the war, in other words, not only as the national effort required to win, but also as the emotional effort required to cope. This includes Anne's helping her daughter Jane (Jennifer Jones) accept the death of her boarder's grandson, Bill (Robert Walker), to whom Jane had been engaged. In helping Jane understand the tragedy that has arrived by telegram, Anne is preparing herself, simultaneously, for the possibility of receiving a similar telegram confirming the fate of her husband, who had been reported "Missing in Action." It was the telegram that more than a quarter of a million American families had already received by the time the film was released.

A year and a half earlier, opening almost exactly one year after Pearl Harbor, *Mrs. Miniver* attracted huge audiences for whom this story of the British middle class enduring the fears, sacrifices, and tragedies of war was both portentous, as *Since You Went Away* attests, and inspirational. Being separated from spouses and losing children, these women demonstrate that, until the war is over, as Garland reminds them in a film released six months after *Since You Went Away*, they will have to muddle through. Significantly, in each of these women's war films, a principal character dies, indicating, as the numerous combat films did, that virtue or likability offers no immunity from war. During wartime, the same values that the Motion Picture Production Code attempted to coerce Hollywood into promoting, along with the implicit assurance that those ("American") values would in general be rewarded, acquired a caveat: like "Have Yourself a Merry Little Christmas," the war effort effects a disruption—hopefully temporary—in the practices comprising normal life. If that normality is a myth, it is a myth that nevertheless delimits the realities of wartime.

SAVING PRIVATE RYAN (AND THE WAR FILM GENRE)

Saving Private Ryan, made more than twenty years after the US evacuation of the collapsed South Vietnam regime, resurrects "the good war" and thus does the cultural work of restoring in the public imaginary the link between the imposition of war and the objective of peace. In this respect, the film not only forges a bond between the American soldier and the domestic audience but also creates a site of common identification between the World War II audience and the post-Vietnam audience. It not only removed Vietnam from the history of American warfare, therefore, but also exorcised ruptures that Vietnam effected in American domestic relations.

New York Times film critic Janet Maslin, feeling that director Steven Spielberg had restored "passion and meaning to the genre with such whirlwind force that he seems to reimagine it entirely, dazzling with the breadth and intensity of that imagination," deemed the film "the finest war movie of our time," and *Entertainment Weekly*'s Owen Gleiberman, reflecting the critical consensus, called this "World War II epic" a movie "of staggering virtuosity and raw lyric power, a masterpiece of terror, chaos, blood, and courage." On this point, most reviewers agreed, even those whose response was more tepid, finding the technical power and pure filmmaking skill extremely impressive. Critics also agreed that Spielberg had consolidated (or rehashed) the tropes and conventions that had become clichés of the World War II combat film genre.

Less agreement existed, however, over whether his handling of the traditional combat unit reflected the film's limitations (Travers) or showed how Spielberg was reinvigorating the genre, whether the stock characters dumbed down the moral and ethical issues he aspired to engage or productively employed the classic tropes to make "the finest war movie of our time." The disagreement over the success or failure of the film, in other words, was lodged in the general agreement that Spielberg had made a quintessential World War II film, rather than a contemporary film set in the 1940s.

Importantly, champions and detractors alike felt, for the most part, that the film's energy was relentlessly retrospective: it returned the audience to World War II. The lauded verisimilitude[5] of the first twenty-five minutes that made the viewers feel as though they were *there*, on Omaha Beach, thus returned them to D-Day, and by inference to everything that motivated average Americans to hazard Omaha Beach; at the same time, the film's homage to D-Day's contemporaneous war films helped return the audience, both emotionally and ideologically, to the experience of watching those films. It is hard to escape the skill with which Spielberg merged, in that way, the experience of the battle-front and the home front.

Spielberg is able to accomplish this not only because, as Basinger aptly points out, "World War II seems to be the combat that speaks to the American soul" (75), but also because Spielberg, perhaps the most deft of those contemporary directors with reverence for classical Hollywood,[6] has, as Phil Landon underscores, "long been a master of American film genres" (62); his canon of films are virtual templates for the kinds of movies that defined the studio era. Epitomizing the traditional American war film genre, *Saving Private Ryan* does not restore war but, rather, reasserts it as Hollywood represented it in the popular imaginary, for "Hollywood's resilient imaginary, reconceptions of past and current wars," Elisabeth Bronfen explains, "make up our cultural possession, functioning as one of our most salient measures of national identity" (4). Each director in the tradition of American war films, she notes, "reimagines the war by commemorating the men who fought it, but also by paying homage to those who came before him in bringing battle to the Hollywood screen" (139). Central to that tradition's notion of war and wartime is, as I have noted, that its purpose is to reestablish the world of domestic norms. Using a powerful depiction of the D-Day invasion as his touchstone, Spielberg underscores the crucial turning point that the Normandy invasion marked in the campaign for a German surrender that would, thereby, allow Americans to return stateside. As Bodnar points out, "at its rhetorical core, the story's argument would have seemed very familiar to audiences in the 1940s: the common American soldier was fundamentally a good man who loved his country and his family. He went to war out of a sense of duty to both, and he wanted to get it over with as quickly as possible. Rather than being a natural-born killer, he was a loving family man who abhorred the use of extreme force but could inflict it when necessary" (806).

Within that narrative arc, the specific mission of a company led by Captain Miller (Tom Hanks) gives purpose and shape to the events involving the search to rescue Private Ryan (Matt Damon) from combat, as well as Ryan's refusal to be rescued, and the film's concluding battle against advancing German forces. The opening D-Day invasion's symmetry with the film's closing battle in the fictional town of Ramelle identifies the latter as an exemplary instance of the former, uniting all the actions of the film into the single objective of defeating Germany, thereby substituting the rescue of the sole surviving son of an American family for the objective of blocking Nazi advances on Cherbourg, so that the two missions enter an economy as equivalent examples of the values that the war is being fought to preserve.

Miller articulates several times a theme iterated by many characters and events: defeating Hitler is requisite to returning to civilian normality, that is, to the American way of life. As Albert Auster points out, "Miller never wavers in his devotion to duty because, in the ultimate sense, the real 'mission' of all World War II platoons is nothing less than the defeat of barbarism" (209). By vigorously asserting this point, Spielberg's "good war" film reconnects the goals of warfare to the objectives of peace. In this way, Spielberg negated the Vietnam era, when war was the alternative to peace, rather than its agent. In so doing, *Saving Private Ryan* not only forged a bond between the American soldier and the domestic audience but also created a site of common identification between World War II audiences and post-Vietnam audiences, one that effaced rifts and fissures Vietnam had inflicted on American norms.

In *Saving Private Ryan*, Spielberg seems not only to have drawn on the same narratives as Basinger but also to have done so in such a way as to gloss her archive, exemplified by five prototypical World War II–era films, *Destination Tokyo*, *Bataan*, *Air Force*, *Sahara*, and *Guadalcanal Diary*, which Basinger uses to outline the tropes and details on which she bases her analysis of the genre. The fundamentals she identifies include that "the credits unfold against a military reference" (67), that "a group of men, led by a hero, undertake a mission which will accomplish an important military objective" (68), that "the hero has had leadership forced upon him in dire circumstances" (68), that episodes alternate "in uneven patterns . . . contrasting patterns of night and day, action and repose, safety and danger . . . comedy and tragedy" (68), that "military iconography is seen and its [use] demonstrated" (69), that "conflict breaks out within the group itself" (69), that "rituals are enacted" (69), that "members of the group die" (69), that "a climactic battle takes place" (69), and that "the audience is ennobled for having shared their combat experience" (69). Binns notes that the way *Saving Private Ryan* aligns with Basinger's rubric suggests that the film is "an archetypal World War II combat film" (39).[7]

FIGURE 2.01. *Sun shining through a washed-out portion of the American flag.* Saving Private Ryan *(1998).*

The military reference that begins *Saving Private Ryan* is an American flag flying over the site of the D-Day invasion. The flag, waving in a breeze, is situated between the camera and a light source (ostensibly the sun) so intense that the colors of the flag seem thin, washed out. The flag overwhelms the screen; we can only see a portion, perhaps two-thirds of it. The image is simultaneously very familiar—we immediately recognize the stars and stripes—and uncanny, too drained of color to be real, too cropped to have a comprehensible context. Is it supposed to suggest the battle-worn image that Francis Scott Key saw "by the dawn's early light" or some faded version thereof? And with whom do we share this gaze, a vision of the red, white, and blue, pallid almost to extinction? These questions—where is the flag? what does it stand for? to whom?—establish the film's impetus, and their answers unify its motifs.

As the sequence that follows indicates, the flag is flying on the Normandy coast, not far from a French flag, more than half a century after D-Day, over the vast graveyards of Ally casualties. An old man—Private Ryan, we later learn—who has returned to France, accompanied by his wife, children, and grandchildren, is in search of a specific grave. He walks ahead of his family, with difficulty but determination, as if on a mission. In their formation and exact number this group echoes the shots of Captain Miller's combat unit, which we will subsequently see crossing the French countryside in search of Ryan, whose three brothers had been killed in combat over the preceding week. The mission of this older Ryan is to pay homage to Miller, Basinger's "hero" upon whom the war had thrust "leadership." Looking for Miller's grave marker amid thousands of identical white crosses, Ryan recapitulates Miller's search for him, half a century earlier, "a needle in a stack of needles." Although Ryan's war is long over, his mission remains incomplete. He must find Miller in the same way that Miller found him; that is, he must come full circle, so that in finding Captain Miller, he can complete the mission of recovering himself, without which the saving (rescuing) of Private Ryan, lacking its commensurate saving (salvation) of Private Ryan, remains incomplete.

Completion is very much the issue in this film, in the same way that completion's absence is central to post–Mission Accomplished films. The attempt to preempt the complete destruction of Private Ryan's family or, perhaps more thematically important, the decimation of his generation—all the siblings— motivates the plot as well as the characters' metacommentary on that narrative. Ryan is the sole surviving son; his three brothers have been killed, and we do not know if his father is still alive. Confronted by the fact that his mother will, in the same day, receive three telegram notifications of her sons' deaths, General Marshall (Harve Presnell), referring to a letter written by Lincoln during the Civil War, decides they must spare Ryan's mother further grief.[8] If Marshall is moved by Lincoln's (not historically verified[9]) letter, he is more generally motivated by the spirit that Lincoln expressed in the Gettysburg Address, which very aptly glosses Spielberg's opening at the Normandy graveyard. About the men there, like those buried at Gettysburg, we can say: "from these honored dead we take increased devotion to that cause for which they gave their last full measure of devotion—that we here highly resolve that these dead shall not have died in vain."

This theme, rather than the visit to Normandy that symbolizes it, is what makes completing Ryan's mission possible, because his mission is to complete Miller's mission, so that the story of Miller's seeking to save the sole surviving Ryan begins and concludes with the surviving Ryan seeking to save his soul. John Biguenet initially concurred with the critics, even those who reviewed the film very favorably, who took issue with what they felt was the heavy-handed sentimentality of the film's opening and closing frame in the contemporary Normandy graveyard.[10] He explains succinctly, however, what he concluded in retrospect was so important about the scenes:

> As a grandfather and his son and grandchildren pay homage to those
> whose deaths we have just witnessed, the living are called not merely to

bear witness to the achievement of fallen heroes; the living are, in fact, the achievement itself. Like Private Ryan, we cannot help but ask what we've done to deserve such sacrifice by others and beg their forgiveness for what we have cost them. And like James Ryan, all we can do to justify that sacrifice is to live our lives as well as we are able.

In making his transition from the Normandy graveyard to the D-Day invasion half a century earlier, Spielberg establishes the connection between Miller's and Ryan's missions by suggesting their shared vision: The camera moves closer and closer to the elder Ryan's eyes. Although Ryan seems to be looking directly into the lens, Spielberg carefully observes the rule of the classical Hollywood style that generally avoids the direct reciprocal gaze between the character and the viewer, because establishing such reciprocity threatens to dissolve the cinematic fourth wall and, with it, the viewer's limited omniscience. Although we may be seeing Ryan's world, he does not see beyond the diegetic frame. Exactly the opposite: he is not remembering events but rather looking into the reality the film will present, attempting to penetrate the vision we will encounter, which memory and history have obscured. The camera pans very slightly to the left to prevent the elder Ryan from looking directly at us; so that, as the camera inches in on Ryan's face, it becomes clear that we are not being invited to look *at* Ryan, whose focus is elsewhere, but to look *with* him, seeing World War II not as he did in its presence, but as he does retrospectively, in a place as far from his home as his present perspective is from the war that has twice brought him to France.

A graphic match between the pattern of white crosses rhythmically arranged across a grass field and the crossed iron obstacles, known as "Czech hedgehogs," deployed along the Normandy beaches to impede amphibian assaults, connects the Normandy graveyard with the D-Day invasion. Although the cut implies that this beach is what Ryan is looking (back) upon, he cannot be doing so, because Ryan, a member of the 101st Airborne, parachuted into France (unlike one of his brothers, who, we subsequently see, had been killed on the beach). The camera's attention to Miller's eyes, echoing our intense focus on Ryan's, confirms that the senior Ryan is not recalling what he saw but rather trying to imagine what Miller saw when his unit approached the beach on the rough water beneath the cold gray June sky. The close-ups of Ryan's and Miller's eyes and the matching of the crosses thus imply a false, or at least incomplete, equation, an elaborate mathematics of warfare, that Basinger identified as characteristic of the World War II combat film: What is the cost of a life or the cost of taking one? The film's mission is thus to balance that equation. How do the war's decisions and sacrifices add up? And to what?

FIGURE 2.02A. *Crosses at the Normandy graveyard.* Saving Private Ryan *(1998).*

FIGURE 2.02B. *Czech hedgehogs along the Normandy shore.* Saving Private Ryan *(1998).*

Solving this equation, however, is confounded by the chaos of the invasion scene, in which death is as random as it is gruesome, as arbitrary as it is faceless. The bombs and bullets do not come from discernible enemies; the enemy is in fact completely out of sight. The dead are the victims of war itself, which is everywhere, a barrage of overlapping sights and sounds; rain and limbs and blood shower the GIs with equal intensity and indifference.[11] Slowly the enemy acquires a visible location in relation to those whom they are killing.

Although these specific agents of Hitler have been found, their Medusa-like presence is too dangerous to behold. Those whose natural curiosity overcomes their wartime precautions die, a sign, as Basinger points out, of the resilience of their nonmartial character; despite the war, they cannot shake their insistence on being ordinary, everyday Americans.

And like Medusa, the specific Nazi Gorgon confronting Miller's men is defeated with a mirror. Miller's makeshift mirror, held together by good old American chewing gum, makes it possible to target the Nazis, and the successful destruction of their machine-gun bunker stands in for all the small sites along the body-strewn beaches of France where coherent attacks emerge successfully out of inchoate violence.[12] Miller's unit, in other words, in fulfilling its mission to secure a pathway for some soldiers to get off the beach, represents all the comparable units that advanced the mission of D-Day. They did so by identifying the enemy's location and tactically destroying it. But if they make specific enemies pay for the soldiers killed on the beach, as the final panning of the beach full of ravaged bodies certifies, the incalculable cost makes meaningful compensation impossible. Other factors must be added to the equation before it can be balanced.

Although this pan of the beach parallels the pan earlier of the cemetery (fifty years later), representing the same American soldiers, in the same French location, participating in the same story, the vision Ryan shares with Miller is not what creates the equation between these two sites. Although the editing, organized around close-ups of their eyes, initially implies that the two men see the history that they share, the film reveals that they share very little history, if "history" means common experiences. In this way, "Spielberg signals that his reenactment of D-Day is to be taken not so much as a witness report than as a capacity for historical reimagination: a survivor's ability to reinvoke in his mind an experience that is his own because he is able to empathize with the vision of a man who was actually there" (Bronfen, 141). Thus combined, therefore, their gazes represent not their having common knowledge, but their sharing comparable quests: for Miller, to get home; for Ryan, to understand why he did, and Miller didn't. By inviting us to share their gaze and join in these quests, the film tasks the audience with balancing the equation, that is, with finding the formula that equates the two objectives.

Thus, on D-Day + 3 (replete with the maps, equipment, and paraphernalia that constitute what Basinger details as "military iconography"), when Lt. Col. Anderson (Dennis Farina) asks Miller for the body count of his unit, it marks the point when the film shifts from the question of taking a body count to making one body count, a process achieved by reducing all missions to one mission. This mathematical motif factors into the film's relentless attempt to recalculate the mission, so that, in the end, the equation will balance. After they set off in search of Ryan, Private Reiben (Ed Burns) says to Miller, "Can you explain the *math* of this to me. I mean where's the sense of risking the *eight* of us to save *one* guy?" [emphasis added]. In the same segment, Private Jackson (Barry Pepper), touting his sniper skills, says he thinks the "entire mission is a serious *misallocation* of valuable military resources" [emphasis added].

Later in the film, illustrating the consequences of misallocated resources, a pilot brings Miller to the site where his plane crashed, killing twenty-two soldiers, some of them high-ranking officers. As the pilot explains:

> Some fuckin' genius had the great idea of welding a couple of steel plates onto our deck, to keep the General safe from ground fire. Unfortunately they forgot to tell me about it until we were just getting airborne, so it was like trying to fly a freight train [. . .] I nearly broke both my arms trying to keep her level and when we released, you know, I cut as hard as I could [. . .] can't keep the altitude and keep from stalling. We came down like a fuckin' meteor. That's how we ended up [. . .]. We were just too goddam heavy, grass was wet, downward slope and all. Twenty-two guys dead. All that for a General—one man.

"There's a lot of that goin' around," Reiben responds, after which the pilot gives Miller a large bag of dog tags, "more than I really want to count," on the possibility that Ryan's is among them. For the audience, the transfer of this bag to Miller, because it might pertain to his mission, equates the pieces of tin with the equally anonymous mass of bodies covering the beach in the D-Day episode. In so doing it returns us to the film's distinction between taking a body count and making one body count. For Miller and his unit, the only name that counts in the abundance of tags is "Ryan"; the rest don't count, in the same way that the other three Ryan names didn't either. It was their anonymous deaths, as represented by the close-up of one Ryan, lying face down in the sand, that gives the final Ryan his identity.

Spending the night in the church of a town that, with the help of Miller's men, the Americans secured that afternoon, Miller again fixates on the mathematics of war in general, accentuated by the skewed equation informing their current mission. "When they end up killing one of your men," he says to his sergeant, Mike Horvath (Tom Sizemore), "you tell yourself it happened so that you could save the lives of two or three or ten others, maybe a hundred others. You know how many men I've lost under my command?" "How many?" Mike asks. "Ninety-four, but that means I've saved the lives of ten times that many, doesn't it? Maybe even twenty, huh? Twenty times? And that's how simple it is. That's how you . . . how you rationalize it—making the choice between the mission and the men." "Except this time," Mike says, "the mission is the man," to which Miller replies, "This Ryan better be worth it." There is not one soldier in Miller's unit, however, who does not realize how ridiculous their mission is, and thus how terrifying is the idea that they might not return home to save someone who, similarly, might not return home, for the terror of war is that termination may come before culmination. People sharing the same objective may not share the same outcome. This fact makes the mission to save Ryan less anomalous than representative of the bizarre economy endemic to war and the war film. Its infinite deferral of trade-offs creates a free market wherein the traders become indistinguishable from their tokens of exchange.

In exploring how Ryan is "worth it," Spielberg is doing what, according to Basinger, World War II combat movies typically do: "the attitudes that the audience should take to the war are taught [and the] tools of the cinema are employed to manipulate viewers into various emotional, cultural, and intellectual attitudes to help them achieve all other goals" (57).

The crucial war film attitude that the movie promotes, in this regard, is not toward war but toward home. The calculation, in other words, is not the tally of deaths, the number of uncounted dog tags in the bag Miller acquired, but rather the home life that lies in the balance. The brutal D-Day landing segment, therefore, ends with a cut to the War Office, using both visual and audio editing to equate the two sites. As on the Normandy beach, in the Washington office, sounds seem to come from everywhere, surrounding extreme close-ups of the faces of the women at this war site. Creating a general effect rather than conveying a focused message, rattling typewriters and clicking high-heeled shoes echo, albeit far less violently, the staccato of machine-gun fire amid the blur of overlapping voices, uttering partially heard phrases. Although the War Office is certainly more orderly than the Normandy beach, the death tally in the office is actually much higher and, at the outset, the intense close-ups and montage editing deny us, as the beach landing initially did, a coherent sense of the action or the agents.

The connection between the present-day Ryan, who opens the film at the site of D-Day, and the younger version of himself, who was part of the invasion that site commemorates, is further underscored in the War Office through two allusions to Bob Dole, a well-known public figure in 1998, having run unsuccessfully for vice president as Gerald Ford's running mate in 1976, and having lost to Bill Clinton for president just two years before *Saving Private Ryan* was released. Because Dole's heroic World War II service and his severe war injury, which had left one arm visibly incapacitated, were common knowledge, the sight of Colonel Bryce (Bryan Cranston) in the War Office with no left arm

FIGURE 2.03B. *Bob Dole. Source:* Topeka Capital-Journal. *Photographed by Pablo Martinez Monsivais at the Associated Press.*

FIGURE 2.03A. *Harve Presnell.* Saving Private Ryan *(1998).*

would no doubt elicit for many in the 1998 audience thoughts of Dole, reinforced by the very strong facial resemblance between Dole and Harve Presnell, portraying General Marshall, to whom Colonel Bryce brings the information about the dead Ryan brothers.

If these elements connect the War Office to the war front, nothing does so more than the barrage of rapid-fire deaths they both encompass. Both sequences, moreover, culminate their onslaught of mortality by focusing on the name "Ryan," first stenciled on the backpack of a soldier lying face-down on the wet sand and then typed on letters at the War Office.[13] In both cases, the imprinting reduces the person named, through an act of mechanical reproduction, to a label.

THE MISSION AND THE RIGHT TO GO HOME

From the moment in the War Office on, the film is organized around the tension between the need to restore Ryan's aura and the cost of doing so, as the characters, including Ryan himself, ask what is so special about him. One thing, referenced by several characters, that makes him special is his mother—ironically so, in that everyone has a mother—because she connects Ryan to a specific family and community, in fact, a small, agrarian community, where people know their neighbors. The sight from her kitchen window of the road winding to the door of her Iowa farm tells us immediately that she lives outside a town where anyone could tell you where the Ryan farm was. And if that farm represents the inhabitants of all American small towns, the winding road to the farmhouse, evoking as it does the path to an Iowa farm in the immensely successful *Field of Dreams* (1989), represents, as well, the cinematic symbolism ascribed to such places, the farm's quintessential "American" character.[14] Many of the shots in the short farmhouse sequence, as well as the details of Mrs. Ryan's domestic life shown in the moments before a car delivers news of the fatalities, feature Andrew Wyeth-like glimpses of a simple kitchen, views from dim interiors onto spreads of grass, through rustic windows, sometimes adorned by simple lace. The cast of light in these shots helps replicate the Wyeth palette: simple, muted, weatherworn earth tones, pale gray, tinged white, faded blue, the pervasive hues of unpainted wood, worn plaster, and grass muted to the verge of tan. When Mrs. Ryan sees the car slowly approaching, she opens the front door to greet it. From her dimly lit hallway, we see the dark silhouette of her entire body. It wobbles slightly as a man in uniform gets out of the front passenger seat, and, when a priest emerges from the back seat, her body falls to the floor, replicating the s-shape of the figure in Wyeth's most famous painting, *Christina's World*. Christina's world thus meets death on the field of dreams, in a collaboration of visuals that brand this moment pure Americana, that is, the thing every man in Miller's unit is fighting to preserve, the place, at least in spirit, to which each of them is trying to return, or, as the film puts it, to *earn the right* to do so.

Although at various moments the men lose sight of that point, they are reminded repeatedly that returning home is their ultimate mission, and that the right to do so must be earned by defeating Germany. Two scenes, one midway through the film and one near the end just prior to the Nazi attack on Ramelle, reiterate this point. In the first scene, Miller's unit has come across a Nazi machine-gun nest, which they could easily sneak around, as his men advocate doing, so that they can chance the fewest possible casualties in completing the mission to rescue Ryan. Miller, however, insists that they take the bunker out rather than ignore it because doing otherwise would permit the Nazis to kill other American soldiers.

Again, mathematics comes into play. If the mission is to rescue Ryan, then each man they lose in the process—they had already lost Caparzo (Vin Diesel) to sniper fire in the town they had just left—makes the equation harder to balance. Caparzo, reflecting one of the caveats identified by Basinger, confuses the combat zone with normal life back home. Attempting to rescue a nine-year-old French girl, who resembles his niece, from a partially destroyed

FIGURE 2.04. *Mrs. Ryan, fallen to the porch floor of her farmhouse.* Saving Private Ryan *(1998).*

building, Caparzo allows himself, despite his ostensible toughness, to confuse the normal behavior of peacetime with the contradictions imposed by the extraordinary conditions of wartime. Standing with the girl in his arms instead of taking cover, he falls prey to sniper fire. "Seems like an unnecessary risk," Melish (Adam Goldberg) says about taking out the machine-gun nest, "given our objective." But Miller responds by reminding Melish, along with the other men, all of whom are still smarting from the loss of Caparzo, that "Our objective is to win the war."

The loss of the medic, Wade (Giovanni Ribisi), in the successful assault on the nest further complicates the issue because the successful action, which was, arguably, ancillary to their mission, skews the math enough to threaten the efficacy of the entire mission, even more so when Miller blindfolds a captured Nazi and sends him down the road with instructions to surrender to the first American unit he finds. That they are burying Wade while sparing one of the Nazi soldiers responsible for his death makes the equation, for some of the men, untenable. When Reiben refuses Miller's order to go on, Mike threatens to shoot him if he disobeys it. To end this near-fatal impasse, Miller once again rebalances the equation by replacing the mission to defeat Germany with the objective of earning the right to go home. Having refused, up until this point, to reveal any information about his own background, that is, about his peacetime identity, he interrupts the altercation between Reiben, who is about to abandon the unit, and Mike, who has a gun pointed at Reiben's head.

"I'm a schoolteacher," Miller says. "I teach English composition, for the last eleven years at Thomas Alva Edison High School. Coach the baseball team in the springtime. Back home, I tell people what I do for a living, they say, well that figures. But over here, that's a big, a big mystery. So I guess I've changed some. Sometimes I wonder if I've changed so much my wife isn't going to recognize me, whenever it is I get back to her . . . I mean, how I'll ever be able to tell her about days like today. Ah—Ryan. I don't know anything about Ryan. I don't care. That man means nothing to me. It's just a name. But if going to Ramelle and finding him so that he can get home—if that earns me the right to get back to my wife, well then . . . then that's my mission. [. . .] I just know every man I kill, the further away from home I feel."

In defining the mission this way, Miller once again unites his small unit, a task that must be undertaken one more time when they find Private Ryan and he rejects the objective of their mission. Standing beside the ravaged remains of his own unit, which, until reinforcements can secure the strategic site, is desperately attempting to protect a bridge from imminent Nazi assault, Ryan raises the same question posed by Miller and his men: "It doesn't make any sense to me, sir. Why? Why do I deserve to go? Why not any of these guys? They all fought just as hard as me." If saving Private Ryan helps *earn* Miller's men the right to go home, then Ryan hasn't done anything to earn that right for himself. As he points out, he has done nothing more than the other men, whom he will be leaving behind in what amounts to a suicide effort to keep General Rommel from blocking the Allied advance on Paris. Asked what they should tell his mother, Ryan says, "Tell her you found me. I was here, and I was with the only brothers I have left. And there was no way I was gonna desert them. I think she'll understand that." In other words, Private Ryan discounted the War Office's attempt to make his body count more than the total body count of the battle of Ramelle, or of D-Day, or of World War II.

This leads Mike to reconsider the mission to save Private Ryan in light of the lessons that Miller has been teaching the men. "Part of me," Mike tells Miller, "thinks the kid's right. What's he gonna do to deserve this? He wants to stay here, fine. Let him stay, and let's go home. But another part of me thinks, what if by some miracle we stay and actually make it outta here? Some day we might look back on this and decide that saving Private Ryan was the one decent thing we were able to pull out of this whole Godawful, shitty mess . . . Like you said, Captain, we do that we all earn the right to go home."

In effect, what Ryan did, via Mike, was to teach Miller his own lesson.

Home is what is earned by protecting it. Until there is peacetime, there is no home—part of the point of films such as *Mrs. Miniver* and *Since You Went Away*—and peacetime is only earned through warfare. In the film's concluding battle, most of the men in Miller's unit, including Miller, who have earned the right to go home, die in the process of doing so. Of the unit, only Reiben and the translator, Corporal Upham (Jeremy Davies), survive the battle, along with the "saved" Ryan, who returns stateside with the knowledge that he has reaped what the men who died saving him and protecting the bridge at Ramelle have earned. Miller, with his dying breath, charges Ryan with the burden of that knowledge: "Earn this! Earn it!"

Miller is telling Ryan, in other words, to earn after the war what Miller and most of his unit have earned in saving him. If, throughout the film, Ryan's life was so overvalued as to make the mission irrational, Miller's demand to him devalues it in comparison to the lives of Miller's men, such that Ryan is charged with balancing the equation by making the rest of his life equal the loss of theirs. Whatever burden this places on Ryan, however, the audience's perspective on the story allows it to know that none of the men who died did so saving Ryan. Each of the events that cost lives—the encounter in the first town, which they help secure, the machine-gun nest that they take out, and the battle at Ramelle—were all in the interest of defeating Hitler instead of saving Ryan.

We can see, therefore, that the equation finally makes sense because the men never really lost sight of the war's true mission, which was to force the Axis surrender that leads to peace. In this way, Spielberg not only underscores the symbiosis of wartime and peacetime but also the way in which peacetime serves as the ostensible cultural norm only because it exists as the spoils of war. For this reason, the "mission" remains the crucial concept in defining wartime. Without it, risks are rent from their purpose, turning the body count into an infinite regress, and thereby making the equation between the sacrifices of wartime and the rewards of peacetime impossible to balance.

The point that I have been making is that the traditional American war film, as indicated by its prolific infusion of the domestic, required that war not be professional. For American soldiers, war was always an aberration, one that could not, that must not, eliminate inscriptions of the peace that remains normalizing and normative. One aspect of meeting this requirement is the knowledge that each moment of combat is part of a larger mission, whether it is to bomb a target, take a hill, or invade Normandy or Guadalcanal, and achieving that objective is part of the greater narrative of restoring the peace. Ultimately, therefore, all marches and movements are, in effect, peace marches, anti-war movements.

CHAPTER 3

LOST IN IRAQ AND THE COLLAPSE OF WARTIME

Although *Saving Private Ryan* consolidated the quintessence of classic studio-era war films, it did so only a few years after the first Iraq War, Desert Storm, in 1991. That brief war, remembered by many as much for its abrupt withdrawal as for its rapid conquest, seemed to reject the narrative arc of wartime despite succeeding at its military objectives. Meeting with little battlefield resistance, US troops advanced rapidly toward Baghdad without ever reaching it or engaging the Iraqi Army delegated to protect it. Instead, without completing the conquest, receiving (or even demanding) a surrender, a ceasefire paved the way for the half million US troops to leave the country, its leadership intact and in charge. Although Kuwait's sovereignty had been restored, the enemy had not really been defeated, and the story had no arc.[1] The history of that war, in other words, could not provide a scaffold for any of the conventions of wartime (either on the home front or the battlefront) that would be consolidated seven years later by Steven Spielberg. As James Fallows points out, in our history, "When fighting not organized enemies but stateless foes, we have underestimated our vulnerability" (5).

Five years after *Saving Private Ryan*, a second Iraq War, in very different and much more complex ways, would also prove incapable of supporting the themes and tropes of the American war film that *Saving Private Ryan* essentialized. Because that incapacity is the subject of this book, it is necessary to understand in some detail the Iraq War and the narratives surrounding it. Most significantly, Iraq was defeated—as President Bush (George II)'s proclamation "Mission Accomplished" announced—and simultaneously liberated: "We gave them freedom. What else do they want?" pondered Rumsfeld. These classifications, "defeated" and "liberated," however, were not only rhetorical but cinematic. The administration had in effect imported them from traditional war films tropes meant to truncate the denouement in accordance with the codes of cinematic representation endemic to the classical Hollywood style.[2] Thus, just as the imagery of cheering civilians showering the invading army with flowers metonymically represents the trappings of surrender and the gradual, controlled return to sovereignty, the post–Iraq War rhetoric attempted to produce the narrative that culminates in a postwar nation, without the requisite surrender and its attendant measures for stabilizing civic order. These bureaucratic activities do not make for compelling film-watching, and clearly the planning for the post–Iraq War effort was based not on the principles of military procedure, international law, or common governance practices, but on the principles that structure Hollywood films. For cinematic purposes, the end of war films makes no distinction between the liberated and the conquered so that the filmmakers can dispense with the visually boring labor of obtaining an unconditional surrender, negotiating a treaty, and administering an Occupation.

The confusion of military planning and moviemaking is evident in Rumsfeld's disappointment that, in the postwar chaos, "There were precious few Mr. Smiths (as in the Jimmy Stewart movie) in the world" (Rumsfeld, 506). If Rumsfeld's citing a cinematic character betrays a troubling inability to distinguish movies from reality, his choice of *Mr. Smith Goes to Washington* suggests the even more disturbing revelation that Rumsfeld had not been able to follow the plot of a Frank Capra movie. The film is about a naïve freshman senator who uses a one-man filibuster to secure a summer camp for inner-city children, foiling his senior colleague's real estate scheme. Certainly, Rumsfeld did not think Iraq's rampant looting, sectarian violence, guerrilla warfare, and economic collapse could be remedied by an Iraqi idealist, like Stewart's Mr. Smith, with the courage to stage a lone filibuster? And certainly he knew that securing land for a summer camp was not analogous to securing street safety in a city of eight million, with tens of thousands of unemployed soldiers who had neither surrendered nor turned in their arms. Rather, he seems to have turned to the comforting neatness of a Hollywood narrative structure to avoid the messiness of tactical complexity and intricate planning. The Hollywood style was designed exactly for the purpose of giving viewers respite from the tactical demands of their personal lives by providing a couple of hours during which they did not have to work to secure rewarding outcomes.

Because the traditional American war film, as we have noted, highlights the GIs' having earned the right to go home, the Hollywood ending announces the normal life Americans will resume; it is unconcerned with the conditions of the defeated country and the measures for restoring orderly civil governance con-

FIGURE 3.01. *President Bush's "Mission Accomplished." Photographed by Stephen Jaffe.*

sistent with political stability, international security, and human rights. Since, when a film ends, the characters cease to exist, the obligations of the victor are immaterial to the filmmaker. (Just as we do not have to worry, after Hamlet dies, about the measures that Fortinbras takes to establish his rule in Denmark, or how his actions contribute to the country's welfare.) The Fourth Geneva Convention (1949) delineates the duties—e.g., preserving the peace, protecting hospitals—to which an occupying power is obliged.[3] International law thus makes the victors in a war accountable for the condition of the vanquished, while filmmakers are only accountable to the audience, a group that leaves the theater and movie-time shortly after the action ceases. And clearly playing to an audience—certainly the American audience, possibly the world audience, and less likely the Arab world or the Iraqi audience (the only audience directly impacted by the absence of Occupation plans)—Bush-Cheney-Rumsfeld simply claimed the role of "liberator" in place of "occupier." By reducing the war's denouement to a scriptwriting and casting decision, Bush-Cheney-Rumsfeld rid the nation of its legal and moral obligations.

THE "GOOD WAR" OCCUPATION

Given the radical difference between a war and a war film, Bush-Cheney-Rumsfeld should have had no trouble differentiating a movie theater from a theater of operations. But the administration's disdain for creating the conditions that make Occupation possible indicates that was not the case, especially when contrasted with the elaborate negotiations entailed in Japan's unconditional surrender and the detailed planning of the Japanese Occupation.

The general terms of the surrender, first issued by Truman and Churchill on July 26, 1945, were, after deliberation and negotiations, assented to by Emperor Hirohito on August 15, 1945. That public assent provided the basis for the post-surrender agreements prior to the actual surrender ceremony, which took place two weeks later, aboard the USS *Missouri*, docked in Tokyo Bay. At that ceremony—immediately preceded by nearly two thousand American aircraft flying in formation overhead—a delegation headed by the Japanese foreign minister in formal attire (striped trousers and morning coat) and the chief of the Imperial Army, also in formal attire, was met by General Douglas MacArthur, wearing casual summer khakis, at the forefront of an assembly of leaders from eleven Allied countries. The flag that had flown over the White House on Pearl Harbor Day flew from the *Missouri*'s mast, and encased in glass was the Stars and Stripes that had been on Commodore Perry's flagship when his 1853 voyage marked the "opening" of Japan to the West. MacArthur, a great showman, understood how the scene vividly captured the diminution of Japanese power, the extent of enemy capitulation, and the historical parameters that framed American domination of the vanquished. This ceremony did not end the war—as it might have ended a movie about the war—but rather served as symbolic confirmation of hard-fought and costly military victories, of rigorous demands, and of unconditional compliance.

In the case of the Iraq War, however, instead of ending the war diplomatically or militarily, Bush-Cheney-Rumsfeld concluded it cinematically, with the image of a jet landing on an aircraft carrier and a commander-in-chief in costume. Unlike the USS *Missouri*, the carrier was not anchored in waters captured from the enemy but at the periphery of a vista borrowed from the San Diego Padres. Absent were most other members of Bush's "Coalition of the Willing"; absent was the American flag that had been flying over the White House when hijacked airplanes were used in a massive foreign attack on America soil neither planned nor executed by Iraq, which was not at that time developing weapons of mass destruction. And crucially absent was the enemy from whom the United States had extracted an unconditional surrender, requisite for legitimizing any ceremony symbolizing the accomplishment of the war's mission, the bilateral confirmation of a victor. Rather than an accomplished mission, these omissions made the landing in San Diego a staged commercial for one, an unintentional parody of the ceremony in Tokyo Bay half a century earlier.

The defects involved in simulating the end of the war, however, pale in comparison to the folly of occupying a country that has not surrendered. Again, comparison with World War II proves instructive. "America's pre-surrender planning for Japan," according to Takemae Eiji, "began in a general sense with a declaration of overreaching principles formulated more than a year and a half *before hostilities broke out*. . . . They laid down a framework that delineated basic rights and obligations and was anchored in international law. By the time of Japan's surrender, a detailed master plan for occupation tailored to that country's precise conditions and requirements had been perfected" (202) [emphasis added]. In 1942, to implement this plan, the War Department set up the School of Military Governance at the University of Virginia; in 1943, at Columbia University; and in 1944 at Princeton. These schools offered instruction in the geography, history, culture, economy, government, and language of the areas slated for occupation. In 1944, Civil Affairs Training Schools were instituted at Harvard, Yale, Chicago, Stanford, Michigan, and Northwestern, allowing officers to study with the premier scholars in Asian studies. After six months, the officers were required to write a specialized paper—something akin to a master's thesis—and after graduating to spend two months studying at an Army-Navy Affairs Staging Area. The government produced numerous special handbooks, guides, and teaching materials for the occupying officers and administrators that contained both facts and "policy alternatives" (208). The occupation plans created an extensive organization of separate offices charged with overseeing Japanese governmental affairs, Japanese economy, industry, finance, labor relations, science, technology, information, education, natural resources, public health and welfare, communications, and transportation. This was all implemented with the cooperation of the defeated regime, such that "MacArthur wielded his authority indirectly, via *existing* civil administration" (212) [emphasis added], with an elaborate table of organization in which the Japanese reported to and took instructions from the occupying force. The Japanese assumed responsibility for disarming their own soldiers and kept detailed records of the process.

"America's two most successful occupations embraced the idea the military officials must play political roles," James Fallows pointed out. "Douglas MacArthur, a lifelong soldier, was immersed in the detailed reconstruction of Japan's domestic order [but] today's Joint Chiefs of Staff would try to veto any suggestion of a MacArthur-like proconsul. . . . The first month, therefore, [Iraq's] occupiers would face a paradox: the institution best equipped to exercise power was a local government—the U.S. military—but it would be the one most reluctant to do so" (27).

LOST ON RUMSFELD

This reluctance was just one symptom of Rumsfeld's abhorrence of planning. In describing the run-up to the war, Thomas Ricks explains the reason several generals were not "happy with the war plans [General Tommy] Franks was bringing back from his meetings with Rumsfeld" (75). Army Lt. Gen. David McKiernan "couldn't get Franks to issue clear orders that stated explicitly what he wanted done, how he wanted to do it, and why. Rather, Franks passed along PowerPoint briefing slides that he had shown to Rumsfeld. . . . '[T]hat is frustrating, [McKiernan felt] because nobody wants to plan against PowerPoint slides.' That reliance on slides rather than formal written orders seemed to some military professionals to capture the essence of Rumsfeld's amateurish approach to war planning" (75). If the planning of the war was "amateurish," even more so was the nonplanning for what followed. According to Maj. Isaiah Wilson, "who served as an official Army historian during the spring 2003 invasion . . . 'there was no Phase IV plan' for occupying Iraq after the combat phase" (Ricks, 110). The reason, Ricks explains, is that the plan "was founded on three basic assumptions, all of which ultimately would prove false" (110). These were that a large number of Iraqi security forces would be willing to support the occupation, "that the international community would pick up the slack from the U.S. military," and that "an Iraqi government would quickly spring into being" (110).

The lack of adequate planning for managing postwar Iraq can be costed out in numerous ways, including the enormous hole it left in the American national debt and the number of American lives lost after the Non-Occupation commenced. While there were no casualties during the Occupation of Japan, the United States lost more than four thousand troops after the May 1, 2003, "Mission Accomplished" declaration. If this statistic indicates the war's incompatibility with wartime, it also explains why the war was unsuitable for movie-time, since incoherent themes and objectives are best dramatized by an open-ended television series.

Although many television series have reflected the consequences of 9/11, none seems as dedicated to the moment of impact itself as does the first season of *Lost*, which mirrors the dilemmas and contradictions of the post–Mission Accomplished war, its confusing and conflicting goals, and its inability to coordinate plans for dealing with these problems. Several factors impel limiting the focus of this discussion: It is not only impractical to discuss fully *Lost*'s one hundred-plus hours of events and characters, but it is also impossible to reconcile responsibly the 121 episodes, each containing several narrative threads, to a coherent set of cultural narratives without accounting for the exigencies of a network television series with its array of writers, directors, and producers, all attempting to retain old viewers while attracting new ones, and also dealing with the financial impossibility of filming twenty-four episodes a year with large casts on location in Hawaii.

The series also had the need to remain open-ended while not appearing to have loose ends. This appearance was facilitated by a duplicitous relationship between the sponsoring network and the series's creators, who promised "that [each episode] requires NO knowledge of the episode(s) that preceded it . . . there is no 'Ultimate Mystery' which requires solving," a promise that categorically belied their true intention.[4] Instead, the creators insisted on a coherent objective—a mystery full of questions and clues—without any formulated plan or solution. In this regard, the series all too closely resembled, from inception to conclusion, the Iraq war fiasco, so dubbed by Ricks's acclaimed book on the war.

It is worth briefly noting, however, that *Lost*, like the Iraq War, manifested a proliferation of attacks and retributions, an aura of dubious or absent culpability, and an escalating loss of purpose in attempting to deal with its inability to make long-term plans over its six-year run; it presented a mayhem of divided leadership and an unending search for villains, caches, insurgents, and sources of sectarian violence. The ongoing debates about whether to destroy or save the place the survivors had occupied served, moreover, to muddy rather than clarify the issues, while the escalating violence and the omnipresent threat of violence, not to mention the tacit indifference in the series to outright homicide, seemed to justify physical and psychological torture, unrestrained by legal precedent or civil convention. And if the legitimacy of the numerous leaders over the six *Lost* years is as murky as is their judgment, sense of justice, or respect for democracy, what remains clear is that *Lost*'s leaders could no more devise a successful exit strategy than the US military in Iraq. Testifying at a Senate hearing, General Anthony Zinni told the Foreign Relations Committee that they should abandon the idea of an exit strategy "because there isn't going to be one" (Ricks, 87).

Although *Lost* did not allegorize the disastrous US entanglement with Iraq, its production continued to adhere to a common cultural narrative about an inability to produce a validating narrative or to narrativize a successful way to deal with that inability. As Fallows has pointed out, with the failure of each justifying narrative for the war, a new one was foregrounded. The absence of WMDs undermined the narrative that the United States invaded to seize them; the growth of insurgency when Saddam was captured discredited the "next Hitler" narrative; the insistence that Iraq was being liberated rather than occupied was refuted by the exigencies of daily life in the country. When these narratives lost their credibility, the next reason for invading Iraq was to make it a beacon of democracy, even though, before the war, Fallows points out, claims about establishing Iraq as an Arab democracy "had taken a very, very distant second place to warnings about the immediate threat of Iraq's weapons" (11).

THE SECOND PEARL HARBOR

In February 2004, in preparation for filming the two-hour pilot of *Lost*, thousands of tons of a cut-apart Lockheed L-1011 began arriving in Hawaii. The series, which premiered September 22, 2004, follows the survivors of a plane crash who find themselves stranded on an apparently uncharted island, a mysterious South Pacific place resembling "Bali Ha'i" because there, à la the Rodgers and Hammerstein song, "Your own special hopes / Your own special dreams / Bloom on the hillside / And shine in the streams."[5] This magical place, both inviting and menacing, has provided the *Lost* characters a setting where they gradually discover that a second chance entails not fleeing one's past but returning to it. Like Bali Ha'i, also an escape bracketed by an ongoing war, this place seems to be saying "Here am I your special island / Come to me . . . Come to me."[6] In the same way that the characters in *Lost*'s wide-body airplane return both on the island and in their memories to the conflicts that led them to this place, the airplane body parts that would constitute the show's 9/11 mise-en-scène must pass through Pearl Harbor, the site of the only other substantial foreign attack on US soil.

Underscoring *Lost*'s connection to the heart of the Iraq War's darkness, the opening segment, with smoke, fire, airplane fragments, dazed or bloody men and women in sooty business attire, alternately staggering and running, dodging debris and secondary explosions, creates a tropical collage of the imagery associated with 9/11. The fourth episode even concludes with a memorial service in which Claire (Emilie de Ravin), a young, pregnant Australian girl,[7] provides brief bits of information about the departed. Because Claire, like the other survivors, hardly knew the departed, her comments ("Judith Martha Wexler, from Denton, Texas. I guess she was going to catch a connecting flight. She wore corrective lenses, and she was an organ donor, or at least would have been. Steve and Kristin . . . I don't know their last name, but . . . ah . . . they were really in love and were going to be married. At least wherever they are now, they're not alone") echo truncated versions of the short obituaries gleaned from available details run by the *New York Times* after the attack.[8]

This focus on the initial impact is also reflected by several "first-responder" events, interspersed with flashbacks raising questions about the collision of personal crisis with mass catastrophe, the implicit search to connect biography and history that characterizes much post-9/11 narrative. *Lost* also typi-

FIGURES 3.02A *and* **3.02B.** Lost *(2004–2010) characters amid 9/11-like plane crash debris.*

fies the post-9/11 moment's obsession with the ongoing threat, represented by the mysterious forces—beasts and, later, humans—that inhabit the place into which an incident of terror has plunged the survivors. These current threats often seem connected with their past, but in an uncertain way, conflating projected fears with imagined retribution, just as Bush and many of his aides and supporters—who saw what he regarded as his father's inability to eliminate saddam Hussein as emasculating—fetishized Iraq as both the source and the object of retribution.[9]

Because, in the War on Terror—by definition, a war impelled by a narrative of imagined violence—the weapons of mass destruction are missing objects that focus the violence that has never occurred, the Iraq War functions as a fetish, that is, a concrete object—in this case, a concrete place—that attempts to replace the violence elsewhere, thereby remasculinizing its consequences. Lest the toppling of the nation's tallest erections prove to be a literal as well as a symbolic emasculation, the Bush administration immediately diverted its eyes, denying the anxiety 9/11 evoked by investing an alien object with power that it did not inherently have. As former CIA Director James Woolsey told Fallows on *September 12*, "'We don't know where this attack came from . . . [b]ut the response has to involve Iraq'—by which," Fallows explains, "he meant not that blame had to be pinned on Saddam Hussein but instead that the United States had to go to the root of its long-term problems in the Middle East, which to Woolsey and others . . . meant Iraq" (xi). Echoing this fetishism, in the summer of 2003, Condoleezza Rice called Paul Bremer III, who led the US occupation of Iraq from May 2, 2003, until June 28, 2004, "to ask how she could help. 'Colin and I are convinced that Iraq has become the decisive theater in the war on terrorism, and that if we can win in Iraq, Islamic terrorism can be defeated" (Bremer, 143).

In that context, *Lost* reflects an American cultural narrative that fetishized Iraq. As Leo Bersani and Ulysse Dutoit point out, however, "the fetish can't replace or re-place anything, since it signifies something that was never any-where" (69). Thus, by extending to its logical limits the necessarily arbitrary selection endemic to the act of fetishizing, the administration turned Iraq into the matrix of terrorism, the site of the imaginary violence that threatened to emasculate the United States or, at least, its largely chicken-hawk leadership. As *Lost* makes clear, this policy made Iraq virtually indistinguishable from an off-the-charts Pacific fantasy island.

SURVIVOR MEETS CLUB MED

Within its broad parallels with the war, *Lost*'s first season seems more emphatically to retain the post-9/11 sensibility informing its inception, for the show's title describes not only the marooned air travelers, but also everything that these travelers cannot find. Because the flashbacks indicate that most of the travelers were engaged in psychological as well as physical flight, their air trip tropes their ontological status; they have lost their future—as represented by unachieved goals, missed appointments, unfulfilled desires—and they have lost their direction. Moreover, they have lost—or so it initially appears—their lifestyle. Scattered on the beach is the wreckage of an affluent civilization at sea.

The fate of this wreckage, resulting from a miraculous crash severing the plane into three parts, focuses chiefly on the middle section. This relatively unscathed middle class (in flashback, two of the travelers complain about having been bounced from first class) endures its beach limbo that merges *Survivor* with Club Med. In fact, throughout the first season, the survivors behave as though they were participating in a task-driven competition meant to insure they survive the short, temporally delimited parameters of a game show on which they have been made unwitting contestants. Thus, they undertake a series of defined tasks, such as hiking a mountain, catching fish with a spear, or placing an antenna on the top of a tree. In the evenings they have periodic campfire gatherings resembling the tribal votes on *Survivor*, and at one point four survivors tasked with constructing a raft have an internal disagreement. When this almost leads to the replacement of Sawyer (a good-looking, irreverent con man), he directly alludes to *Survivor*, asking, "Are you voting me off the raft?"

At the same time, the first season of *Lost* retains the aura of a quasi-rustic tropical resort. Although that environment may seem antithetical to the world of the reality game show, Club Med bears an interesting kinship to *Survivor*. As with *Survivor*, where the bare necessities of the competition and the abundance entailed in victory become indistinguishable, the antimaterialism at the original Club Med, a French resort founded in 1950, was itself highly commodified. Sleeping on cots in Army surplus tents at a resort on Majorca, provided with sports equipment and a small orchestra, the guests "swam, played sports, ate at tables for eight, and were entertained at night by flamenco dancers. Yet, after varying troubles, including a hurricane, people met and demanded their money back" (Furlough, 67). As Ellen Furlough astutely explains, "Club Med's 'formula' expressed, and helped consolidate, the orienting practices, attitudes, and values of the 'new' French middle class during what has been termed 'the postwar regime of accumulation'" (66). Like the contestants on *Survivor* and their 1950s predecessors at Club Med, the *Lost* characters inhabit a *pseudo-Darwinian* world.

As Mark Andrejevic has pointed out about *Survivor*,

In the crudest terms, we are faced with the opposition between naturalized ideology and the reality of human contrivance as such. The standard assumption is that the process of fetishization—whereby a product of human activity is misrecognized as a force of nature—operates on the basis of this opposition. Against [this] background . . . a third stance emerges [that] concedes the contrivance of reality, while nonetheless refusing to entertain the possibility that "things could be otherwise." We are left with the defining formulation of contemporary capitalism: the "jungle" of the marketplace is a human creation, but it is beyond human control. (204)

Andrejevic's analysis of *Survivor* strikingly glosses both the War on Terror and the tenets of *Lost*. The circumstances framing the invasion of Iraq were as contrived as was the reality of *Survivor*. The contrivances included not just the invention of the WMDs or the casting of Saddam as Hitler, but the construction of generic terror, like generic survival, as a totalizing environment. Wherever one attacks, one is attacking terror; whatever the mechanisms of acquisition, one is enacting the marketplace's survival of the fittest.

Thus, the *Lost* survivors, even though plunged into terror, retain the trappings of their consumerist lives. As *Survivor* graphically illustrates, the two conditions are interdependent aspects of the marketplace narrative. It is as if *Lost* had captured the midsection of the Boeing 757 just as it struck the World Trade Center, leaving the (predominantly) American travelers to contemplate what led to this collision and what to do in its wake, and empowering them, at the exact moment of impact, to heed both of President Bush's post-9/11 dictates: accept the ethos of the security state *and* don't let that alter your life. In his November 2001 speech on homeland security, Bush said: "Our nation faces a threat to our freedoms, and the stakes could not be higher. We are the target of enemies who boast they want to kill: kill all Americans, kill all Jews and kill all Christians." In a speech he delivered at O'Hare Airport a little over a month earlier, he urged Americans to "Fly and enjoy America's great destination spots. Go down to Disney World in Florida, take your families, and enjoy life the way we want it to be enjoyed." As *Time* writer Frank Pellegrini said in *praise* of Bush's post-9/11 speech, the president urged Americans to "be patient, patient, patient, at airports and skyscrapers and landmarks and hotels and traffic stops and bus stops and train stations and anywhere else it is possible to imagine a public vulnerability, which of course is everywhere. And for God's sake keep shopping."

The vagaries of Pellegrini's praise, in relation to the public's responsibilities, are consistent with those aspects of Bush's speech ("I ask you to live your lives and hug your children . . . I ask you to uphold the values of America and remember why so many have come here"), vagaries echoed in *Lost* episode five in an announcement by Jack (Matthew Fox), a doctor who is bringing the body of his deceased, alcoholic father back the United States, to the assembled survivors: "If you don't want to go to the cave, then find another way to contribute."

WAR AS A FAITH-BASED INITIATIVE

Lost started shooting not only after Bush's speeches in the wake of 9/11 but also after his "Mission Accomplished" speech and after the failure to find WMDs. In fact, five days after shooting began, Bush, at a black-tie Washington event, showed a slide of himself looking under furniture in the Oval Office. "Those weapons of mass destruction have got to be somewhere," he told the audience, then made similar remarks about two more slides. Once again, Bush was inadvertently engaged in fetishizing 9/11, embarking on the pointless search for the source of the terror that emasculates him. The ostensible mission in which the Iraq War was grounded was actually a mission impossible, an attempt to discover and retrieve not the instrument of the violence against the Twin Towers, but the emasculating violence in the American psyche that the attack instrumentalized. If Bush's obsession with nonexistent weapons may have been particularly puerile, as the harsh criticism of this presidential frat-boy-with-a-twang frivolity demonstrated,[10] the aim of his humor was as lost on the general public as was the aim of his policy on the people who were making it.

"[General Tommy] Franks, [Donald] Rumsfeld, [Paul] Wolfowitz, [Douglas] Feith . . . and other top officials," Ricks notes, "spent well over a year planning to attack Iraq, but treated almost casually what would come after that. 'I think people are overly pessimistic about the aftermath,' Wolfowitz flatly stated" three months before the invasion (78). If Wolfowitz's lack of pessimism stemmed from a surfeit of ignorance, his attitude was not accidental but rather consistent with Rumsfeld's management philosophy. As Fallows emphatically states, "On the basis of all available evidence, it appears that the very people who were most insistent on the need to invade Iraq were most negligent about what would happen next" (222). Feith, Rumsfeld's undersecretary of defense for policy, explained to Fallows, "We don't exactly deal with 'expectations.' Expectations are too close to 'predictions.' We're not comfortable with predictions" (Fallows, 45). Rumsfeld, he emphasized, "is death to prediction" (Fallows, 45).

In the absence of predictions and of the process that formulates them (commonly known as "planning"), the administration was in the de facto position of putting more than one hundred thousand American soldiers and the entire American economy at risk, based purely on faith. In the preface to his eight-hundred-page memoir, *Known and Unknown*, Rumsfeld quoted his now infamous engagement with uncertainty:

. . . as we know, there are known knowns: there are things we know we know. We also know there are known unknowns: that is to say we know there are some things [we know] we do not know. But there are also some unknown unknowns—the ones we don't know we don't know. (xv)

That this mélange of tautologies sounds like gibberish is less interesting than that the gibberish is not epistemological but *theological*, as it has little to do with the nature or limit of knowledge but with everything for which knowledge proves inadequate, that is, the world of the Unknown, which lies beyond the scope of empirical discovery. By definition, "unknown unknowns" cannot be hypothesized and thus cannot be subject to legitimate empirical tests.

As Feith noted, "You will not find a single piece of paper . . . If anybody ever went through all of our records . . . nobody will find a single piece of paper that says, 'Mr. Secretary or Mr. President, let me tell you what postwar Iraq is going to look like, and here is what we need to plan for.' If you tried that, you would get thrown out of Rumsfeld's office so fast—if you ever [said] 'let me tell you what something's going to look like in the future,' you wouldn't get to your next sentence" (quoted in Fallows, 45). Operating from this Zen-of-ignorance perspective, Rumsfeld understandably disdained predictions, which infringed on the Unknown, that is, the realm of faith.

Faith, coincidentally, underpinned the mode of policymaking with which the Bush administration was most comfortable. "Not long after taking office in 2001," James Hoopes notes, "[Bush] began opening cabinet meetings with a prayer" (85). After he took office, Bush created by executive order the White House Office of Faith-based and Community Initiatives, the aim of which was to facilitate funding of (ostensibly nonreligious) community organizations run by religious groups. This initiative came under criticism from secular groups such as the ACLU, which held that the office violated the establishment clause of the Constitution.

Of Bush's many faith-based initiatives, the most grotesque, I believe, was the Iraq War. Although the war, like the religion-supported activities that the administration funded, was figured as charitable—liberating Iraqis—Bush often used language evoking the (Christian) Crusades. According to former CIA intelligence officer Michael Scheuer, moreover, Rumsfeld defined "self-determination" in Iraq "as the creation of any government as long as it is not Islamic" (Fallows, 46). Most significantly, Blackwater, a major mercenary force of private contractors that augmented the US military action (without commensurate accountability) overtly sought to advance Christianity by killing Muslims.[11]

Tragically for both the Iraqis and the American GIs, the war's planning was as faith-based as its impetus. It was expected, for example, that "Iraqi commanders in the south would surrender and even bring their forces over to the side of the Americans by the thousands [but] not one commander did so" (Ricks, 118). Similarly, faith precluded detainees. "The War plan had called for the Iraqi population to cheerfully greet the American liberators, quickly establish a new government, and wave farewell to the departing American troops" (Ricks, 291). Subsequently, "'the realization dawned . . . that pre-war planning had not included . . . detainee operations,' [an] Army report noted" (Ricks, 291). A report from the Third Infantry Division explicitly blamed the catastrophic power/authority vacuum in the aftermath of Saddam's fall on the "chain of command, leading to Franks to Rumsfeld to Bush: ' . . . there was no timely plan prepared for the obvious consequences of a regime change'" (Ricks, 151). In place of the plan was faith that the Iraqis would play their part in a World War II movie version of the invasion, which negated having to meet the responsibilities of an occupying force, as delineated in the Fourth Geneva Convention. As Fallows explains, because "American troops would be 'liberators' rather than 'occupiers' . . . the [occupiers] obligation did not apply" (71).

In the administration's world of the Unknown, cause and effect dissolved comfortably into one another, such that the effect of the war—discovery of WMDs and proof that Saddam was supporting terrorists set to use them—would justify faith in its cause. Faith in not having to plan an occupation, moreover, morphed into a faith-based rebuilding process, the staffing for which was run from Jim O'Beirne's office in the Pentagon. As Rajiv Chandrasekaran explains,

> To pass muster with O'Beirne . . . applicants didn't need to be experts in the Middle East or in post-conflict reconstruction. What seemed most important was loyalty to the Bush administration.
>
> O'Beirne's staff posed blunt questions to some candidates . . . Did you vote for George W. Bush in 2000? Do you support the way the president is fighting the war on terror? Two people who sought jobs with the U.S. occupation authority said they were even asked their views on *Roe v. Wade*.
>
> Many of those chosen by O'Beirne's office . . . lacked vital skills and experience. A 24-year-old who had never worked in finance . . . was sent to reopen Baghdad's stock exchange. The daughter of a prominent neoconservative commentator and a recent graduate from an evangelical university . . . were tapped to manage Iraq's $13 billion budget, even though they didn't have a background in accounting. ("Ties to GOP")

Nor was faith shaken by facts. For example, Franks (who, according to Ricks, was not a deep thinker) called Feith "the fucking stupidest guy on the face of the earth," a point supported by the fact that as late as 2007 Feith alleged a connection between Saddam and Al Qaeda,[12] just as *Lost* did in 2005, when a flashback shows Sayid (Naveen Andrews), a former member of Saddam's Republican Guard, coerced into penetrating an Iraqi terrorist cell in Australia: "Last week 300 pounds of C4 explosives were stolen from an army base outside Melbourne," he is told. "The men responsible are members of a terrorist cell intent on disrupting the coalition presence in Iraq." While nothing makes clear how the Iraqi terrorist cells are intent on disrupting the coalition—or how stealing explosives in Australia would do so—the terrorists are clearly Iraqi agents. In this flashback, the 9/11 terrorism that motivated the invasion thus becomes synonymous with the guerrilla resistance to that invasion, and these Australian cells provide fictional support for Bush's bogus choice between fighting them "over there" and fighting them "over here."

Like the logic of Bush's here/there argument, when *Lost* premiered, other lost things (in addition to policy and purpose) included the whereabouts of Osama bin Laden and the credibility of the administration's latest justifying narrative, that Iraq would become a beacon of democracy. By fall 2005, American objectives were as unrecoverable as were vast treasures of Persian art, about which, Rumsfeld announced a month after the invasion,

> I read eight headlines that talked about chaos, violence, and unrest. And it was just "Henny Penny the sky is falling." I've never seen anything like it! And here is a country that's being liberated, here are people who are going from being repressed and under the thumb of a vicious dictator, and they're free. The images you are seeing on television . . . it's the same picture of some person walking out of some building with a vase, and you see it twenty times and you think, "My goodness, is it possible that there were that many vases in the whole country?" (Bremer, 14)

In addition to "countless" vases, also lost were Iraqi lives—by 2004 more than ten thousand of these, expeditiously liberated from the thumb of the vicious dictator by means of mortality. Add to that more than one thousand American liberators, whose lives, like American credibility and the validity of international law, were fatally lost. According to the Council on Foreign Relations, Al Qaeda had recruited forty thousand fighters since 9/11 and expanded "from rural Afghanistan into North Africa, East Africa, the Sahel, the Gulf States, the Middle East and Central Asia."[13] Therefore, if one evaluates the

War on Terror by comparing Al Qaeda's presence in Iraq in 2004, its worldwide membership, or the percentage of people on the planet who wished Americans harm at that time, we could say the entire War on Terror was lost, or at least that it had failed to justify the faith based on the administration initiative.

A NEOCONOMIC UTOPIA

But *all* was not lost, for the core values of the Republican Party—that the free market cures all woes, that government *is* the problem—carried Bush past his unfortunate jokes to reelection a little more than a month after *Lost*'s premiere, with the same surety that these values persevered among the *Lost* survivors. Even years later, neocons such as Feith, Richard Perle, and John Bolton insisted that the *only* problem with the Iraq War was too much government regulation after the invasion. After removing Saddam, they argued, America should have immediately let flourish the democracy that the marketplace produces. In August 2003, Bremer sent a memo to Rumsfeld explaining that "[w]e have to bridge the gap between a dysfunctional economy and one where the private sector provides self-sustaining growth" (Bremer, 123).

As Naomi Klein explains in a September 2004 *Harper's* article,

The honey theory of Iraqi reconstruction stems from the most cherished belief of the war's ideological architects: that greed is good. Not good just for them and their friends but good for humanity, and certainly good for Iraqis. Greed creates profit, which creates growth, which creates jobs and products and services and everything else anyone could possibly need or want. The role of good government, then, is to create the optimal conditions for corporations to pursue their bottomless greed, so that they in turn can meet the needs of the society. The problem is that governments, even neoconservative governments, rarely get the chance to prove their sacred theory right: despite their enormous ideological advances, even George Bush's Republicans are, in their own minds, perennially sabotaged by meddling Democrats, intractable unions, and alarmist environmentalists.

Iraq was going to change all that. In one place on Earth, the theory would finally be put into practice in its most perfect and uncompromised form. A country of 25 million would not be rebuilt as it was before the war; it would be erased, disappeared.

Erased, in other words, like the trauma of 9/11's emasculation, disappeared, in other words, like the violence that erased it. "In its place would spring forth," Klein goes on,

> a gleaming showroom for laissez-faire economics, a utopia such as the world had never seen. Every policy that liberates multinational corporations to pursue their quest for profit would be put into place: a shrunken state, a flexible workforce, open borders, minimal taxes, no tariffs, no ownership restrictions.

Bremer's attempt to turn Iraq into this Milton Friedman fantasy[14] was, as some neocons claimed, too little too late. In his defense, Bremer explained that "[w]e recognized that a full transition to a market economy was beyond the scope of the Coalition mission" (115–116). It was also, he failed to note, beyond the mandate for the war. Could Bush have convinced the nation that American security was threatened by an Iraqi single-payer health plan or Saddam's over-regulation of the price of sheep? Here we have one more example of how "Mission Accomplished" morphed into "mission impossible."

A few months after taking over Iraq, at a World Economic Forum in Amman, Jordan, an undaunted Bremer stated: "Saddam Hussein had been crushed by . . . 'misguided state planning'" (Bremer, 77). Thus, Bremer persisted relentlessly with his neoconomic agenda at the expense of such necessities as transportation and running water. Instead of restoring electricity and safety on the street, he prioritized, in his own words, "creating momentum toward a market economy. . . . We would seek to liberalize Iraq's commercial and investment laws" (116).

Bremer, Klein points out, therefore

> pushed through . . . wrenching changes in one . . . summer . . . [He] fired 500,000 state workers, most of them soldiers, but also doctors, nurses, teachers, publishers, and printers. Next, he flung open the country's borders to . . . unrestricted imports: no tariffs, no duties, no inspections, no taxes. Iraq, Bremer declared two weeks after he arrived, was "open for business."
>
> . . . "Getting inefficient state enterprises into private hands," he said, "is essential for Iraq's economic recovery."

Bremer's impetus to privatize, it turns out, was not just a neoconomic canard but also a symptom of the disastrous neoconomic philosophy that took hold of America with the ascendency of Bush-Cheney, exacerbated by the broad leeway given for implementation without planning, accountability, evaluation, or reflection, that is, without any of the criteria used to assess strategies. In place of strategies was the notion of faith-based initiatives, a concept much broader, as we have seen, than serving as a rationale for funneling public dollars into religious organizations (i.e., circumventing the establishment clause of the Constitution). More generically, faith-based initiatives characterized the entire Bush administration agenda, whether in regard to the under-regulation of Wall Street or Fannie Mae, "No Child Left Behind," or the Iraq War. At the most quasi-pragmatic level, they all put faith above reason: "If we do it, it will work. If we ignore it, it will flourish."

Perhaps no one, not Bush nor Cheney nor Bremer, embodied this faith-based initiative ethos more than Rumsfeld. If Bremer tried to privatize Iraqi businesses, Rumsfeld attempted to privatize the war itself. "The key to understanding the staggering level of incompetence," Jonathan Alter succinctly explains, "is the privatizing of the Iraq War" (Rasor and Bauman, xi). KBR (Kellogg, Brown and Root), a Halliburton subsidiary, for example, was hired to supply US soldiers in Iraq, a move that proved both a financial and strategic disaster. KBR's $16 billion no-bid contract was "structured so that the more the company spends, the more it keeps" (Rasor and Bauman, xiii). (This was on top of the $7 billion no-bid contract that Halliburton received to restore Iraq oil fields.)[15] Highly paid KBR employees, safely organizing supply shipments from Kuwait, occupied luxurious resort villas overlooking the Persian Gulf. Running up a hotel tab of at least $1.5 million per month, they enjoyed swimming, hiking, windsurfing, and deep-sea fishing, while billing the Department of Defense for eighty-four hours per week (i.e., twelve hours per person, per day, six days per week). At the same time, KBR often delivered broken, outdated, or substandard equipment, or, if transporting supplies was too dangerous, they delivered nothing, leaving troops in the field short of food, water, and ammunition. If privatization is the cornerstone of freedom, then what better example could the liberators provide to Iraq's fledgling democracy than the success of KBR? Americans free to choose working for KBR (or the Blackwater mercenary force) over working in the military were clearly much better off than the typical government-dependent Iraqi under Saddam. Or, as the post–Mission Accomplished films illustrate, under Uncle Sam.

THE IRAQ MINI-CAMP

The comparable absence of governmental impediments makes *Lost*'s island an Iraq mini-camp. Governed by no rules, the forty-eight survivors scavenge the plane's remains and rifle the pockets of the dead, finding handy gadgets, bottled water, and luggage filled with stylish beach wear, expensive makeup, and paperback books. Significantly, this unsystematic process recognizes no regulations and produces no obligations. (The *Lost* island is the ultimate duty-free port.) As a group, therefore, the survivors do not assess their circumstances, make plans, allocate responsibilities, acknowledge rules, or (ever!) pool resources. As Kate (Evangeline Lilly), the central female character, a tough, attractive woman running from the police, points out about Locke (Terry O'Quinn), a survivalist adept at hunting with knives who catches boar for the survivors: "It's a lot of mouths to feed. If the boar's thinning out, then why should he feed everyone else at his own expense?" Similarly, Sawyer at one point shouts at Jack, "Look I don't know what kind of a commie share-fest you're running over in Cavetown, but down here, possession's nine-tenths." Sawyer never completes the cliché—nine-tenths *of the law*—which would acknowledge the existence of a law that could govern property, when the show holds axiomatic that property *is* the law, a position Sawyer affirms by indicating that other rights flow from it: "and a man's got a right to defend his property." Because private property is sacrosanct, any scavenged item on the *Lost* island belongs to the scavenger, even if the luggage from which it was appropriated belonged to one of the other survivors. Almost instinctively, moreover, everyone seems to recognize the scavengers' inalienable right to trade looted booty. (The logical extension of this premise, to the point of puerile irrationality, was Donald Trump's 2016 assertion that when we left Iraq we should have taken the oil.)[16]

The point is that the *Lost* island's accepted practice of looting was not only corrosive to the principles of civil society but also symptomatic of the void in leadership and authority, which sharply, and increasingly, diminished the potential to establish a functional society, a condition grotesquely magnified in Iraq with a population more than five hundred thousand times larger than the community of *Lost* survivors:

> The looting spread, destroying the infrastructure that had survived the war and creating the expectation of future chaos. "There is this kind of magic moment, when you can't imagine until you see it," an American civilian who was in Baghdad during the looting told Fallows. "People are used to someone being in charge, and when they realize no one is, the fabric rips." (102)

Yet, shortly after assuming control of the country, at a meeting in Jordan, Bremer told members of a World Economic Forum, however counterintuitively, "It is an axiom that political and economic freedom go hand in hand" (Bremer, 77).

On the *Lost* island, however, from these lawless, laissez-faire principles, a mutually beneficial economy seems to emerge naturally, consistent with Bremer's predictions for Iraq. As Jack states about the economy into which he has fallen, he is "bringing water down to the beach and bringing fish back." Like the private contractors in Iraq, he and all the other *Lost* survivors are, in Friedman's sense of the phrase, free to choose. Thus, as Rumsfeld explained, even the looting in Baghdad was a symptom of freedom: "On April 11, when asked why U.S. soldiers were not stopping the looting . . . Rumsfeld said, 'It's untidy, and freedom's untidy,' he said, jabbing his hand in the air. 'Free people are free to make mistakes and commit crimes and do bad things. They're also free to live their lives and do wonderful things, and that's what's going to happen here'" (Fallows, 101). But what actually followed from the looting was $12 billion of destruction—"the gutted buildings, the lost equipment, the destroyed records, the damaged infrastructure"—and even more catastrophic intangible effects, such that "Iraq's first experience of freedom was chaos and violence" (Packer, 139).

In maximizing their freedom, the private contractors and the looters were on the same page, choosing with Rumsfeld's blessing to commodify every aspect of the war. Since commodities are foundational to neoconomic freedom, the invisible hand of the market masks the invisible army that sustains the marketplace. Therefore, in *Lost* the violence of the crash and of the island's perils is displaced onto fetishized objects, at first those salvaged or retained, and then also those supplied by an island that continually produces supplements.

Marx uses the concept of the fetish to define that "which attaches itself to the products of labour, so soon as they are produced as commodities, and which is therefore inseparable from the production of commodities" (83). As Linda Williams notes, both Freud and Marx "offer an economic application: . . . For both, fetishization involves the construction of a substitute object to evade the complex realities of social or psychic relations" (105). Most important, within the framework of neoconomics, the tactics of the *Lost* survivors operate in an ad hoc psychic and material economy. Appropriating the Darwinian principle of adaptation to multifarious social environments, neoconomics turns Darwinism into a form of Panglossian destiny that valorizes all American actions as fulfilling the best interests of humankind. This reasoning renders the fact of American exceptionalism simultaneously inductive, deductive, and a priori. As both the mode of explanation and the means of self-propagation, the Darwinian marketplace, in neoconomics, constitutes a factual verity foundational to every aspect of American life (with the sole exception of biology, where Darwinism remains a "theory" comparable, albeit insufficiently so, to Intelligent Design).

In *Lost*, the character most strongly advocating Intelligent Design is ironically named John Locke. (I'm assuming his name is ironic, although possibly the erudition implicit in the allusion reflects the same level of knowledge as the intelligence guaranteeing WMDs.)[17] Inspired by an act of faith-healing—he boarded the plane in a wheelchair but reacquired the use of his legs after the crash—Locke constantly attempts to convince the other survivors that they are on the island for a divine purpose. Thus, when he is unable to open the hatch that he discovers with Boone (Ian Somerhalder), the young man who runs his mother's wedding business and is on the island with his attractive stepsister, Shannon (Maggie Grace), he gives the same explanation as creationists when confronted with fossils: "Our faith is being tested," which also describes the neocon response to the failures in Iraq. When Locke's faith-based initiatives fail, he lies and/or uses his superior command of weaponry to enforce his faith in the Unknown.

Confusing faith with planning, therefore, makes Locke virtually indistinguishable from Rumsfeld and Bush:

> One of Bush's advisors once explained to the journalist Ron Suskind the worldview of the White House. Whereas the nation-building experts and the war critics and Ron Suskind lived "in what we call the reality-based community" where people "believe that solutions emerge from your judicious study of discernible reality," unfortunately, "that's not the way the world really works anymore." The way the world now works amounted to a repudiation of reason, skeptical intelligence, the whole slate of liberal Enlightenment values. "We're an empire now, and when we act, we create our own reality . . ." (Packer, 390)

If philosopher John Locke was a cornerstone of Enlightenment thinking, his ideas are lost on his *Lost* namesake, who, echoing Rumsfeld, privileges the Unknown over the Enlightenment. It is not surprising therefore that Locke's scheme for the *Lost* island makes his mission undefinable, and hence, by definition, its accomplishment impossible, exactly the situation of Bush-Cheney-Rumsfeld's war architects, who were, Packer explains, "working deductively, not inductively. The premise was true; facts would be found to confirm it" (107). Feeling that the record of mainstream analysts of the Middle East was poor, a "new method was urgently needed, starting with the higher insights of political philosophy rather than evidence from the fallen world of social science" (107).

This marketplace that trades faith for morality allows all the principal characters comparably to invest, divest, and reinvest. Although the examples are prolific, a few can well illustrate *Lost*'s neoconomic ethics: Jin (Daniel Dae Kim), a Korean businessman, violently attacks Michael (Harold Perrineau), an aspiring artist bringing his estranged young son, Walt (Malcolm David Kelley), back to the United States and one of the only Black survivors, because Michael is wearing the Rolex watch given to Jin by the father of his wife, Sun (Yunjin Kim). Because Jin cannot speak English, he cannot claim the watch, which in any case would violate the free-market rules that all those who *do* speak English understand and accept because they are antithetical to what Sawyer summarized as "commie share-fest" rules. Nor can Jin learn that Michael found rather than stole the watch. Outside of language, that is, of the mediation that can displace the violence, the fetishized watch produces pure violence—Jin tries to kill Michael—which fetishism normally defers through an economy of substitution. The watch represents the exchange that permits and also undermines Jin's marriage to the daughter of a Korean mobster. Jin had entered Sun's father's employ, ostensibly as a corporate manager, but also as an enforcer. Thus, protecting the watch is Jin's way of honoring the law of the father.

For Sayid, who thought he had disavowed the torture he practiced in Iraq, Shannon's asthma inhalers become the fetishized objects that, in this neoconomic utopia, afford him a second chance to choose torture, when it appears Sawyer has looted the inhalers from Shannon's luggage. If Sayid and Jack use coercion and then Kate pays Sawyer for the inhalers with a (long, wet) kiss, the core point is that whether the torture or the bribe succeeds, the community as a whole has neither the means nor the right to make Sawyer give up anything. Thus, when it turns out that Sawyer never had the inhalers, neither the duped Kate nor the tortured Sawyer has any recourse.

These obvious flaws, however, do not threaten the authority of *Lost*'s free-market environment. The only real threat comes from the lurking terror, at first unnamed but then shamelessly identified as "The Others." Angrily noting the sectarian violence besetting the survivors, Locke shouts, "We're so intent on pointing a finger at one another, that we're all denying the simple, undeniable truth, that the problem isn't here. It's there. They've attacked us, sabotaged us, abducted us, murdered us. Maybe it's time we stopped blaming us and started worrying about them." Locke's speech focusing antagonism on the Others thus articulates both the reason for attacking Iraq and for continuing to defend it. (If the problem is out "there," not in "here," Bush must be right that it is better to fight them *there*.) The onslaught of violent Iraqi death was caused by the Others, Others who now have to be protected from other Others, who otherwise might do other things to one another.

Fortunately, the survivors can create their own mercenary force because they find a metal Halliburton case with a number of handguns, but of course they never devise a policy regulating the right to bear arms. Rather, because Jack has the key to the case, he decides who uses the weapons and when, so when one of the Others kidnaps Claire, Jack hands out the guns to his own small coalition of the willing, and when they find the subversive Other, Ethan, without either consultation or consequence, Charlie (Dominic Monaghan), a former British rock star with a heroin addiction problem, summarily executes Ethan, "Because," Charlie explains, "he deserved to die." This confusion over the authority for and implementation of policing was comparable, albeit exponentially more prolific, in Iraq. On the second day of the war, a civil affairs officer at the Iraq-Kuwait border asked a USAID worker about the plan for policing.

> "I thought you knew the plan," he said.
> "No, we thought you knew."
> "Haven't you talked to ORHA [Office of Reconstruction and Humanitarian Assistance]?"
> "No, no one talked to us."
> [The officer] wanted to run away. He remembered the incident as "a Laurel and Hardy routine. What happened to the plans? This is like the million-dollar question that I can't figure out. There was planning—I know there was. I saw it, I took part in it. It was a failure either to accept those plans or communicate them down to where it mattered, on the ground." (Packer, 134–135)

One reason *Lost*'s anarchy can pass for freedom is that the survivors have limitless resources: a jungle rich with fruit, an ocean full of fish, an airplane full of liquor (in two-ounce bottles), and batteries to power their CD players. From tarps and dislodged seats, they fashion beach cabanas, or, for those who prefer, alternative living quarters in caves provide shelter from the tropical storms and fresh running water. Lovely coves allow recreational swimming; scenic hiking trails abound, and the evenings end in luaus, complete with roasted boar. When Charlie runs out of heroin, he conveniently finds a stash, neatly wrapped in small plastic bags. In one episode, Sawyer and Kate even use the bottled liquor to play a drinking game. Endlessly supplied with pop novels and toenail polish, these lost people can enjoy their makeshift resort, with uncrowded beaches and no waiting at the golf course that Hurley (Jorge Garcia), an affable, overweight young man who has won a lottery, fashioned to make good use of salvaged golf clubs.

Thus, *Lost* enacts the War on Terror within the parameters Bush established. The plane's middle class survives the shock of the unpredictable crash by going to Disney World while also constantly suspecting Others and fearing terrorism. Nor can this tacit practice of viewing otherness as equivalent to relentless violence—potential indistinguishable from proactive—be tempered by reason. Jack's demands for rational explanations seem as preposterous as it would be for one of the contestants on *Survivor* to ask why they can't eat the same catered food that the crew does down at the canteen, or for the GIs in Iraq to ask why the Pentagon failed to provide them with Kevlar jackets or to hire contractors who would supply them with food and water. The answer is that in America, survival is not a process of natural selection; it is a game, a summer resort game, a fraternity game, a political game. In the *Survivor* game show, as in presidential elections, what you say or do doesn't matter, so long as they vote in your favor, as Richard Hatch, the infamous victor of *Survivor*'s premiere season proved. In *Survivor*, as Andrejevic makes clear, "life on the island is not a back-to-basics, 'survival'-level existence, but the deployment of imaginary knowledge about back-to-basics survival as a means of competing according to the stylized rules of a costly, exotic game show" (210).

If *Survivor* is *about* the contrivance of danger—survival as a game—then in conjunction with *Lost* it helps make apparent the board-game attitude of the Iraq War planners, who required no Occupation strategy for the same reason one does not need to build detention centers for the captured pieces in a chess game. Hence the bewilderment that Bush-Cheney-Rumsfeld experience when the Iraqi people failed to conform to their roles in the American War on Terror game show. Instead, they found the Iraqis incomprehensibly reacting as citizens of an invaded nation, a point implicit in Bremer's senior assistant Hume Horan's blaming the occupation failures on Iraqi ignorance: "The Germans and the Japanese may not have liked being occupied," he said, "but they knew occupation is what happens when you lose a war" (Bremer, 37).[18]

Horan is, however, categorically wrong on all counts. The Germans and the Japanese knew that Occupation is not what happens when they lose a war but when they unconditionally surrender, because surrender is Occupation's necessary precondition. That is why, in *Saving Private Ryan*, the soldiers and the audience are constantly reminded that their mission is Hitler's surrender.

GOOD DAD, BAGHDAD

The rationale for *Lost*'s game, reflected by the personal agenda of virtually every principal in the series, entails a problematic father. Jack was transporting the corpse of his alcoholic father back to the US, after his father disappeared on a binge, when Jack's testimony about his father's performing surgery while drunk caused his father to lose his license. Sawyer's father committed suicide after having lost all his money to a con man named "Sawyer," after whom Sawyer modeled his life while still seeking to avenge the death of the father whose name Sawyer had renounced. Walt, stranded on the island with his father, Michael, is a nine-year-old boy trying to build a relationship with Michael, with whom he has had no contact since infancy. Locke, raised in foster homes, is contacted by his estranged father only so that his father can con Locke into donating a kidney to him; after the surgery, Locke's father again cut off all contact with him. Hurley, devoted to his mother, seems to have grown up in a single-parent household. Kate had been running from the law for years because she killed her abusive father. And the collapse of Sun and Jin's relationship is inextricably linked to Sun's domineering, mobster father. This pervasive theme brings the endless struggle with the Others back again to President Bush, whose troubled family relationship may be the referent of episode 10: "All the Best Cowboys Have Daddy Issues." "After all," Bush proclaimed about Saddam Hussein, as part of his buildup to the war, "this is the guy who tried to kill my dad."

> If Cheney and Rumsfeld were the bureaucratic heavyweights, the leading intellect of post-9/11 policy was Wolfowitz. In the weeks after the terror attack, there was a surprising convergence between the former oilman president, whose favorite philosopher was Jesus and who could mock his own submediocre academic record because it didn't matter when your last name was Bush, and his brilliant deputy secretary of defense, a secular Jew with a Cornell BA in mathematics and a Chicago PhD in political science . . . Bush and Wolfowitz—both of them now free of the stifling authority of Bush's father—saw the world the same way. They believed in the existence of evil and they had messianic notions of what America should do about it. . . . but on Iraq it was Bush himself who seized the chance to cast off the Oedipal burden and prove that he was his own man, better able than his fallen father to deal with an old enemy." (Packer, 44–45)

If for Freud the fetish "remains a token of triumph over the threat of castration and a protection against it" (154), *Lost* acts out the narrative uniting Bush's war and Freud's fetish, the story of imagined castration that alienates son from father. Conflict over Jin's fetishized watch therefore glosses numerous exchanges in *Lost*'s community of implicit post-9/11 survivors. The watch, by also signifying reward for labor, unites alienation from the products of production to alienation from the potentially violent father. Therefore, the show may illustrate how, by fetishizing Iraq, neoconomics has reified the violence that, by remaining both imagined and unimaginable, material and utopian, permitted Bush and his administration, at the expense of national security and international law, to restore their "potency."

The more extensively Iraq functioned in this way, the more it was linked to an unachievable mission, as hard to articulate as to ascertain because the mission involved retribution for a terror that cannot be identified, a violence attached to the imagined intentions of an absent father who can never be captured, only reimagined, repurposed, reified. This condition of infinite deferral precludes the war's having a final stage, which transitions from the end of hostilities to the restoration of nonbelligerent sovereignty. In this regard, the declaration of "Mission Accomplished" in the absence of a surrender became the United States' surrender to the absence of a mission, substituting in its place a hazardous and pointless occupation.

THE GREEN ZONE—THE *LOST* ISLAND FOUND

If *Lost* reflects the general chaos of the Iraq War, its setting is actually more akin to the Green Zone, a unique island at the center of Baghdad. Bobby Yen, a member of the Army Reserves who was stationed in the Green Zone, "was astonished by the comfort inside and the misery outside it. The Green Zone— Saddam's former palace and surrounding grounds—was lush and tropical, with contractors swarming all over to serve the needs of military and civilian officials. It was gold-plated and unrealistic—the Club Med of Iraq" (Rasor and Bauman, 75). In other words, it bore much of *Lost*'s resort ambiance:

> A four-square-mile area that felt very different from the rest of Iraq, a novel mix of palm trees and third-rate Iraqi palaces . . . It was isolated from the city's traffic jams and shaded by many more trees than grew elsewhere in Baghdad. It also was attuned to different realities that prevailed beyond its blast walls. . . . "It's almost like being at a Walt Disney version of *Arabian Nights*," said [an Army Reserve major] who spent a year working on civil affairs issues in the zone. "I lived in a villa that was originally owned by a Republican Guard colonel. It featured six bedrooms, a hot tub on a balcony and three Iraqi maids. We lived very large." (Ricks, 206)

In addition to being heavily fortified and thus insulated from the violence that surrounded it, the Zone featured swimming pools, a state-of-the-art gym, television (no power shortages in the Zone), and an active nightlife with alcohol and seven bars (including a disco). Like the survivors on *Lost*, the occupants of the Green Zone seemed miraculously supplied with all the trappings of a luxury vacation site. And, like the *Lost* survivors, they were marooned: any attempt to leave their island engaged the risk of violence, failure, or death.

> Nor were some of the zone's inhabitants much connected to the country they were ostensibly remaking. "There was just a level of ignorance" that was surprising, [retired Army Colonel Ralph] Hallenbeck, a contractor dealing with Iraqi communications infrastructure, said. "There were maybe seven thousand people in the Green Zone, and very few spoke Arabic or ever got out." Even if they wanted to get outside . . . their protected area, CPA rules made it difficult. (Ricks, 207)

The surfeit of regulations, emanating from sundry sources of authority, neither rational nor consistent, rendered this Baghdad island's conditions tantamount to the lawless situation faced by the *Lost* survivors. For example, if one wished to leave the Green Zone, it was necessary to apply for armed guards and escorts, but even if the application's approval had been confirmed at 11:00 p.m. one evening, the next morning it could turn out to have been superseded. Most of the fifteen hundred Coalition Provisional Authority employees rarely left.

It was very safe inside and very dangerous outside. In addition, inside everything worked; electricity, running water, and air conditioning were constant, while outside these basics were erratic and often rare. The Green Zone had laundry service, swimming pools, sports bars and cafés, internet, a business center, a gym, nightly movies in the palace's movie theater, yoga lessons, and a cafeteria where "everything, even the water in which hot dogs were boiled [was] shipped in from approved suppliers in other nations. Milk and bread were trucked in from Kuwait, as were tinned peas and carrots. The breakfast cereal was flown in from the United States" (Chandrasekaran, *Imperial Life*, 9). "A pleated skirt decorated the salad bar and dessert table, which was piled high with cakes and cookies. The floor was polished after every meal" (Chandrasekaran, *Imperial Life*, 10). Saddam's palace was Versailles on the Tigris, the centerpiece of a walled city within the city, renovated into Baghdad's Little America.

Each switch in Occupation administration brought new groups into the Green Zone family of bureaucrats and special interests, doing little to clarify America's objectives or sort out, much less accomplish, its mission. The same lack of clarity in *Lost*—especially complicated by the unclear source, power, and legitimacy of the numerous agents asserting authority—characterized the series's last season such that, for many viewers, it left the show in the same condition that the United States left Iraq: devoid of a credible purpose, its characters with no comprehensible missions, and with even the story's time and space completely at sea.

CHAPTER 4

IT'S NOT AN OCCUPATION, IT'S WAR, AND WAR IS A SHIT OCCUPATION

In the traditional war narrative that moves from attack to conquest to surrender, a formal Occupation is a form of dénouement, wherein war is designated "over" and the objectives designated "won." It thus marks the transition from the hostile sovereign state, now vanquished, to the peaceful sovereign state, now reconstructed in terms congenial to the victors, so that the period (meaning both "time span" and "caesura") of Occupation makes possible the destruction and resurrection of the vanquished state. Having the traits of war—the occupying of alien ground—without the action of capturing that alien space, Occupation signifies war without warfare; having the traits of peace—a daily life absent of imminent or actual martial aggression—without internal governance, it signifies peace without the independence of a state at peace. In this way, an Occupation is a Lyotardian *differend*, the space between that belongs to neither side and to both. In Lyotard's conception, the *differend* is crucial to the possibility of difference, in this case, the difference between war and peace. It must be remembered, moreover, that in a war, peace comes to both belligerents, or it comes to neither: there are no wars with only one side.

Yet this is exactly the condition that Bush-Cheney-Rumsfeld wished to effect in imagining a war without a surrender. In substituting the notion of "liberation" for that of surrender, Bush-Cheney-Rumsfeld was relying on a figurative conversion to replace a material one, such that the invaded state ceased retrospectively to be the enemy, in that liberation marks the end of (enemy) occupation. In World War II, for example, the Allies liberated France, but they defeated Germany. France, therefore, was not required to surrender, while Germany had to, unconditionally.

THE CONDITIONS OF THE JOB

Coexisting with and structurally dependent upon ongoing hostilities, Bush-Cheney-Rumsfeld's (unofficial?) Occupation of Iraq changed what should have been the final phase of a war into the job of sustaining it. Rumsfeld had "decided to invade Iraq with as few troops as possible, so that the troops would quickly enter Baghdad and topple Saddam Hussein, and then, just as quickly, win the peace and leave. The Pentagon civilian hierarchy imagined that the troops would be welcomed with flowers and cheers and that stability would be quickly achieved" (Rasor and Bauman, 4). (Rumsfeld's noted antipathy to predictions may emanate, this example suggests, from how inept he was at making them.)

When the Pentagon's cinematic version of Iraq failed to materialize, Rumsfeld had no Plan B to compensate for the fact that he never made a Plan A. In the lead-up to the invasion, Rumsfeld was so averse to the traditional (meaning "intelligent" or "logical") war narrative, he threatened to fire staff who suggested creating an Occupation plan. These threats left him in the middle of an occupation-without-surrender, which turned the US invasion into a war without fronts, or movements, or long-term objectives: since culminating active hostilities is Occupation's *pre*condition, it cannot also be Occupation's objective. In an imploded narrative structure, which pasted, like a mobius strip, the beginning to its inverted end, the United States found itself fighting a war not to occupy Iraq, but *because* it had done so. As everyone in the media knew, to the point where it morphed from a punch line to a hackneyed cliché, the mission was not accomplished.

For years, therefore, Bush-Cheney-Rumsfeld attempted damage control. On the fifth anniversary of "Mission Accomplished," White House spokesperson Dana Perino said that "President Bush was well aware that the banner should have been more specific." Asserting that the phrase "mission accomplished" referred to the sailors on the ship, she explained that "[w]e have certainly paid a price for not being more specific on this banner," without acknowledging the much higher price American troops paid, who, instead of occupying Iraq, were fighting a war converting Iraq into a lethal occupation. As AP journalist Judy Boysha pointed out regarding Perino's May 2008 statement: "More than 4000 members of the military have died there since the beginning of the war, in March 2003."[1]

But their deaths advanced no mission. Most of the American military were not occupying Iraq because they had been drafted into the service of their country or had enlisted to fulfill a patriotic mission, but because, in the twenty-first century, they had chosen soldiering as their occupation. The US contingent in

Iraq, following Rumsfeld's privatization initiatives, also included nonmilitary workers who had chosen a job that entailed soldiering or, in general, contributed to the war effort. While in 2003 the starting salary for an enlistee was $1,065 per month ($21,000 per year in 2024 dollars),[2] these private contractors received large, often exorbitant salaries. It was assumed the war would be brief, the invasion joyfully received, and a new (pro-American) regime rapidly in control. But because no plan existed to achieve these conditions, things got bad, until they got worse. From the war's start to the moment when its mission was accomplished, the United States had only lost 139 lives; in the three and a half years after "Mission Accomplished," 2,700 more were lost, and 22,000 more had been wounded (Bailey, 227). "In the first decade of the twenty-first century," Beth Bailey explains,

> the modern army faced, for the first time, the challenge of recruiting during an extended war with no threat of conscription to motivate volunteers. And the war in Iraq posed a particular set of challenges. In Iraq, it was not only those in the combat arms that were at risk. There was no clear battle front. The insurgents did not wear uniforms; their weapons-of-choice were improvised explosive devices, or IEDs, which exploded without warning and with no regard for combat destination. In this war there were many fewer "safe" MOSs for which to volunteer—and those, of course, were not the ones that carried enlistment bonuses of twenty or thirty thousand dollars. Once in the army, soldiers faced repeated tours in Iraq, while stop-loss provisions could prevent them from leaving the military when they completed their terms of enlistment. And those who joined the US Army Reserve, with its recruiting promise of "one weekend a month," were not exempt. Controversy over the war itself also made recruiting difficult. (229)

Thus, maintaining troop levels required recruitment adjustments. These included greatly increasing enlistment and reenlistment bonuses, lowering qualification standards for acceptance into the service, and reducing the amount of training time for recruits before they were sent into combat zones.

In contrast to this situation, even the Vietnam War distinguished between the occupation of serving in the US military and the occupation of continuously fighting a war, that is, service endlessly suspended between active and imminent violence. In the Iraq War, however, the flow of new recruits, which allowed soldiers to rotate steadily and permanently out of wartime, declined significantly. In consequence, those who chose the military as their short-term or long-term occupation were forced to serve two, three, or even four tours in the war zone. To maintain troop levels, the mandated amount of time between tours in war zones was significantly decreased, which, in effect, made military service a job of nearly continuous war. Because they are available for national mobilization, members of the National Guard had to augment the troops in Iraq, often leaving an inadequate number available for their domestic duties. This practice redefined the National Guard, a state-based military force, primarily intended to address state emergencies caused by natural disasters or by civil unrest. One difficulty in responding to the damage caused by Hurricane Katrina, for example, was that more than a third of the Louisiana National Guard at the time of the hurricane was in Iraq, leaving the governor with only four thousand of the Guard at his disposal.[3]

Service in Iraq was thus bracketed neither by the war's duration nor the length of a tour of duty, but by the conditions of their contract as nonunionized workers doing hazardous work at substandard pay. Their job required waiving several Constitutional rights, including freedom of speech and assembly (First Amendment), a point explicitly articulated in one of the first post–Mission Accomplished war films, *Jarhead*, which follows Marine recruit Anthony Swofford (Jake Gyllenhaal) from basic training through his deployment in Kuwait in the buildup to Operation Desert Storm (the 1991 Iraq War) to that brief war's conclusion. Just prior to the start of Desert Storm, the company's Staff Sergeant Sykes (Jamie Foxx), in preparing the men for being interviewed by television journalists, instructs them specifically about what they can say, and threatens them with retribution if they deviate from their proscribed scripts. One soldier objects, calling the instructions "censorship": "You're telling us what we can and can't say to the press. It's un-American." When Swofford agrees ("What about freedom of speech? . . . It's in the Constitution"), Sykes corrects him: "No. You signed a contract. You don't got any rights. . . . You are a Marine. There is no such thing as speech that is free. You must pay for everything that you say."

This scene emphasizes the hypocrisy—that the soldiers lack the American rights they are allegedly fighting to defend—less than it does the fact that they are workers whose contracts waive those rights, including freedom of assembly (First Amendment), right to trial by a jury of their peers (Sixth), and protection from cruel and unusual punishment (Eighth). Even their right to bear arms, despite being part of "a well-regulated militia" (Second), is more curtailed than it is among the vast, unregulated American population.

Nor have they the same latitude to sue their employer regarding workplace safety, as illustrated by an episode when the soldiers, during basic training, crawl through mud, under barbed wire, with live machine-gun fire just above their heads. The soldier next to Swofford, undergoing a panic attack, starts screaming

"I can't do it! I can't do it!" Jumping to his feet in a hysterical attempt to escape, he is killed by the gunfire. Instead of questioning the legitimacy of a training procedure that could kill a trainee, Sykes blames the victim.

Military recruiters, moreover, in this age of the "all-volunteer" army promise recruits career training and attractive travel, then deploy them as grunts in war zones such as Iraq. Although only a small percentage of the enlistees receive the training advertised in recruitment commercials, and very few go where they were promised, they have no legal recourse for challenging these bait-and-switch practices, outlawed in most civil transactions, because, according to the enlistment/reenlistment contract, "Laws and regulations that govern military personnel may change without notice to me. Such changes may affect my status, pay, allowances, benefits, and responsibilities as a member of the Armed Forces REGARDLESS of the provisions of this enlistment/reenlistment document."[4]

Although most World War II soldiers operated under similar restrictions on their Constitutional rights, their sacrifices, as noted, accrued to the special conditions of wartime, just as during wartime, some civilian rights are also suspended in the interest of securing victory and, thereby, expediting the return to peacetime. No such exigencies applied to troops sent to Iraq. They had not enlisted to occupy a distant, hostile land indefinitely, nor joined the National Guard to fight in a Middle Eastern desert, nor become Reservists to spend numerous tours in harm's way, occupying a hostile Arab country. Upon invading Iraq, the United States created ongoing threats for the military rather than marshalling American forces to end them.

Because the Iraq invasion initiated a war lacking the conditions for its culmination, it is worth reiterating that an Occupation plan is *not* a plan for running a defeated country (such plans are called "annexation" or "colonization"), but a plan for leaving the defeated country in a condition that makes the cost the victor paid to defeat it meaningful and (relatively) enduring. The overwhelming problem, pursuant to "Mission Accomplished," therefore, was how to leave the country without a plan or any criteria for evaluating what had been done. This left the men and women employed in the US military with no way of knowing when they had completed their jobs. Nor could the war be reengineered to give it a purpose. Each ersatz "mission" made prior actions unreconcilable to the new alleged goals. What was reengineered instead were the public relations campaigns to represent situations that were never the case as having always existed.

THE IRAQ WAR (MOVIE) JOB

Looking at *Jarhead* and *The Hurt Locker* as exemplary of an array of post–Mission Accomplished American war films illustrates how a war without a mission is a quotidian job inimical to the role soldiers play in traditional war narratives, such as *Saving Private Ryan*. This disparity between the war's aim and its enactment is particularly glaring, moreover, because Bush-Cheney-Rumsfeld's war was planned according to cinematic conventions. (Troops would train intensely, deploy rapidly, engage enthusiastically, encounter early triumphs, then some daunting setbacks, followed by hard-earned victory, joyous celebration, and triumphant departure, either for home to reap the fruits of peace or on to the next mission in pursuit of it.) Serving without either main or contingent plans for the real situations in Iraq, those in the US Armed Services, instead of being citizens enlisted in the service of restoring peace, became employees doing the jobs their bosses demanded. Like the bots that explore bomb sites or the workers on industrial assembly lines, they performed tasks—hazardous or mundane—with dehumanizingly mechanical regularity.

Jarhead was one of the first Iraq War films made after the revelation that nothing had been accomplished that could end the war or justify its beginning. Although the film takes place during Desert Storm, it is a clear product of its post–Mission Accomplished moment. Following Private Swofford through Marine basic training to his deployment in the Gulf and, finally, in Iraq, the film presents a series of excruciatingly debasing and emphatically pointless tasks.

From the outset, Swofford indicates that he considers joining the Marines a bad job decision. When his abusive drill sergeant asks him what he is doing in the service, he screams, "Sir, I got lost on the way to college, Sir!" He then tells us that "it was after meeting Drill Instructor Finch that I realized joining the Marines might have been a bad decision." We immediately learn Swofford's job training entails a new vocabulary: "Now my hands were dick-skinners, a flashlight was a moon beam, a pen was an ink stick, my mouth a cum receptacle, a bed was a rack, a wall a bulkhead, a shirt was a blouse . . ."

While this privileged jargon, like all professional jargon, helps establish Swofford's service in the Marine Corps as a distinct occupation, it also makes clear that the profession's lexicon serves no discernible purpose other than the degradation of its users, and if professional jargon is intended to provide a shorthand (e.g., lawyers use words such as "executory," "exculpatory," or "estoppel") to accomplish tasks more efficiently, it is clear from Swofford's lexicon that his occupation has little need to accomplish things efficiently or, perhaps, to accomplish anything at all. Acquiring the new vocabulary, in other words, is a masturbatory exercise, as suggested not only by some of the phrases but also by Swofford's manual-like list of ways to cope with the boredom of his job after the company arrives in the desert: "Suggested techniques for the Marine to use in avoidance of boredom and loneliness: Masturbation, reading of letters from unfaithful wives and girlfriends, cleaning your rifle, further masturbation, rewiring Walkman, arguing about religion and meaning of life, discussing in detail every woman the Marine has ever fucked, debating differences, such as Cuban vs. Mexican, Harley's vs. Honda's, left-handed vs. right-handed masturbation. Further cleaning of rifle. Studying of Filipino mail-order bride catalogue. Further masturbation . . ."

Arranged in this way, the list converts masturbation from a singular job activity to the job's informing rubric; like the vocabulary that specifies the items as job-related, their objective is solely autoerotic. The rote itemizing, moreover, renders the list an occupational routine, which it is, one Swofford crucially associates with military service through reference to his rifle. The opening lines of the film establish the rifle as a defining instrument of phallic power and masculine identity: "A man fires a rifle for many years, and he goes to war, and afterward he turns the rifle in at the armory. He believes he's finished with the rifle. But no matter what else he might do with his hands, love a woman, build a house, change his son's diaper, his hands remember the rifle." He gets his rifle from the Marines, and it changes his life forever. As his list of job activities affirms, the rifle is both his defining piece of equipment and the source of autoerotic pleasure that compensates for his occupation's degrading routine. Thus, the list juxtaposes cleaning his rifle with further masturbation, as though the two were synonymous; that the rifle has already been identified as part of his hand thus gives meaning to the debate over right-handed vs. left-handed masturbation.

This implies that in an occupation with no clear objective, compensation for boredom and degradation is necessarily autoerotic. Masturbation, cleaning his rifle, attaching his rifle to his hand, thus occupies his time and his imagination, instead of his imagining, as he might in a traditional war film, that he will soon go home. Home, in this film, is not the site of the welcoming families of *Mrs. Miniver*, *Since You Went Away*, or *Tender Comrade*, but of a barren absence, as one item on the list—"reading of letters from unfaithful wives and girlfriends"—makes clear.

At one point, the men have a few days of R&R, which they spend on a base with nice barracks and recreational facilities. There the company gathers in a large room to watch a video one of the soldiers has received from his wife. When he puts the video in the VCR, believing it is *The Deer Hunter*, the company sees, instead, homemade porn that, as the soldier quickly realizes, features his neighbor having sex with his wife. Swofford, who believes his girlfriend is cheating on him, wants to watch the video again so that, he explains, "I can imagine what it feels like seeing your girlfriend fuck someone else."

The Marine's autoerotic connection to the rifle is further strengthened by the fact that Swofford becomes a scout sniper, ever more emphatically merging his hand, his rifle, and his occupation, so that in the film's climactic scene, after months in the desert he is finally cleared to kill an Iraqi military "higher-up" squarely sighted in his crosshairs. Consistent with the representation of missionless military service as an autoerotic enterprise that psychically even more than physically merges rifle, hand, and job, this sniper kill, the first combat shot in his Marine career, is set up to be the film's money shot,[5] a shot his partner wants even more desperately than Swofford. As Swofford is about to squeeze the trigger, however, Major Lincoln (Dennis Haysbert) bursts into his position to abort the order because an airstrike is about to take out the entire building complex where the targeted Iraqi is situated. Swofford and his partner object violently. "Requesting permission to take the shot," Swofford says and is again denied. Swofford's contention is based, paradoxically, on his agreeing with Major Lincoln that the shot is pointless. If the entire building is about to be leveled, they both agree, "what difference does it make" if he completes the assassination or aborts it? This Catch-22 epitomizes not just Marine life in *Jarhead*, but wartime in general in a world where the job of being a Marine is divorced from any mission. Whatever job they do, it makes no difference.

This final moment confirms what the Marines had discovered months earlier, when they first arrived in the desert, as they engaged in a series of pointless activities that came to represent everything that brought them to the Persian Gulf:

> Six times a day, we gather for formation. We hydrate. We patrol the empty desert. And we hydrate. We throw hand grenades into nowhere. We navigate imaginary mine fields. We fire at nothing. And we hydrate some more.

The setting for this voice-over list of activities is a nearly white desert, with a mist of sand often dulling the images of figures in camouflage uniforms that are shades of beige and tan only slightly darker than the sand. Even when their images are sharper, their background suggests that they are in Nowhere. At one point, they are hitting golf balls over a sand berm into that Nowhere. Figuratively and literally, they are on a course without a target; no holes, or fairways, or putting greens, only sand traps. They labor in sand, and they are trapped in it. As the bright sand is replaced by a dark shot of the sun, blood-orange, on the

FIGURE 4.01. *Playing a football game in 112-degree weather, wearing chemical protective gear and gas masks.* Jarhead *(2005)*.

edge of the horizon, with a dark sky behind and a darker desert beneath, we are told, "And we look north toward the border, and we wait for them. *This is our labor: we wait*" [emphasis added].

That labor also includes playing a football game in 112-degree weather, while wearing thick chemical protective gear and gas masks, in order to demonstrate for the media how the gear works. When the game degenerates into brawling, followed by the men's ripping off their gear and simulating for the press an array of homoerotic acts and positions, the media are quickly ushered away. This is just one instance of how brutality, homoerotic roughhousing, and celebratory playfulness merge into one another, clearly in lieu of a sense of occupational purpose or domestic gratification.

We see another conflation of the celebratory and the violent during a Christmas Eve party, when one of the recruits, Ferguson, has switched assignments with Swofford so that Swofford can party with the other men, drinking the contraband alcohol that he has acquired. Ferguson's attempt to cook some sausages, however, starts a fire that enflames his tent and envelops some boxes of flares and rockets, which launch and explode in the night sky over the camp, disrupting the semi-clad, drunken soldiers dancing together in another tent.

Because he switched shifts and brought the liquor into camp, Swofford is busted to private and put in charge of burning all the excrement produced each day by the encampment. This entails removing several large metal barrels full of shit from beneath the outdoor latrines, adding kerosene and setting the putrid mixture aflame, all under the scorching desert sun. After doing this for a few days, Swofford in a crazed moment verges on killing Ferguson with an M-16, and then hands the terrified Ferguson the gun, puts its barrel in his own face, and screams at Ferguson to pull the trigger. In this instance, for Swofford, who is spending his days in the desert sun over barrels of shit, shooting and being shot amount to the same thing: they are both ways to terminate his employment.

The pointlessness of their work is particularly disturbing in light of the extensively brutal and degrading training that prepared them for it. After basic training, when Swofford reported to his barracks, he was attacked by the other men in his new unit, who beat him, tied his hands, and attempted to brand his leg with "USMC." If, at the last second, they switched out the hot iron for a cold one, they did so to make two points: his on-the-job training involves equal portions of physical and psychological abuse, and failing to burn him does not signify their compassion but his inadequacy. "You got to earn the hot branding iron," they tell him.

The roughhousing becomes an increasingly brutal release for the pointless boredom, and the two in combination make clear that being a Marine is a shit occupation, a message underscored by the film's scatological motif. In basic training, Swofford tells us we can see him taking a dump. When they first arrive in the Persian Gulf, he quickly determines that "We need to get out of this shithole soon," to which another soldier responds, "Fuck politics. We're here. All the rest is bullshit." Later, when Swofford is cleaning the latrines, Major Lincoln orders him to return a shit-filled barrel that he has just removed from under the latrine, so that the Major can take his morning dump. Upon leaving, he tells Swofford, "I left you a little gift in there—not too hard, not too soft: perfect." As the episode underscores, Swofford's shit occupation is the job of receiving shit and disposing of it.

Significantly, killing—the ostensible objective of their job—is treated as a task, no more a necessary consequence of fulfilling a mission than cleaning a pot of shit. Divorced of its mission, a sniper shot becomes the point where autoerotic pleasure and shitwork merge under the rubric of their "real" job. But instead of arriving, that reality operates in an economy that constantly exchanges the shit they have to take for the kill they will never accomplish. If the final war episode shows that Swofford's shot makes no difference, the preceding episode makes clear the Marines' occupation is not defined by military missions, but by everyday shitwork. Swofford's unit, in pursuit of retreating Iraqi soldiers, finds itself showered by oil from exploding Iraqi wells, oil so dense and profuse the Marines seem to be covered in shit, which stands for all the vile fluids and human detritus defining their life. In basic training Swofford

FIGURE 4.02. *Swofford's unit showered by oil from exploding Iraqi wells.* Jarhead *(2005).*

endures chronic, laxative-induced diarrhea to feign a stomach virus and thus escape the torture of his job. In both his daily life and his dreams, he regularly vomits. Following on the heels of US air strikes, he finds immolated bodies: "The whole desert is shitting dead ragheads!" When the Marine who panicked during basic training was killed by machine-gun fire, Staff Sergeant Sykes screamed "Halt," ran over to the body and screamed "Shit!" At this moment, Sykes is not only exclaiming his frustration and ire, but also identifying the dead Marine for what he is, military excrement, the detritus of a shit job.

Under that shower of oil that has blackened the sky, the sand, and everything between, Sykes tells Swofford:

> I could be working for my brother right now. Dry wall business in Compton. I would be his partner . . . See my wife every night, fuck her, maybe . . . take my children to school. If I ran his crews too, probably increase productivity 40 . . . 50 per cent. Like a hundred K a year. Do you know why I don't? . . . *Because I love this job!* I mean who else gets a chance to see shit like this!

Although Binns argues that Sykes "remains patriotic" (97), nothing Sykes says indicates loyalty to his country or dedication to a cause, but if he, as Binns claims, "snaps the other figures out of their delusions of home" (98), in doing so he is making clear that they are not there to protect the homeland or establish the conditions that will make returning home possible. The connection between their warfare and the home front is, as Binns understands, delusional. This is the antithesis of love of country, taken to its limits: loyalty to one's job as opposed to one's home.

The chance, as Sykes puts it, to see "shit like this," on the one hand, or to clean barrels full of it, on the other, was not Swofford's mission but the perks and hazards of his occupation, a point underscored by repeated time-and-troop signatures that provide the film's structure in lieu of a mission-based narrative:

TIME IN THE DESERT 14 MINUTES,
TROOPS IN THE DESERT: 5000

TIME IN THE DESERT 122 DAYS, 5 HOURS, 22 MINUTES,
TROOPS IN THE DESERT: 390,000

TIME IN THE DESERT 175 DAYS, 14 HOURS, 5 MINUTES,
TROOPS IN THE DESERT: 575,000

BRAVO'S ROTATION: A DISARMING JOB

This time-card approach to military service also structures *The Hurt Locker*, which reduces the military service purely to a clock, divorced from any larger troop actions:

Days Left in Bravo Rotation: 38
Days Left in Bravo Rotation: 37
Days Left in Bravo Rotation: 16
Days Left in Bravo Rotation: 2

The film opens with a black screen, with a quote in white: "The rush of battle is often a potent and lethal addiction, for war is a drug."[6] After a few seconds, the first clause disappears, leaving "war is a drug" to fade slowly into the blackness. As an addiction, the rush of battle attributes no gratification to the end goal because addiction, like Swofford's handling his rifle, is a self-gratifying practice, necessarily concentrated on its self-perpetuation, making it the antithesis of warfare's mission to end wartime. That goal gives soldiers at war a long-term, but clearly limited, trajectory, whereas the addicted, whether clean and sober or actively indulging, take things one day at a time. Like the time stamps that order the film's episodes, the idea that war is a drug runs counter to the narrative differentiating the aberrant wartime from normal peacetime because drugs substitute sensation for narrative. For this reason, as Burgoyne points out, the film "has none of the ordinary rhythms that have shaped the dramatic structure of the war film for over a century" (3).

The quote also misleadingly directs our attention to the significance of battle, a misdirection that the rest of the film corrects. In the context of that correction, it seems clear that emphasis should be placed on the *rush* rather than the battles that produce it, as battles are absent from *The Hurt Locker*, a symptom of a greater absence. *The Hurt Locker* not only lacks combat but, more importantly, lacks anything that would give battles meaning. The men we see have no objective other than to stay alive, which cannot, technically, be a soldier's mission, since it is accomplished most easily by not being a soldier. In an all-volunteer army, one can avoid death from combat by not volunteering. But, as the ending of *Saving Private Ryan* reminded us, avoiding death is not the traditional soldier's objective, since most of the soldiers in Miller's unit die in the process of accomplishing their mission. Thus, for the film's opening quote to apply, the film has to disaggregate the "rush" from the "battle" by turning the rush into an essence rather than an end.

This becomes apparent in the film's first minutes. On the masterfully orchestrated soundtrack, we hear a voice—anxious, urgent, scared—giving what sounds from its rhythm to be orders or instructions, spoken in what we presume to be Arabic. These commands or pleas mix with blaring horns and rapid footsteps, a clamor of harried voices, the hum of a mobile bot, and the rumble of its metal treads over gravel. "Here," as Burgoyne aptly notes, "an ancient metropolis and its ingrained rhythms of daily life are crosshatched by the sounds and sights of modern war" (4).

A tracking shot from ground level follows the device—a mini tank on steroids—as it rushes toward an object, while Iraqi civilians, being cleared from the street, race in the opposite direction. The bot's motor seems to be getting louder and faster as it approaches the thing everyone else is escaping. The frenzy grows as more elements join the crescendo: armored Humvees, troops deploying from them, orders being shouted, a merchant in the marketplace yelling at soldiers who are driving him from his shop. At the same time, rapid cutting juxtaposes fragments of these events with the view from the camera on the bot, showing a pixelated image of the ground across which it races.

The background sound starts to recede as we switch from the bot's view to the remote-control screen where the bomb disposal team, perhaps seventy-five yards away, is controlling the device. Unlike the other voices we have heard, these are clear and calm, allowing extremely tight framing, rather than the hectic soundtrack, to express the sequence's intensity. We see the eye of a Black soldier, Sergeant Sanborn (Anthony Mackie), part of his nose (sharply enough focused to reveal the pores), fringes of his helmet and chinstrap. He is operating the bot together with the team leader, Sergeant Thompson (Guy Pearce), a fragment of whose face we see in another tight, sharply focused shot. They operate the bot while they crack dick jokes, as though on a fraternity couch, playing a video game. When a wheel falls off the bot's wagon, which is carrying explosives to destroy the bomb it has located, Thompson routinely dons the heavy, thickly padded protective outfit and headgear, and heads down the street to complete the bot's job. The calm banter on the headphones, between Thompson and his team—Sanborn and Specialist Eldridge (Brian Geraghty)—is undermined by ominous music, which intensifies when Thompson places the explosives at the bomb site. As Thompson starts to walk back, Eldridge spots an Iraqi man in front of the butcher shop, apparently having evaded the soldiers who had cleared everyone else. The man holds a cell phone, which can be, Eldridge knows, a remote triggering device. He alerts Sanborn, who tells Thompson to leave the bomb site rapidly, while Eldridge rushes at the man with the phone, but before Eldridge takes a shot, the man detonates the bomb, and Thompson, prevented by the protective gear from moving fast enough to clear the kill zone, dies from the blast's percussion.

In capturing a battle's rush—both its adrenaline surge and its haste—without actual combat, this first episode glosses the opening quote by encapsulating the problem of a war without a mission. Extracted from battle, the rush, in acquiring an existence independent of the war, becomes wartime essentialized. Similarly, the occupation of serving in the military in a foreign country can be divorced from serving the military Occupation of that country, just as a rush of battle can be simulated by a video game as easily as remote controls, video screens, and bots can produce the act that a video game simulates. And in the same way that a player hits "reset" when the game blows up their avatar, the film resets with the arrival of Thompson's replacement, Sergeant James (Jeremy Renner), an experienced bomb disposal expert, one addicted to that rush of battle in ways that terrify Sanborn and Eldridge.

The rest of the film follows the activities of this three-man bomb squad, led by James, whose job clock ticks at exactly the same pace, regardless of specific accomplishments or failures. Even more tautly organized than *Jarhead*, the film forgoes not only the mission but everything leading up to the team's task on a given day, and almost everything following from it. Most of the film consists of six separate jobs. Working in Iraq years after the invasion and its alleged victory, the men have as little sense of their mission as we do. Each day they go out, somewhat like fishermen, to use their professional equipment. What we see of the day's work begins as they approach a suspicious object in some tenuously secured Iraqi street while locals watch for unspecified reasons. These apparent Iraqi civilians may be planning to detonate an IED (improvised explosive device), or shoot at a team member, or simply film the team's work; they may be caught up in their daily chores or businesses. Humvees or tanks pull into their street, Marines with guns aggressively give them instructions in a language they do not understand, threaten to shoot them, or do shoot them. These locals surreptitiously detonate bombs or try to; they shoot and are shot or are not shot; they escape or fail to. "Who or what is the U.S. fighting against," Robert Sklar asks, "or more pertinently, who is fighting against the U.S., planting those IEDs that the squad is assigned to defuse? Why do Iraqis sometimes target other Iraqis?" (56). These differences are minor, given that *The Hurt Locker* does not make clear the Iraqis' identities, their missions, or how they relate to the film's narrative structure. As pertains to the team's job specs, their stories do not matter. "Not part of the story," Sklar points out (56).

The first vignette begins with the team navigating heavy traffic on a Baghdad street to respond to a call from soldiers they find huddling in an alley, a block away from a suspected bomb. Clearly, the soldiers fear that, exposed in the street, they are vulnerable targets. James, shunning the bot, dons the protective gear and walks the block to explore the suspicious material, dropping smoke bombs to create "a diversion," he says, but also blocking the view for Sanborn and Eldridge, who are supposed to provide protective cover.

A taxi speeds at James from a side street and slams its brakes a few feet from him. Without budging, he points his pistol at the driver and commands him to back up. The driver sits motionless, even after James shoots a bullet on the ground, close to his tire, then shoots out his windshield, and then places a gun against the driver's temple. Either the driver doesn't understand James's gestures or is frozen with terror, until, after James clicks the hammer, he places the car in reverse, but he goes no more than fifty yards before another group of soldiers pull him from his car at gunpoint. That is the last we see of him. "If he wasn't an insurgent," James quips, "he is now." After James disables the bomb, he follows a wire to a cluster of six bombs buried in the street, such that when he tugs the wire, he is surrounded by explosives. On hands and knees, he crawls within the circle, severing each bomb's connection to its detonating source.

This activity is intercut with shots of Iraqis looking down on James from surrounding buildings. One man rushes downstairs and out of his building, where his eyes meet James's. James holds up the disabled detonator as the man flees. If the previous scene forces us to understand that James might have been blown up by this man, more significantly, we understand little else, such as why and how the man is connected to the IED, what motivated him to run, and more generally toward what objective these bombs were planted. We get only a handful of gestures and acts, a cluster of glimpses. His motives are as opaque as those of the hapless taxi driver. *If* the driver was an insurgent, was he in any way connected to the man who ran from his apartment, or *might* they have been from rival factions? And what about the other people, whom we have seen even more briefly viewing James's bravado from their windows? Compared to these insufficient glimpses, the time we spend with James, Sanborn, and Eldridge should provide more information, but it does not. Nor do any of the subsequent workdays further clarify their situation.

DAY TWO

In the second vignette, the team is called to inspect a suspiciously sagging car, probably weighed down by explosives. When they arrive, a shooter fires at the car from an unspecified location, attempting to detonate those explosives. But, with a handheld fire extinguisher, James extinguishes the fire before the car explodes. While James tears apart the car's guts in search of its hidden wiring, Sanborn and Eldridge try to give him cover, exposing themselves to possible snipers who could be sighting them from any direction. Despite their pleas to abandon the site, leaving the car to a demolition team, James persists in attempting to figure out the wiring, while they continue to spot more Iraqi observers, one using a camera to photograph the events and others apparently in communication with the cameraman from a distant minaret. They do not know, nor do we, whether any of these Iraqis initially shot at the car, whether any of the observers are armed with guns or an even more lethal detonating device, which could kill James and possibly Eldridge, who is not far from him. If that happened, what chance would Sanborn have of getting out alive?

Although the shot at the car seemed to be initiating a battle sequence, instead of a firefight we get a battle of nerves emanating from the team's ignorance: not knowing who or where the enemy is, they are at war with everything and nothing. If each Iraqi they spot means they are in more danger, then so are the Iraqis, perhaps even more than the soldiers. The Iraqis are (or may be) in their homes, homes that could be destroyed if a car bomb explodes. Therefore, they are (or may be) hoping that James disables the bombs. If so, they have no way of communicating this to the soldiers pointing automatic rifles at them, not only because they may lack English communication skills adequate to convey their support or lack of hostility, but also because any attempt to do so could be fatal, as it nearly was for the cab driver who encountered James, or for the man who attempted to talk to Eldridge the day Thompson died. A more frightened or simply more trigger-happy soldier might have shot him after he ignored the first order to leave. And if that man was an accomplice of the man with the cell phone responsible for Thompson's death, shooting him might have been correct, and if the man were innocent, shooting him would have been tantamount to cold-blooded murder.

Thus, even those who welcomed the United States' deposal of Saddam and its promise to liberate Iraq have come to realize, by 2008, that the US had made no plan to establish a system of governance replacing Saddam's despotic regime, nor had any interest in the work of making Iraq a beacon of democracy, despite that objective's being asserted more aggressively by administration die-hards after the threat of WMDs proved bogus. In 2006, Peter Baker reported, "While President Bush vows to transform Iraq into a beacon of democracy in the Middle East, his administration has been scaling back funding for the main organizations trying to carry out his vision."[7] Instead, US "liberation" brought to Iraq more than 150,000 armed, frightened men, generally ignorant of Iraqi language, culture, or religion. Empowered to kill civilians, these men were incapable of distinguishing the people for whom they were fighting from the enemies of American forces or other Iraqis who might be sectarian foes or just collateral damage.

The team's ignorance of one another's motives or objectives in this episode compounds the confusion. Eldridge, having spotted a man on another rooftop recording his actions with a video camera, wants to know whether he should kill the man, as he should have killed the man who detonated the bomb that killed Thompson, or whether the trauma of not having done so would lead him to kill a man and/or initiate a firefight that could leave him trapped in a crossfire, as a crossfire is always a potential threat when one is surrounded by buildings without knowing who is in them or how to figure out, until it is too late, who is friend and who is foe. Sanborn, on the rooftop, farther away from James and Eldridge, although in less danger from a car explosion, is more vulnerable to sniper fire. He wants to leave the site, which he sees as becoming increasingly dangerous, and leave the car to the engineers, whose job it is to dispense with it.

But the biggest enigma is James, who seems reckless in ways that befuddle his team. After standing with a fire extinguisher a few feet from a car that could explode, he becomes obsessed with the hidden detonation box to the point of tearing the car apart, checking and, to the extent possible, disassembling every section of the car, even taking off his headset so that he cannot hear Sanborn's increasingly intense demands that they leave. He seems indifferent to the fact that in addition to putting himself in danger, he is also endangering his team, who cannot leave because they are obliged to provide cover for his obsessive, and in many ways pointless, search of the vehicle. Although he is the team leader, he seems not to regard its safety as part of his mission. In orchestrating danger rather than minimizing it, he seems to use the rush of battle to replace his mission instead of to help him accomplish it.

DAY THREE: 23 DAYS FROM THE END OF THE ROTATION, PART 1

The third vignette, two weeks after the second episode, takes place someplace in the desert, where the team is detonating explosives from about a quarter of a mile away. Between detonations, when James drives to the explosion site to retrieve his gloves, Sanborn holding the detonation trigger says to Eldridge, "You know these detonators misfire all the time." When Eldridge asks, "What are you doing?" Sanborn replies, "I'm just saying shit happens—they mis-fire." Grasping that Sanborn is suggesting they trigger the device when James reaches the explosion site, Eldridge says, "He'd be obliterated to nothing."

This scene thus rereads the film's opening, in which, because of a technical failure, Thompson had to approach undetonated explosives, and Eldridge saw the detonating device in the hands of a man about to trigger the fatal explosion. Only this time, the trigger man is Sanborn. Both Sanborn and Eldridge acknowledge that little would be left of James. "A half a helmet, somewhere, bits of hair," Sanborn notes with distant calm, replicating, albeit not as jovially, the ironic repartee between him and Thompson as Thompson had prepared to approach the bomb site. "Be a change of protocol," Sanborn says to Eldridge, "Make sure this kind of thing never happened again, you know." The menacing irony of this comment pivots on the phrase "this kind of thing" because the kind of thing Sanborn wants to prevent is the need to kill a team leader so addicted to the rush of battle that he recklessly disregards standard protocol.

In this instance, as in all the other vignettes, the paramount issue is identifying the enemy. Because Sanborn now is the potential trigger man, he expresses this sentiment as an American soldier in Iraq, and also implicitly speaks for the Iraqi who killed Thompson. For both Sanborn and that Iraqi, the leader of the US bomb disposal team is the enemy. As Yossarian says about his commanding officer in *Catch-22*, "the enemy is anyone who is trying to kill me."

When Sanborn tells Eldridge that he (Eldridge) would have to write the report, Eldridge, realizing Sanborn's job may have eroded the boundary between dark irony and unchecked desperation, says, "Are you serious?" At the micro level, Eldridge is asking Sanborn the same question that should have been raised to President Bush when he confused personal revenge ("The guy tried to kill my Dad") with his fantasy of completing the war his father left unfinished by fabricating WMDs as a rationale for violating international law and thereby causing the deaths of more than a quarter of a million innocent Iraqis.[8] Sanborn responds to Eldridge in much the way that Bush-Cheney-Rumsfeld and the seventy-seven senators who authorized the administration's actions treated the issue of the war as procedural rather than moral. "I can't write it," Sanborn matter-of-factly states. But Eldridge clarifies—"I mean are you serious about killing him?"—forcing Sanborn to face the implication of proceeding as though his fantasy that James's death by "accident" were a fait accompli, with the knowledge that Eldridge, unlike Bush-Cheney-Rumsfeld, would not be his accomplice in finding protocols to turn his fantasy into actual bloodshed.

DAY FOUR: 23 DAYS FROM THE END OF THE ROTATION, PART 2

Returning from this desert explosion site, the team encounters an immobile, armed Humvee with some men in Hadji outfits, whom they approach with their weapons aimed because, in their line of work, it is not always possible to distinguish enemies from "friendlies." It turns out, however, that these are British contractors transporting prisoners back to their base. They cannot repair a flat tire because one of them had, in a fit of rage, thrown the tire iron at someone. As James's team finishes helping them change the tire, a sniper bullet kills one of the contractors, and they all begin shooting in multiple directions, once again starting what, in a traditional war film, might be a combat episode, but that instead quickly devolves into a scene of trapped men with little shelter, attempting to locate the source of the threat. In the process, two more of the contractors, including the leader (Ralph Fiennes), are killed by fewer than a half dozen insurgents with telescopic lenses a half mile or more away, who are pinning them down. In an excruciating process, the men spend several hours immobile under the desert sun, lest any motion reveal their location to the snipers, while James uses binoculars to help Sanborn fix them in the crosshairs of his telescopic lens and, eventually, kill them. Not until sundown does James say to Sanborn, "I think we're done."

Both of the day's events fall within the scope of their workday: their job in the morning was to detonate explosives and, in the afternoon, to kill a cadre of snipers, each task with its own dangers, one more safe, the other less so. The completion of neither task accomplished any objective beyond allowing them to return to the base after a busy workday.

FIGURE 4.03. *Immobile for hours under the desert sun, James helps Sanborn target the snipers.* The Hurt Locker *(2008).*

DAY FIVE: THREE WEEKS LATER ("16 DAYS LEFT IN BRAVO COMPANY'S ROTATION")

This episode starts with Colonel Cambridge (Christian Camargo), the base therapist, requesting to go out with the team on this workday. We first saw Cambridge speaking with Eldridge about his fear of being killed and about the soldier's guilt over failing to kill the Iraqi before he detonated the bomb that killed Thompson. Cambridge urges Eldridge to "stop obsessing." "Right now," Cambridge asks him, "what are you thinking about?" to which he responds by shooting his empty rifle. Pulling back the hammer, he says, "Here's Thompson—he's dead"; then, pulling the trigger, he says, "Here's Thompson—he's alive." He repeats this sequence three times in rapid succession, leaving his therapist speechless.

During his second conversation with Cambridge, Eldridge is working on the engine of his Humvee the day after the episode in which the team waited anxiously in a Baghdad street, with the growing number of Iraqis observing them from buildings on all sides, while James traced wires in the car full of bombs. When Cambridge asks Eldridge how he is doing, he replies, sounding at least minimally sincere,

"Fine. Feeling great."

"Getting along with the other men in your unit?"

"Yeah. Men are great. Team is great," Eldridge replies, this time with a level of enthusiasm that, for Cambridge, strains credibility.

"Are you being sarcastic, soldier?" he asks. With the addition of the word "soldier," Colonel Cambridge reminds Specialist Eldridge of Eldridge's position in a chain of command that requires him to supply militarily appropriate answers to his superior officer, even while sharing his personal anxieties with his therapist. Because addressing the colonel sarcastically would be insubordination, Eldridge denies he was sarcastic, actually an honest response in that what sounded like sarcasm was more an attempt to follow military protocol than to ridicule Cambridge. To navigate this impossible situation, Eldridge elaborates by oscillating between factual details and official cant.

"He's going to get me killed. Almost did yesterday. At least I'll die in the line of duty. Proud and strong."

"You know it doesn't have to be a bad time in your life," Cambridge responds, attempting to reconcile his therapeutic role with his oath of office. "Going to war is a once-in-a-lifetime experience. Could be fun." That Cambridge is transparently ludicrous is particularly galling because he seems sincere, evoking a now clearly sarcastic response:

"You know this from your extensive work in the field, right?"

"I've done my field duty."

"Where was that? Yale?"

At this moment, Cambridge, who has been speaking with the authority conferred by his rank and his educational training, finds these foundations challenged. His formal training has kept him from acquiring the experience necessary to do the job the military has assigned him, such that attempting to get Eldridge to conform raises more questions about his own fitness for duty than about Eldridge's. Because Eldridge's responses again leave the colonel speechless, Cambridge exercises his authority to extricate himself from defending the indefensible. Were he not fighting a missionless war, he could commiserate with Eldridge, in the same way, in *Saving Private Ryan*, Captain Miller acknowledges that they all want to go home and return to normal. Miller agrees that many people will die to defeat Hitler, while reminding the men that if they fail at that mission, all the sacrifices will have earned them nothing. With the mission accomplished, however, Cambridge cannot stress the importance of keeping it in sight. Nor can he ask Eldridge to consider the "fun" side of seeing his old team leader killed or being trapped in a Baghdad street by the reckless actions of his new team leader. To extricate himself from giving advice that invites self-humiliation, Cambridge blames Eldridge for Cambridge's own failures:

"Look, you don't want me to come around, I won't come around. These talks are voluntary."

Cambridge has confronted Eldridge with another of the Catch-22s that proliferate post–Mission Accomplished war films by making clear that the privilege of having someone with whom he can *honestly* discuss his fears requires *he not be honest* about them. Attempting to salvage his (ersatz) relationship, Eldridge apologizes.

"Look, I'm sorry. I appreciate what you're saying. I do. I appreciate our sessions together, but you need to come out from behind the wire and see what we do."

"Well," Cambridge replies, "the circumstance calls for it, I will, just like every other soldier." The irony of this statement is that a missionless war makes it difficult, if not impossible, to identify what circumstances call for what actions.

After two weeks of deliberation, however, Cambridge has decided to follow Eldridge's suggestion. The day's work entails picking up unexploded ordnances in an apparently abandoned factory building. As always, the team enters the site—in this case a large, dark building—with their guns up, cautiously turning every corner in anticipation of an ambush. Although the building is empty, they discover it is a bomb factory abandoned only moments earlier. They also discover the mutilated body of a boy approximately twelve years old, whom James recognizes as "Beckham," the boy who sold him DVDs at the entrance to the base. The boy had been tortured and disemboweled, his innards replaced by a body bomb. Although they should have a demolition squad destroy the entire building, James, visibly disturbed by the boy's death, cannot allow the corpse to be blown up with the rest of the structure. Instead, he disables the bomb wired into the boy's body, despite the wretched odor and extensive gore. After completing this odious job, he carries Beckham's wrapped corpse to an Army vehicle that will dispense with it.

Sanborn and Eldridge find James's behavior "very weird," especially when contrasting his sentimental attachment to someone he barely knew to his normal detachment. Because James's job is bomb disposal, not body disposal, this special attention operates in a pointless vacuum, like all the isolated gestures that constitute his occupation in Iraq. The fact that James is certain the corpse is Beckham does not mean he knows anything about the boy's family, not how to contact them or where the corpse should be delivered. His attachment, in fact, is based on a few trivial encounters in which they haggled about a DVD or, for a few moments, played soccer. That James's insubstantial connection provides one of the film's few narrative threads makes its superficiality all the more significant.

While the team is inspecting the bomb factory, Cambridge tries to steer locals away from the area. His demeanor, in contrast to the troops we have seen shouting at the Iraqis, is almost gentle, as he tries to explain that they should move back. He is attempting to apply his counselor training, even though the people understand little or nothing that he says, just as he understands almost nothing most of them say. He clearly believes he is trying to keep them safe, while betraying no cognizance of another Catch-22: it is his presence in Iraq that has made their lives unsafe. Prior to the US invasion, streets were not cluttered with the IEDs from which he is trying to protect them; there was an active police force and no sectarian violence. These all followed from the invasion in search of WMDs that did not exist, to avert an attack on America that was not being planned, and to revenge an attack on America for which Iraq was not responsible. Nor does Cambridge seem to understand that his government did not charge the US military with replacing the police force that his government disbanded. He does not act, therefore, as though he were policing the area—it's not his job—but as though he were counseling Iraqis about their welfare. "I'm thinking, maybe we should move," he says to an Iraqi man, almost as if he is asking a rhetorical question rather than giving an order.

After convincing the group to move, however, he trips on an IED and is blown to shreds. A distraught and disbelieving Eldridge runs out of the Humvee into the haze of smoke and debris, calling his therapist's name, but finds nothing other than a fragment of Cambridge's helmet. Nevertheless, in denial of the explosion he has just witnessed, Eldridge continues to call "Cambridge" rather than acknowledge that what brought Cambridge to that street was that he had challenged his qualifications. Eldridge knows that, as with Thompson's death, had he behaved differently it could have been avoided.

This moment in the film, when, almost back-to-back, James discovers Beckham's corpse and Cambridge is killed, removes simultaneously the two thin narrative threads running through the film's series of workdays. Otherwise, for the most part, the vignettes could occur in any order, like all the workdays we do not see during the film's thirty-eight-day span covering Bravo Company's occupation defusing bombs in Iraq. As represented in *The Hurt Locker*, the deaths of Beckham and Cambridge suggest the impossibility of finding the plot—i.e., conspiracy—behind the war's mission, just as the film cannot provide a plot—i.e., narrative structure—to describe the war's search to uncover the Iraqi plot, in areas besieged by Iraqis plotting against the United States and against one another. If Cambridge's earlier sessions failed therapeutically because he lacked appropriate experience, in this episode Cambridge's life becomes the cost of acquiring that experience—the perfect Catch-22. In the end, it makes no difference what Cambridge knows, in the same way that it made no difference what Swofford learned. The Marine Corps trained Swofford to be a sniper, wedding his life to his rifle, and also denied him his only opportunity to be one. As both films keep reminding us, "what difference does it make?"

In this war, therefore, James's efforts to make the circumstances of Beckham's death motivate him prove particularly pointless and self-destructive. Attempting to find out who murdered and mutilated the boy, James asks the older man for whom Beckham worked what became of the boy. When the bewildered man, who understands no English, has no idea what "Beckham" refers to, James becomes violent and informs the base guards that the man may be an insurgent: "He's a security risk. We should get rid of him." "All the merchants are cleared," James is told, but James refuses to accept the guards' claims. He persists, furthermore, in believing that the boy's name is actually "Beckham," when it was more or less obvious from the outset that the boy was kidding, a perception confirmed by the older man's incomprehension when James keeps shouting the name.

The man's befuddlement, while confirming that the boy's name isn't "Beckham," more significantly reveals how willfully oblivious James remains to that fact. Forcing himself, at gunpoint, into the older man's car that evening, James demands he be taken to Beckham's home. The terrified man, with no idea what "Beckham" means, drives James to a residential section of Baghdad. When James asks if that is Beckham's home, the man seems to respond affirmatively, then quickly speeds away when James is clear of his car (probably because he didn't know what "wait" meant and probably because he wouldn't have heeded James even if he did. What sane person would?).

James then breaks into the house, where a sophisticated, English-speaking Iraqi, who identifies himself as a professor, warmly greets him, invites him to sit down, and calmly urges him to put his gun down. But James, lacking the poise or the rational processing to react appropriately, keeps demanding information about Beckham. Yet Beckham is simply a fictional character in a story that James created to give his occupation some meaning, his military service some semblance of a mission. Even with no language barrier, however, James continues to react as though he had stumbled into a terrorist cell; he demonstrates no understanding that the only threat in the house is him. Neither the old man selling DVDs, nor the soldiers guarding the base, nor the professor's behavior comports with James's fictional reason for being in this house, or in Iraq, or at war.

James is obviously confused, but he refuses to be disabused. Although he and his team repeatedly identify themselves as "friendlies," the Iraqi professor, not James, shows the friendliness. Still pointing his gun, James, befuddled and frightened, backs into a darkened hallway where the professor's wife hits this dangerous intruder on the head with a frying pan. The injured, dizzy James flees into the dark to commence his long walk back to the base. As he approaches, declaring himself a "friendly," he meets the same suspicious hostility from the perimeter guards as the Iraqis had from his team. Just as each Iraqi was, potentially, the man who killed Thompson, James, despite proclaiming himself "friendly," remained in the guards' view a potential insurgent. First forced to his knees and then thrust to the ground, James is handcuffed and interrogated before he is allowed to return to his barrack, in the same way many Iraqis are when troops search their homes.

At this point, the film mirrors the war in its lack of a plot, of a narrative objective, of an informing mission. Like Col. Cambridge's relationship with the enlisted man, James's relationship with the Iraqi boy was an unsustainable fiction, evoking all the fictional Iraqis whose fictional liberation focused the fictional mission of the war, a fiction tested by the daily occupation of US soldiers with no mission. To fill that void, James takes on the mission of tracking down Beckham's murderers. If the encounter with the professor hints at James's folly, the final episodes expose the absurdity of James's mission as well as the consequences of his attachment to it.

"LET'S GET OUT OF THIS FUCKING DESERT!"

Not long after James returns to base, his team is awoken to inspect the aftermath of a massive bombing that has occurred in Baghdad. At night, within the explosion radius, the only light coming from their flashlights and the flames from several fires, they walk through a living inferno, half-lit, body-strewn, and chaotic. Rushing soldiers shout orders, call for medics, and try to clear debris and manage terrified Iraqis, many crying or screaming. While hearing the blast of horns and the blare of sirens, we glimpse the wounded and the dead, architectural fragments and human fragments, flames and flickers, but the rapid cutting and the camera's movements across a space of pervasive darkness makes comprehension of the scene in its totality impossible. James's team performs its assessment, wandering through the rubble like insurance adjusters in Hell.

When they determine the origin of the blast and the perimeter of its radius, James wants to go beyond that perimeter (and beyond the parameters of his team's job) to locate and capture the trigger man, whom he assumes is nearby enough to observe the damage. Sanborn challenges James's conclusion by raising the possibility that the trigger man was a suicide bomber, in which case "You'll never find him."

"What if it was a remote det?" James responds. As with his attempts to trace Beckham's origins, his adamance about investing his job with a mission drives him outside his occupational constraints.

"This is bullshit!" Sanborn says. "You got three infantry platoons behind you whose job it is to go Hadji hunting. That ain't our fucking *job!*" [emphasis added].

"You don't say no to me, Sanborn. I say no to you," James shouts, using his rank to override rational arguments, as Cambridge had done with Eldridge. Because it's not Sanborn's job to find insurgents, but it is his job to follow orders, being in the military at this moment in Baghdad conflicts with the job assigned him by the military. In traditional wartime, the war's informing mission may help resolve these conflicts, as is the case in *Saving Private Ryan*, where the war's mission made stopping the Germans at Ramelle more important to Miller and to Ryan than, for either of them, following the order to extricate Ryan from combat. But in this case, at a point when even the objective of capturing and executing Saddam Hussein had proved inconsequential, the only mission weighing against the constraints of their job descriptions is one that James contrives: "You know there are guys watching us right now, out there, laughing at this. And I'm not OK with *that!*"

It is clear, moreover, that this contrivance is not motivated by any sense of duty, but in part by James's lingering need to avenge Beckham, and in part by his desire to avenge the humiliation of his last attempt to do so. Nor has James any respect for the organization of military operations or the people strategizing the Occupation. He does not care whose job it is to find the trigger man or to stop insurgents from laughing at the Americans who threw Iraq into lethal chaos. None of the characters give any thought to discovering who the insurgents are, even though, without knowing that, the United States cannot formulate its own mission, any more than James can begin to guess what ends his invented mission serves. If the death of Beckham has turned the war into James's personal fiction, his mission only lasts as long as he accepts that fiction, in the same way that Bush-Cheney-Rumsfeld based their mission on the fictitious WMDs. Thus, like the entire Iraq invasion force, this bomb disposal team, emulating their leader's hunger for revenge and his fictional excuse for it, proceeds on a mission both dangerous and pointless.

Having identified the likely area for the trigger men, James orders his team to split up, each man searching a different narrow street in the dark, with the music cuing us to impending danger. Running toward the sound of gunfire,

James and Sanborn converge on the alley down which Eldridge had gone. Eventually they see two men dragging Eldridge around a corner, and, cutting the men off at the other end of the block, James opens fire, killing one Iraqi and shattering Eldridge's leg.

The next day, James and Sanborn go to see Eldridge off as he is being evacuated by helicopter. As they approach their Humvee, the boy James has called "Beckham" comes running toward him, smiling, with DVDs and a soccer ball in his arms. Instead of showing joy at discovering the boy is unharmed, James scowls with resentment, then turns away. This makes the boy, who is clearly crushed by James's rejection, one more of the millions of Iraqis who discovered that American concern for their liberation was a fiction. Thus, Beckham's mere existence, because it belied James's fiction, signified betrayal.

When they get to Eldridge as his stretcher is being loaded onto a helicopter, he is in great pain and furious with James. "My fucking femur's shattered in nine places. They say I'll be walking in six months, if I'm lucky." When James attempts to comfort him, he screams, "You see that—you fucking see that? That's what happens when you shoot someone in the leg, you motherfucker!" He will have none of James's apology, which he treats as self-serving. "Fuck you, Will! Fuck you! Thank you for saving my life, but we didn't have to go out looking for trouble to get your adrenaline fix. Fuck you!" Eldridge's last words as the helicopter is about to leave serve as a generic renunciation of all the bogus missions constituting the war: "Let's get out of this fucking desert!"

The film then cuts with no transition from a close-up of James and Sanborn walking away from the helicopter to a close-up of Sanborn, with his rifle lifted, screaming, "Don't move!" at a man in a street at midday, who has his hands in the air. This time they have a translator who tells them that the man had approached them saying a bomb was attached to him and begging them to remove it. "Please don't leave me," he begs. But, despite James's efforts to cut all the locks securing the iron bars that bind the man to the bomb, while a timer ticks down to under one minute before detonation, he has to look into the man's eyes and admit, "There's too many locks. I'm sorry. There is nothing I can do." And then he flees from the explosion, managing to survive the blast by getting just a few yards further from the kill zone than Thompson had been able to in the film's opening sequence. James survives to return home to his wife and infant, a domestic life so far from what he has come to consider "normal" that he has to return to work, as indicated by the film's final shot of his boots on the ground under the new time stamp, "365 Days Left in the Desert."

The film's vignettes, in sum, are connected graphically and thematically, but not narratively. Whether or not a civilian detonates the bomb or only tries, whether one escapes or dies, is irrelevant to the film's narrative arc. When James killed one of the men who had captured Eldridge, there was no way to know whether the dead man was the bomber for whom they were looking, nor to determine what they had accomplished by shooting him, other than saving (as well as seriously injuring) Eldridge. When the team had screamed, to no avail, "it's not our job!" they were right, and James's attempt to give their job a mission constitutes the war's true occupational hazard.

CHAPTER 5

US, THEM, AND THE SPOILS OF WAR

In the last weeks of the series *Lost*, *Green Zone*, a 2010 film about the search for WMDs that dominated the first years of the war, received generally positive reviews, with some qualifications, mostly relating to the director Paul Greengrass's attempt to combine an action thriller with a serious engagement with the consequences of the Bush administration's fictions and deceptions regarding the existence of Saddam's WMD program. A. O. Scott ("A Search for That Casualty, Truth") astutely summarized the complexity of Greengrass's intention: "Mr. Greengrass and the screenwriter, Brian Helgeland, deftly glean material from the historical record, and while they compress, simplify and invent according to the imperatives of the genre—this is a thriller, not a documentary—they do so with seriousness and an impressive sense of scruples." While sharing Scott's admiration for Greengrass's ambition, J. Hoberman felt the film's two objectives never adequately cohered: "As black-and-white as [the] script is, the movie may still be too nuanced for mass consumption," and at the same time, "In the end . . . action trumps logic." Kenneth Turan comes to a similar assessment: "Even though it comes awfully close, 'Green Zone' can't totally keep its balance right up to the end. Precisely because so much of this film is so good at verisimilitude, the Hollywood tendencies of its last sections are not as satisfying as what's come before, the forceful and engaging nature of the action footage notwithstanding."

The ambivalence toward the film seems to emanate from its genre inconsistency in that the political exposé genre, often associated with legal intrigue, follows protagonists who pursue leads and accumulate evidence until a clear explanation replaces an array of initial confusions. Such is the case in *Dark Waters* (2019), about the litigation surrounding DuPont's pollution of Parkersburg, West Virginia, with carcinogenic Teflon toxins, or in *The Insider* (1999), about the whistleblower who revealed Big Tobacco's suppression of the harmful effects of cigarettes. Often, instead of litigators, the exposé genre follows journalists who unravel scandals, as in *Spotlight* (2015) or *All the President's Men* (1976). In this genre, truth and clarity triumph even more than the characters who uncover the truth. Action-adventure films, such as the Bourne trilogy (mentioned in most reviews of *Green Zone* because they have the same director and star), rely on clear adversaries whose fast-paced conflicts, chases, and intrigues supply the films' escapist fun. The reviewers of *Green Zone* thus note the difficulty, if not impossibility, of merging these genres, because one genre demands complexity, just as a successful Occupation does, while the other, like an invasion based on cinematic conventions, facilitates action by keeping objectives simple. I am suggesting, in other words, that what some reviewers saw as *Green Zone*'s inability to meld inimical genres reflected the same problem Bush-Cheney-Rumsfeld had in running a war that required top-flight military execution rather than schlock movie direction.

WHICH SIDE OF THE GREEN ZONE ARE WE ON?

In many ways, therefore, *Green Zone*, set in 2003 Iraq, reflected the confusion that surrounded *Lost*'s Others. That TV series started with the plane crash survivors as the island's definitive community, ignoring the fact that the survivors were also intruders. These middle-class travelers seem at the outset to be the unquestionable avatars of Western values (even though they include two non-Enlish-speaking Koreans). Disentangling the shifting allegiances and values that enmesh those survivors and the Others in a world of uncertainty, paranoia, duplicity, and betrayal is less important to this discussion than noting that in the first decade of the twenty-first century, the same uncertainty, paranoia, duplicity, and betrayal infused every aspect of American-Iraqi relations. Fear that Saddam might use weapons that the United States had sold him merged with fear that he might manufacture weapons to retaliate for the oppressive embargoes it imposed on him. (This logic assumed, we should note, that Saddam intended to retaliate for embargoes prior to their imposition.) If Saddam, by having so easily succumbed in the first Gulf War, demonstrated US strength, the failure to topple his regime became emblematic of US weakness: a loss of nerve, a lack of faith, an inability to get the job done. 9/11 thus evoked the specter of weapons that could have (but didn't [but could next time ("We don't want the smoking gun to be a mushroom cloud")]) caused the mass destruction of the Twin Towers (or a reasonable facsimile). What if Al Qaeda's impetus allied itself with Iraq's imagined capacity for destruction (even though Saddam and Al Qaeda were hostile to one another)? What was the risk that a shared hostility toward the United States might turn sworn enemies into conspiring allies? Would liberating Iraq turn it into a US ally? If so, would that abort Al Qaeda's access to Iraq's WMDs (if they existed [but they didn't])? Would eliminating Iraq's WMDs also eliminate Al Qaeda's impetus to align with Iraq (of which there was no evidence)? And, in addition, wouldn't toppling Saddam show the Arab world (which, for this logic to work, must be a monolith [which it wasn't]) that the United States is strong and determined, which would further deter Al Qaeda (which must be part of that monolith [though it wouldn't be (even if the monolith existed)]) from attacking the United States again? And wouldn't this enhance Israeli security as well as be economically advantageous for US firms situated at the center of an oil-rich Iraq economy, after embargoes are lifted and Iraq, to show gratitude for the invasion (and the destruction of its infrastructure, economy, and civil law), becomes a valued US trade partner?

Although the United States could not know the probability of these far-fetched possibilities, not knowing something, according to Rumsfeld's management philosophy, beneficially eliminates the work of thinking about it. Combining Rumsfeld's sanction on planning with Cheney's "one percent doctrine" (threats with even a one percent likelihood must be treated as certainties[1]) made it almost a 99-to-1 certainty that invading Iraq was the best course for the United States. This deductive logic was so persuasive to some of the Rumsfeld crew that they continued to defend it years after the war became a costly, bloody mess. Obsession with the imagined violence threatening American manhood (didn't 9/11 catch the nation with its pants down and flatten its two largest erections?) turned Iraq into the perfect Freudian fetish, the object that would erase the fear of castration by inverting the narratives of cause and effect. The Green Zone was the place where these irrational narratives repeatedly coalesced to cancel one another out. As the political and military hub of the new Iraq, the Green Zone became the revelation of everything that was not there, other than the specter of violence.

This confusing sampling of the ifs and maybes that became certainties effectively glosses the plot of *Green Zone*. The central figure, Chief Warrant Officer Roy Miller (Damon), in the spring of 2003 heads a unit searching for WMDs but finding vacant sites. His fruitless searches entail taking his men through the hazardous streets, where war was tantamount to over but still technically under way (or still raging, albeit technically over, depending on whose talking points prevail at any Baghdad intersection). All the narratives, in any case, leave the status of the Iraqi Army fuzzy. Seemingly defeated but not surrendering, its existence cannot be discounted, although its presence is not apparent. Still regarded as the opposition, its location remains uncertain, its chain of command unclear, and its role and allegiance clouded under the mist of burgeoning sectarian conflicts. The fuzziness surrounding the Iraqi Army therefore necessarily blurs the status of the war in 2003 along with the US role in Iraq.

In contrast to this complexity, Miller's mission, as he repeatedly asserts, is clear, as clear as the intelligence marking WMD locations is bad. The reason Miller can't find the WMDs, as the film's 2010 audience knows, is that they don't exist, but that does not explain why he keeps receiving bad intelligence about their bogus locations. In addition, with the US chain of command rife with infighting, defining the US mission was difficult, if not impossible, because a mission is an authorized goal, and authorization requires a site of authority with a legitimate authority figure occupying that site. Because the absence of a surrender made the war and the Occupation simultaneous rather than sequential, multiple authorities governed US troops. That both the war and the Occupation employed private contractors in several roles compounded the confusion, since the contractors did not answer to military authority or submit to civil jurisdiction. Their behavior, therefore, was governed by their jobs rather than by a mission. Their injuries were occupational hazards, not consequences of a hazardous Occupation. They were not earning the right to go home; they could simply quit.

Civilian officials in the numerous departments and agencies were, similarly, contractors whose goals were governed by their jobs. Rajiv Chandrasekaran describes the "motley bunch" of fifteen hundred American occupational administration employees in the Green Zone in 2003 and 2004: "businessmen who were active in the Republican Party, retirees who wanted one last taste of adventure, diplomats who had studied Iraq for years, recent college graduates who had never had a full-time job, government employees who wanted the 25 percent salary bonus paid for working in a war zone" (*Imperial Life*, 13).

For them, "mission" was a euphemism for career advancement: "liberating" Iraq was a talking point; Baghdad was a post assignment. The film's representative career bureaucrat is Clark Poundstone (Greg Kinnear), a Pentagon Intelligence official, who seems loosely based on Douglas Feith, Rumsfeld's undersecretary of defense for policy, whom General Tommy Franks, we should recall, famously called "the fucking stupidest guy on the face of the earth."[2] A composite spokesman for the Washington narrative, Poundstone insists on ignoring Miller's complaints, based on two Washington mandates: that Iraqi WMDs were real, and that the Iraqi people should not be alienated as they verge on forming a government believed by Washington to be favorable to US objectives. In Washingtonian logic, these two fictions validated one another.

WEAPONS OF MASS DISINFORMATION

At the outset of the film, just after Miller's team has risked their lives to secure a warehouse identified as housing chemical weapons but instead containing rusty machinery covered with pigeon shit, we see Poundstone greeting the heralded landing of Ahmed Zubaidi (a fictional representation of Ahmed Chalabi, the Iraqi exile who conned the war's planners in Washington into believing he would be welcomed as the popular leader of a coalition government). Lawrie Dayne (Amy Ryan), a *Wall Street Journal* reporter who, in the leadup to the war, had published articles attesting to Saddam's WMDs, presses Poundstone for contact with the source upon which his leaks to her were based.[3] Poundstone instead assures her that they will find the WMDs soon. This is the first of many moments when the film indicates the war's official mission is immaterial; both Poundstone and Dayne only care about the role the WMDs play in their own professional advancement.

At the same time that this exchange between Poundstone and Dayne takes place, Miller attends a briefing about the following day's search for WMDs, where he is assured the intelligence is good because, an officer tells the group,

> We have a detailed media plan we've worked out. We coordinated it with the public affairs folks. We have a good plan that involves the top-rated media in the United States and the UK so that they're prepared to cover all aspects of the good news.

Poundstone next reassures his superior that things are going well: "We're convening a Freedom Convention here inside the Green Zone" to be attended by all the Iraqi factions, which, Poundstone feels confident, will select Zubaidi as the leader of the new government. Just like the WMDs, the new government need not exist in Iraq so long as Western media treats it as real. This approach to the job of starting and running a war constitutes the Rumsfeld-Wolfowitz-Feith version of idealism: if the philosophy is correct, the facts will follow. Poundstone, therefore, is adhering to government policy, while Miller is undermining it with facts contradicting the stories manufactured in the Green Zone to echo claims produced in Washington.

In his pursuit of the nonexistent weapons, Miller is tipped off to an Iraqi Army cell headed by Al Rawi (Igal Naor), a former higher-up in the Republican Guard, who is certain the United States will embrace the Iraqi Army, because, as Saddam proved, only a draconian dictatorship can maintain order in a country rife with hostile factions. This fact, however, contradicts the Washington fiction that in a free market released from Saddam's socialist oppression, democratic government would flourish, regardless of the people in charge. There were, moreover, too many unknowns to plan and implement a feasible government. Thus, Rumsfeld's only requirement was that the installed government not be Islamic. The remaining details would fall to the Iraqis, regardless of which Iraqis or how they handled those details. But the Iraqis, embroiled in sectarian violence, were completely occupied by an onslaught of warring militias. Morgues overflowed, while the remnants of the Iraqi resistance, manifest as ambushes, IEDs, and guerrilla action, made life outside of the Green Zone a deathtrap for several hundred thousand Iraqis as well as for thousands of American troops who would die during the short war and long Occupation.[4]

Miller's search, in other words, entailed multiple hazards—WMDs being the least of them—including ambushes and booby traps. For his specific team, these hazards increase when he is tipped off to the meeting between Al Rawi and other leaders of the (former?) Iraqi Army, now constituting a potential insurgency. This results in a raid on their safe house, where, although Al Rawi escapes, Miller captures some conspirators and obtains a book listing other safe houses. This puts Miller in the middle of a Green Zone conflict between the CIA unit that wants to incorporate the Iraqi Army in Iraq's future and the administration agencies that want to vilify everything associated with Saddam. In a heated interchange, Martin Brown (Brendan Gleeson), the CIA bureau chief in Baghdad, tells Poundstone that Zubaidi, who hasn't been in Iraq for thirty years, "has been selling a crock of shit. The guy is not reliable," to which Poundstone replies:

> This is exactly why people are losing confidence in the agency, Marty. You're questioning every single piece of intelligence that's coming in, up to the point where we can't make any progress . . .
> We need to use the Iraqi Army to help us. This place is a powder keg of ethnic divisions. They're the only ones that can help us.

Like Poundstone, this CIA administrator cares about how belief in the presence of WMDs could affect the realignment of power in the region. Poundstone, therefore, does not object to Brown's objective, per se, but to the political ramifications of undermining the Bush-Cheney-Rumsfeld narrative, telling Brown, "We're not selling that to the American people. We beat the Iraqi Army."

"Well they're still out there," Brown emphatically replies.

Strategically, of course, once Bush and his crew used 9/11 as the public motivation to remove Saddam, the only practical course of action was to set up a puppet government replicating Saddam's. Doing so, however, would destroy the claim that the United States went to war to liberate Iraq, a risky admission, given that the other rationale for the invasion was to prevent an attack even more devastating than 9/11. In addition, relying on the same Iraqi Army that Bush-Cheney-Rumsfeld set out to defeat would undermine the desired remasculinization from completing the unfinished Gulf War and avenging the Twin Towers.

Whatever their strategic or philosophical disputes, these warring US agencies shared a transparent indifference to the Iraqis. Rumsfeld's disinterest in Iraq and the Iraqi people, furthermore, was matched by equal indifference to the welfare of US troops. While many US generals claimed their first priority was troop safety, Rumsfeld appeared not to share that concern. Providing troops with food and water was turned over to private contractors who were not held accountable for failing to do so, while costing the government exponentially more than the quartermasters corps that they had replaced. An employee of KRB, a Halliburton subsidiary, who was orienting new employees for work in Iraq, told them, "'Just remember the money.' The new employees were told it would be easy to earn $100,000 [$185,000 in 2024 dollars] a year and that it would be the easiest money they ever earned" (Rasor and Bauman, 13).

Nor did Rumsfeld make sure the troops had adequate protection. At a famous meeting in Kuwait addressing twenty-five hundred National Guard personnel destined for Iraq, a soldier complained to Rumsfeld that "our vehicles are not armored. We're digging pieces of rusted scrap metal and compromised ballistic glass that's already been shot up . . . picking the best of this scrap to put on our vehicles to take into combat" (Ricks, 411–412). Rumsfeld condescendingly replied, "You go to war with the Army you have" (Ricks, 412), resulting in an outcry in the Senate and in the press, pointing out that as secretary of defense, the person in charge of planning the war, he sent the Americans to war equipped according to the plans he had made. Rumsfeld's critics were unaware, however, that his policy regarding "unknown unknowns" made it moot to distinguish between the army you have and the one equipped to execute your plans.

Rumsfeld's privatization did not improve the quality of the goods and services the troops received, nor was it cost-efficient. Rather, it prioritized private businessmen and the well-paid contractors over an underpaid group of government employees. Although they constituted the US military, they were treated more like human fodder, compared to those working under lucrative private-sector contracts. But the welfare of the GIs who were "liberating" Iraq was not treated as any more of an administration priority than the Iraqis who were being "liberated."

A much higher administration priority was affirming the cinematic narrative it had advanced: the United States invaded Iraq to liberate the Iraqis from Saddam and to secure his WMDs before he used them on America. But both the liberation and the WMDs were cinematic plot devices that needed constant supplementation to offset the recurrent evidence of their fictionality. Each day, sectarian rifts grew, consequent deaths multiplied, and quotidian dangers proliferated. No one could claim these direct results of the US invasion were necessary because, as the absence of WMDs proved, no one could (credibly) claim the invasion was necessary. If the lesson the invasion was "teaching to the Arab world" was unclear, it was even less helpful to US security: it increased Al Qaeda membership exponentially, led to the creation of ISIS, and turned Iraq into a pro-Iranian state. No mission statement the State Department and the Defense Department could have formulated would have included any of these outcomes. Early evidence of the disparity between the war's rationale and its outcomes intensified the pressure on Miller to search for WMDs, no matter how pointless and dangerous the process, because, crucial to Washington's script, the search sustained the myth that they existed.

The desires of Miller's translator, "Freddy" (Khalid Abdalla), further complicate Miller's situation. An Iraqi patriot, Freddy hoped the overthrow of Saddam would lead to a genuine regime change, not just a name change or a puppet government promoted by Washington sound bites. Still unsure whether his searches had failed because he was misinformed about the WMDs' location or because their existence was a lie, Miller connects with Dayne, whose reporting lent credence to the WMD story, but her source, it turns out, was Poundstone. In other words, because the WMDs were an administration fabrication, Miller's problem was not bad intelligence but deceit.

In contrast, the CIA, being a largely sub-rosa organization, was less concerned with official narratives than with the secret alliances that those narratives help cover up. Brown therefore pretended to sympathize with Miller's decrying the bad intelligence, only to enlist Miller in connecting him with former Iraqi military leaders. Thus, Brown is eager to acquire the book full of Al Rawi's safe houses, just as Poundstone is eager to destroy the possibility of any contact with Al Rawi, who could reveal that the leak about WMDs had been fabricated by Poundstone, doing his job as a loyal member of Rumsfeld's Defense Department.

The reason even this cursory summary of the film's plot reads like a mess rather than a movie is because it is. If the biggest complaint about the film was that its genres didn't gel, that is, that it lacked the elegance of a movie plot, what *Green Zone* illustrates repeatedly is the disparity between the simplistic cinematic narrative that Washington promoted and the material with which it was dealing. *Green Zone*, in other words, contains everything that Hollywood conventions exclude, which prevented the film from incorporating everything that war films conventionally require. There is no mission, even if Miller thinks there is because it is his job to do so; even if Poundstone pretends there is because it is his job to promote the virtues of the war, despite the absence of a mission; even if Brown wants the idea of a mission because it facilitates his job of forging covert alliances; even if Dayne wants a mission because it would validate her reports and save her job.

IRAQIS HAVEN'T GOT A LEG TO STAND ON

Freddy, the only person who identifies with a real mission, is marginalized, discredited, and frequently dismissed by Miller and the other US officials because his mission interferes with everyone else's job. Having lost half of his leg fighting for Iraq in the Iran-Iraq War, Freddy represents a segment of Iraqis ready to greet the Americans as liberators, believing that the United States was committed to undertaking the tasks involved in occupying a defeated country. Like many of his compatriots prior to the invasion, Freddy assumed the United States was serious about bringing democracy to Iraq and had planned accordingly. Because Iraqis who had longed for Saddam to be deposed dreaded the idea of sustaining the Saddam regime under a new leader, when Freddy sees Al Rawi convening a secret meeting in a safe house, he eagerly informs the US troops, approaching Miller at the risk of being shot. At first skeptical, Miller, in part frustrated by his bad intelligence, decides to let Freddy drive him to this safe house. When the presence of guards outside confirms Freddy's claim, Miller initiates a raid. Although Al Rawi escapes and some of his cohorts are killed, Miller captures the man living in the house and confiscates the book containing the locations of Al Rawi's other safe houses. However, when Special Forces troops under Poundstone's direct command arrive, instead of supporting Miller, they take his captive to an enhanced interrogation site (where he is tortured to death), and they assault Miller in an unsuccessful attempt to find the book, which Miller had managed to slip into Freddy's pocket. While Poundstone's men beat Miller searching for the book, Freddy flees, and when Miller's men subsequently chase him down, they treat him like an insurgent until he shouts at Miller,

> What I have to do for you to believe me? . . . What more I have to do for you? I come to you with information, and you take the information, and is right. You want the book. I have the book. I give you the book. You think I can leave my car? You know what this car, it mean to me? Even you have the key.

When Miller offers him a reward, Freddy replies,

> Reward? You think I do this for money? [. . .] You don't think I do this for me, for my future, for my country, for all these things? Whatever you want here I want more than you want. I want to help my country.[5]

Freddy in effect speaks for the Iraqis, rightfully asking of the troops what Iraq has to do to get the US forces to protect them rather than assault them. Freddy thus focuses the central dilemma of the Iraq War: How can the United States turn Iraq into an ally if it persists in treating the people it is liberating as terrorists? Is the United States' mission to liberate Iraq, to subdue it, or to punish it, to teach the Iraqi people a lesson? And if the latter, what is the lesson: that they should not have attacked the United States on 9/11 (although they didn't)? That they should not be manufacturing WMDs (although they weren't)? That they should not be planning to use them on the United States (although they couldn't)? That they should have never supported Saddam (although the majority didn't)? That they shouldn't be Middle Eastern Muslim Arabs (a question more appropriate for eugenicists and missionaries)? What does the United States want from them?

Bush-Cheney-Rumsfeld had no answers for the broader questions that Freddy's plea typifies because they had refused to acknowledge that the US invasion entailed obligations to the people they purported to be liberating. Put simply, the United States wanted *nothing* from Freddy or the Iraqis because it had no plans to give anything in return. The Iraqis could do nothing to get the United States to do for them what, defying logic and ignoring historical precedent, the United States assumed the Iraqis could and would do for themselves.

The film concludes very shortly after President Bush's declaring "Mission Accomplished," immediately followed by Paul Bremer's disbanding the Iraqi Army and firing all Ba'ath Party members, making it impossible to enlist the Iraqi Army to facilitate restoring order in Iraq, that is, in effecting the orderly transition from wartime to peacetime, which is the purpose of an Occupation. This failure guaranteed widespread insurgency. As Al Rawi says to Miller near the end of the film, "Your government wanted to hear a lie [about the presence of WMDs], Mr. Miller. They wanted Saddam Hussein out, and they did exactly what they had to do. That is why you're here."

Bremer's disbanding of the Iraqi government and army also assured that the civil war between Shiites and Sunnis would blossom into a national catastrophe, the outcome of which would make impossible the formation of a secular democracy. If Bremer's declaration assured the destruction of everything in Iraq outside the Green Zone, it also destroyed the plot of *Green Zone*, at the beginning of which Miller relentlessly pursues his unambiguous mission. He questions the bad intelligence so that he may fulfill his duties. The "Mission Accomplished" moment, which the film shows televised in the Green Zone to an applauding audience, tells Miller in 2003 what the film's 2010 audience already knew: the mission had been accomplished without the war's accomplishing its mission. That fact, however, does not change Miller's job, but merely shifts its context from wartime to workday. The rest of his activities— finding Al Rawi, proving Dayne was manipulated by her "sources," exposing the deception initiated by Bush-Cheney-Rumsfeld, showing how it was abetted by media more interested in job success than journalistic responsibility—all these concerns are, as Miller is told by almost everyone in the film, *not* his job. His job is to navigate the daily perils of everything outside the Green Zone so that everyone inside the Zone can perform the job tasks that will advance their careers.

Because that schema allows no meaningful role for Freddy and all those he represents, a traditional Hollywood combat film would omit Freddy's perspective. He would be a simple functionary, in cinematic terminology a human "prop," that is, an object employed in the film as a necessary plot mechanism (e.g., the ruby slippers in *The Wizard of Oz*). Greengrass, however, makes Freddy's perspective the only one valorized by the film. If Miller wants to expose the truth about WMDs, the importance he places on doing his job is corrected by Freddy's concern with the future of Iraq. Miller's terminating his quest by exposing the war's big lie does not undo the loss of life or the devastation of the Iraqi social and physical infrastructure. It does not stop the looting, rebuild the schools or universities, or restore the country's health care system. Nor does it prevent the years of sectarian violence that followed the conclusion of *Green Zone*'s story or the rise of ISIS over the next decade. History may verify Miller's (fictional) discovery, but the film reminds us that doing so is pointless. If the events transpiring between 2003 and 2010 demonstrated anything, it was that the absence of WMDs did not end the war initiated to eliminate them.

Al Rawi's last words to a captive Miller, before ordering an underling to kill him, are, "You think the war is over, just because you are in Baghdad? The war has just begun." A few minutes later in the film, Freddy's last words, after killing Al Rawi, raise what J. Hoberman calls "the movie's big unanswerable line" (43): "It is not you Americans to decide what happens here!" These two moments, containing the film's last words spoken by adversarial Iraqis, confound our ability to define the sides in post-invasion/post-Saddam Iraq by complicating our understanding of ally and foe in ways that exceed Hollywood conventions.

If Freddy is trying to help the US forces by providing information leading to Al Rawi, that puts him on the *same* side as Poundstone, for the *opposite* reason: Freddy wants Al Rawi captured to see him exposed and punished, while Poundstone wants Al Rawi captured (or killed) to silence him. Freddy is also on the *opposite* side from Brown, who is on the *opposite* side from Poundstone, because Brown wants to empower Al Rawi rather than silence him, while Freddy wants Al Rawi prohibited from regaining power. Freddy, in other words, is attempting to side with the Americans, as represented by Bush-Cheney-Rumsfeld's promises, even though the Americans—Poundstone, Brown, and Miller—are not on the same side as one another. Poundstone is on the *opposite* side from Brown and Miller, who are on the *same* side as one another, for *opposite* reasons. Both Brown and Miller do not want Al Rawi killed, but Miller wants Al Rawi to reveal what both Brown and Poundstone want to prevent him from revealing, in Brown's case so that Al Rawi can replace Saddam, and in Poundstone's so that he cannot reveal Washington's fabrications. To thwart Brown, Freddy sabotages Miller's attempt to save Al Rawi from Poundstone's assassination squad; then Miller saves Freddy to keep him from being punished for killing Al Rawi, even though Miller was trying to prevent Al Rawi's death.

What this all amounts to is that, with so many warring sides, it is impossible to certify who or what defines the US side and the enemy side. In American wartime, the warring parties are either "with us" or "against us," but, as *Green Zone* suggests, the Iraq War has turned "us" and "them" into fluid categories and the Green Zone into a misnomer: like everywhere else in Iraq and in the United States, it is a gray area.

A WAR OF REDACTED MISSIONS

And that gray area renders all the war's conceptual graph-points blurry, making the outlines of "us" and "them" impossible to plot. In Iraq, all that remained perceptible was the gray cloud that emerged in the wake of a war bereft of a mission, a zombie war of sorts, where bodies march without purpose, spread death and epitomize it. This situation negates the kind of war represented by *Saving*

Private Ryan, because justifying war requires identifying "us" and "them" with rigid distinctions that are not merely current or strategic, but historical and characterological. As Basinger has made clear, and *Saving Private Ryan* so well illustrates, in traditional American war films, Americans win because they have earned the right to do so. "Blessed with victory and peace, may the heav'n rescued land," the fourth stanza of the national anthem proclaims, "Praise the power that hath made and preserv'd us a nation! / Then conquer we must, when our cause it is just / And this be our motto—'In God is our trust.'" This is why traditional American war films take the nature of "us" for granted: If it were up to *us,* there would have been no war, but *they* threatened our security, freedom, way of life, so it is up to *us* to fight *them* because *they* asked for it; now *they* are going to get what *they* deserve.

This logic is both explicitly evoked and radically perverted in Brian De Palma's *Redacted* (2007), a film that follows six men for six weeks while they are stationed at a checkpoint in Samarra, during which time two of them break into an Iraqi home, rape a fifteen-year-old girl, then kill her and her mother, sister, and grandfather before burning down their house. After the rape, the other men in that squad, who for several reasons are afraid to report it, come forward, impelling an in-house investigation that produces no serious repercussions.

If "Mission Accomplished" initiated the attempts to represent the war as accomplishing a mission with the conditions of employment typified by *Jarhead,* it is not surprising that the issue of representation itself would move to the foreground, as it does aggressively in *Redacted,* a film made when the nation was still strongly divided, with 51 percent in mid-2006 indicating it was a mistake to invade Iraq and 44 percent feeling it was the right thing to do;[6] a year earlier it had been divided equally, 47 percent/47 percent, a steep decline from the year before that, when under 40 percent of the nation thought the war was a mistake.[7] The failure of the war had been apparent for several years (early in 2005, a majority of Americans disapproved of Bush's handling of the war, and by September of that year more than two-thirds disapproved), but it was not until mid-2006 that a majority of the country felt the invasion itself was a mistake. When *Redacted* was released, in other words, general acceptance was emerging that the war was a military and political fiasco, but the majority of Americans were only just starting to see that the continuous attempts to represent it otherwise were rife with comparable blunders.

Redacted reflects this situation by denying the viewer any unmediated access to the Iraq War. It is presented as a compilation documentary, using footage from numerous sources, including one soldier's video recordings of his tour in Samarra along with some footage shot by other soldiers, portions of a French documentary about the checkpoint at which the soldiers are stationed, clips from Iraqi television news, black-and-white surveillance footage at the entrance to the Army post, screenshots and Skype conversations from various computer screens, terrorist videos distributed to broadcast media, and video recordings made by Army investigators and a therapist while conducting interviews. The fact that all these mediations are fictional further undermines the viewer's ability to judge the veracity of what they are seeing, especially since, as Ken Provencher points out, "Every scene is a primary source clip, and every sequence edited by an unseen, unknown secondary source" (33). At the same time, A. O. Scott argues, "the measure of Mr. De Palma's artistic seriousness is his willingness to ask not only what it means to take part in an act of murderous sexual violence, but also what it means to represent it and to watch the representation."[8] Scott is correct about De Palma's artistic seriousness, but in this film he seems to be interested in the even more serious task of connecting his artistry to his politics. To that end, one way to understand the film, amid the wide range of reactions it generated, is to examine the connection between the questions De Palma raises about representing and viewing the rape in Samarra (based on an actual 2006 rape and murder in Mahmoudiya of a fourteen-year-old girl and her family by five US Army soldiers), and about mediated representations so dense and prolific as to raise unanswerable questions about every aspect of the war:

When did it start? Was the invasion of Iraq merely the response to the Pearl Harbor that was 9/11? Or was the invasion the conclusion of the war started in 1991? If so, was the first act of war Iraq's invasion of Kuwait, or did the war start when the United States invaded Iraq, or, as some have held, has the United States been at war with the Muslim world ever since Iran took American hostages at the US embassy in Tehran? When did this binary opposition between *us* and *them* start, and how are the consequent battles defined, delimited, and organized? Or is everything just another initiative in an all-encompassing War on Terror, in which case, it has no beginning—was there a time *before* terror? —and can have no end, which means no US action is an initiating act? Terror is the given aggressor to which the United States responds, but only defensively.

Clearly a whole book could be compiled providing partial answers to these questions, which have appeared in copious media in the first decades of a century more exponentially inundated by mediation than any in the history of the world. The issue of hyper-saturated media raises questions not just about the efficacy of a war without a mission but also about the future possibility of agreement about any war's mission. The conditions of possibility in the twenty-first century, in other words, may render impossible the kind of cultural focus and national cohesion that constructed in the national imaginary the World War II notion of wartime.

MEDIATED BEYOND RECOGNITION

Whether or not current conditions of mediation may at some future time alter or abate, however, is less important for this discussion of *Redacted* than recognizing the relentless self-consciousness with which De Palma calls our attention to the mediation from which some version of reality must be extracted and/or redacted. The title, in other words, plunges the viewer into the mire of mediation. The film opens with a printed paragraph:

> This film is entirely fictional, inspired by an incident widely reported to have occurred in Iraq.
> While some of the events depicted here may resemble those of the reported incident, the characters are entirely fictional, and their words and actions should not be confused with those of real persons.

This passage creates a compromised relationship with the authority created by the cinematic apparatus to which an audience must yield in order to access the imaginary space that comprises the film's narrative. If, when watching a movie, we refuse to accept anything we see, then in effect we see nothing, an experience akin to watching with the sound off and our eyes shut. Watching films, therefore, requires training ourselves to resist our resistance to its authority. When a scene is very dark, we gravitate toward hints and glimmers of the visible, listen closely for revelatory sounds, try to connect what we are grasping to what we have seen and what we already know. If the words tell us this is a fiction, we accept, however tenuously, the bracketed reality of the film's diegesis. In the case of *Redacted*, we accept that diegetic space as one presenting "fictional" representations of "real" events. That condition may seem contradictory until we realize that De Palma's preface could be applied to all mediation. *Redacted* is significant, therefore, because as a fiction initiated by real events, it counterpoints the Iraq War, a real war initiated by fictional events. *Green Zone* underscores that theme at the end, when Miller emails documents to a long list of media outlets, revealing how the Americans were deceived into believing in fictitious WMDs. The email and the film conclude, "Let's get the story right, next time."

In this regard, made three years earlier, *Redacted*, figuratively picking up where *Green Zone* left off, turns *Green Zone* into its prequel. More generally, both films address how media, in facilitating the substitution of fiction for fact, exacted a horrifying price for *us* and for *them*. De Palma uses one incident—a rape and murder—to exemplify that price by examining its effect on the violated family, on the people who violated that family, on those who failed to stop the violation, on those who redacted the investigation of it, and on the American nation that actively arranged and tacitly condoned that violation under the rubric of wartime.

But as quickly as *Redacted* presents statements that demand the viewers' mediation, it redacts them. One black smear after another covers up portions of the statement on the screen until nothing but eight isolated lower-case letters remain, which are visually extracted and rearranged to spell "r e d a c t e d." Before our eyes, the passage we have seen turns a rearrangement of its sparse remnants into a single word that reduces the passage's content to nil: a message about the absence of a message. This rearranging actively revokes the authority invoked to assert the veracity of its diegetic imaginary. The "r e d a c t e d" is augmented by a message beneath it, so that it appears as:

r e d a c t e d
visually documents
imagined events before, during and after
a 2006 rape and murder in Samarra

Recontextualized in this way, the word is converted into a title, a proper noun without an authorizing capital, initiating a sentence that tells us the film documents events that cannot be "documented" because they are "imagined." For the same reason, they cannot be fixed in time, either before, during, or after anything. The real event did not occur in Samarra, where this imagined documentation of the imagined event that resembles it occurs. Prior to any images, the viewer is asked repeatedly to mediate the tension between imagined representations of reality and real representations of the imaginary.

The film then plunges into an abundance of mediated representations, starting with one soldier, Salazar (Izzy Diaz), narrating the footage he is shooting on his camcorder by describing the intense heat on the street and the even more intense stink. Recording the men in his unit at leisure, he introduces each one while explaining his own dual purpose: to convey the reality of the war and to produce a documentary, the impressive realism of which will assure his admission to USC film school.

Footage from his amateur film is followed up by a segment of a professional documentary, *Barage*, made by fictional French filmmakers. While drawing on aspects of cinema verité, the footage, accompanied by haunting music, begins with aesthetically composed shots of dawn at this Samarra checkpoint. The orange hues of sunrise that silhouette the soldiers, their weapons, and the makeshift fences suggest, in some ways reminiscent of shots in *Lawrence of Arabia*, Arabia's beautiful solitude. To contrast this romanticized opening with the war's crude imposition of unappreciative invaders, the (fictional) French filmmakers cut to footage in the intense brightness of midday, devoid of beauty. The soldiers give their French interviewers unsatisfactory answers about the checkpoint's security and the safeguards provided for the Iraqi civilians.

If these soldiers have the same dangerous, tedious jobs as the soldiers in *The Hurt Locker* or *Green Zone*, their daily experiences are more excruciatingly dreary and uncomfortable, their perspective more limited, their sense of purpose more vague, and their insignificance more consistently apparent to them. The unit oversees a checkpoint where they stop cars and pedestrians (or shoot Iraqis who fail to stop). On one afternoon, in the brutal heat—made more punishing by the heavy gear the men wear—a car speeding through the tight maze of wood and barbed-wire fencing ignores numerous orders to halt, until a soldier opens fire. Only after they have disabled the car and the passengers remove the bullet-riddled body of a pregnant woman do they discover that she was in labor, and her brother was speeding to the hospital. Private Flake (Patrick Carroll), who shot her, has no regrets about the woman's death: "Waxing Hajis is like stomping cockroaches."

Private Rush (Daniel Stewart Sherman), an overweight brute with a nonexistent moral compass, agrees: because the car passed the trigger line without slowing down (and because, it is implied, she was Iraqi), they had no choice. He also has no compunction, we later see, about stopping each day the fifteen-year-old girl (whom they will eventually rape and kill) on her way to school so that he can "thoroughly" check her body for concealed weapons. If his buddy, Flake, shows signs of being a homicidal sociopath, Flake is nevertheless more able to assess accurately the situation of the American soldiers in Iraq than the better educated and morally grounded McCoy (Rob Devaney), who is idealistic enough to believe the Bush-Cheney-Rumsfeld clichés.

Thus, when Flake and Rush first formulate the rape plan, the debates among the men, which encapsulate many dynamics of the war, frequently focus on whether *they* (the Iraqi family, or by extension all the Iraqis) are with *us*, or whether *they* are the people who asked for it (a long-standing—bogus but too often successful—defense for rapists). This crucial scene illustrates how little the soldiers agree upon their role in Iraq, and how hard it is for them to align their job with any definitive notions of "us" and "them" so as to connect their role to any mission on behalf of "us."

One night, when the men are playing poker with large cards featuring pictures of naked women, and drinking heavily, Flake and Rush, expressing their horniness, suggest that the unit rape the teenaged girl who lives in a house they had raided earlier. At first, their talk seems like crude fantasizing, but as their plans solidify, McCoy, a more mature soldier—the only married man in the group—argues that they can't be serious. Flake replies, "She's a spoil of war." Pointing out that Flake is drunk, Blix (Kel O'Neill) and McCoy say, "You're not seeing things clearly."

"What the fuck am I supposed to see clearly?" Flake asks, "I mean, what are we doing here?"

"You know what we're doing here. We're trying to help the Iraqi government survive."

"And what do you think is so important about that?"

"I think there's a lot that's important about that," McCoy insists, then backs away from pursuing a political argument. "You know, we're just doing our job. We're not supposed to think about it. We're just following orders."

"These people don't want us here."

"Yes they do."

"No they don't," Flake insists. "They want us dead and gone, and when those fucking Beltway clerks finally figure that out, we're gonna be boats. So, in the meantime, Rush and me and Gabriel [Blix] . . ." But Blix refuses. This argument resembles crucial disagreements in *Green Zone*, but in this case the debate is not among policymakers and their white-collar functionaries, but among combat soldiers whose occupation exposes them daily to myriad forms of actual or potential violence. A few days earlier, before their eyes, their sergeant had been blown up by an IED.

McCoy, who objects to the idea of raping the girl, believes the war has a mission, while Flake sees through the administration propaganda, and therefore does not see rape as inimical to his job in Iraq, which he perceives, correctly, is pointless. His implicit reasoning is that if the men acknowledge they are pointlessly fighting multiple enemies, conducting checkpoint shootouts, and destroying Iraqi homes and families, in other words, if they recognize they are risking their lives to rape a country, then how can raping one of its citizens fall outside their job description? This reasoning, more immoral than irrational, is incompatible with the tenets of the traditional war films, where atrocities not only lie outside of the war's mission but also negate it. Why risk lives to stop Hitler if we are no different from him?

When Flake and Rush leave the tent to carry out their rape mission, McCoy goes with them, half-believing they will not go through with it, and half-believing that if they attempt to, he can stop them. Salazar also goes on this mock military raid, in part because he is titillated and curious, and in part so that he can film the event, in keeping with his commitment as a self-appointed documentarian.

The scene in which the US soldiers break into a civilian house is typical of many Iraq War films. Several such segments appeared over the eight-year run of the Showtime series *Homeland*. In *The Hurt Locker*, the home James breaks into at night resembles the safe house in *Green Zone* where Miller confiscated Al Rawi's book. In all these scenes, a narrow entranceway opens on a small living room and a hallway leading to other parts of the house. In each case, soldiers thrust themselves through an entranceway at the center of that architectural body, leading to a tight corridor that connects the home's vital organs, many unseen, all directly or indirectly assaulted.

Unlike *Saving Private Ryan*, which represents wars primarily as fighting across battlelines, these Iraq War films often feature assaults on homes and apartments, suspects rather than combatants, civilians rather than enlistees. These attacks, in which heavily armed soldiers raid a household, resemble an act of terror more than a search for terrorists. Unarmed women, children, and the elderly are thrown against walls or pushed into corners at gunpoint. Orders are screamed at civilians, who are shoved, hit, and threatened, often for failing to comply with instructions they cannot comprehend. Men—husbands, fathers, brothers—are plucked from their families, bound, hooded, dragged away, along with photos, letters, personal documents, which are most often unintelligible to those confiscating them. Behind, on the floors and in the peripheral crevices of the ravaged homes, the inhabitants not abducted scream, cry, and shudder. What motivates this assault? How do personal items and family keepsakes pertain to the soldiers' mission? The soldiers usually seem viciously purposeful while, oxymoronically, lacking a clear sense of purpose. They appear less to be fulfilling a mission than desperately trying to justify their jobs.

In their first raid on the house, while rifling through the family's letters and photos, Rush tells an Iraqi television reporter, "We're looking for evidence right now." "Evidence of what?" she asks, to which he responds, "Evidence of anything that's going to help us fight the war." "This is really important stuff," Rush tells her. Pointing out that Rush can't read Arabic, she asks how he knows it is important.

"Well," he responds, "we're going to find out if it's important because I've got people who can translate this for me."

"How do you know if it's evidence?"

"We're going to find out if it's evidence."

On their return—the second rape of the house—Rush mockingly parodies the first, claiming, as he molests the girl, "We're here and we're gonna fucking find these weapons. We're searching for evidence. We're looking for weapons of mass destruction. I don't care what anybody says. They're here. We're gonna find them."

More terrifying than Rush's crude parody of his day job is that, in the buildup to the war, comparable assertions were made by Bush-Cheney-Rumsfeld, none of whom were held accountable for the resulting deaths of one hundred thousand times as many Iraqi civilians. When McCoy urges Flake to stop—"She's a fifteen-year-old girl!!!"—Flake ignores him. And when McCoy refuses to participate in the rape, Flake, like Rush, employs the Bush-Cheney-Rumsfeld talking points that saturated the media to stifle criticism of the war: "Are you not supporting the troops? Are you not supporting the troops!" As in *Green Zone*, weapons are not the object of the search but the excuse for invasive terrorizing.

YOU'LL FIND *US* OUTSIDE THE *GREEN ZONE*

Although Jordan Peele's 2019 film *Us* is not specific to the Iraq War, it echoes this trope of Iraq War films. *Us* follows the events of a day when people living in California are invaded by an army of the "Tethered," who live in abandoned tunnels beneath the surface of middle-class American life. On the first evening of their summer vacation, the Wilsons—a father, Gabe (Winston Duke), a mother, Adelaide (Lupita Nyong'o), a teenage girl, Zora (Shahadi Wright Joseph), and a preteen boy, Jason (Evan Alex)—find themselves assaulted in their vacation home by four of the Tethered. They are grotesque distortions of the Wilsons, played by the same actors. Although the Wilsons' summer home is larger and more modern than the Iraqi civilian homes, the scene of the break-in has all the key traits of the Iraq War film raids: the Tethered's assault is sudden, brutal, and apparently unmotivated. Armed with lethal weapons (in this case, large scissors or shears), the intruders physically overwhelm the family, whose members are beaten, thrown to the floor, handcuffed to a table, and, in general, terrorized. Although the Tethered seem to speak the family's language, their enunciation is poor, their vocabulary limited, their expression heavily reliant on grunts, gestures, and brute force. They also manifest a perverse interest in the family's personal items.

FIGURE 5.01A. *The terrified Wilsons.* Us *(2019).*

FIGURE 5.01B. *The Wilsons' terrifying doppelgangers.* Us *(2019).*

"I love the idea of subverting idyllic locations," Peele has said.[9] It is almost as if he is asking the audience to imagine relaxing one evening when armed, uniformed intruders burst through the door to assault and terrify the entire family. As in the Iraq films, the father, who in this case has his knee smashed by a baseball bat, is kicked, beaten, and dragged out of the house by a man who, it appears, intends to kill him. As in so many of the war films, the helpless family looks on in terror, fearing they will never see their loved one again. When Adelaide asks these intruders, "Who are you?" her double, Red, responds in horrifying tones, reminiscent of Regan (Linda Blair) in *The Exorcist*, "We're Americans," evoking an uncomfortable comparison between this break-in and the house raids typifying films about the American "liberation" of Iraq.

This is one of Peele's many decentering strategies. Despite the supernatural context of a horror film, it is hard to tell whether the Tethered's identifying themselves as Americans means we have entered an alternate universe where Americans are not the people who resemble *us*, or proves that these invaders are psychotically delusional. By the same token, the Tethered *do* resemble their American victims in uncanny ways, implying that being "Americans" is just another aspect of that resemblance, or perhaps, we might shudder to think, the definitive aspect. These considerations of liminality operate not only between the Wilsons and the Tethered but also between the audience and its sites of identification. And they reflect Peele's approach to horror: "One reason I love genres is because they push their visceral reactions, these involuntary reactions that ultimately teach you something about yourself, if you want to look."[10]

Even though this is a horror movie, it is also a war film in that the attack on the Wilsons is one of hundreds or thousands across America by a uniformed army. We see in graphic detail the Tethered attack that eliminates the Tylers, a family of four, who are friends of the Wilsons. The Wilsons escape their assaulters and flee to the Tylers' home, only to find their bodies and fend off the Tethered who have killed them. Like people living in a war zone (contemporary Ukrainians, for example), they hear television reports of other attacks and, the next morning, they see the streets strewn with victims. The emergency vehicle that the Wilsons appropriate—the EMTs, apparently, have been killed—looks like a brightly painted version of the military Humvees that rumble through Iraq in wartime. When the vehicle turns a corner, the street is blocked by a flaming auto resembling those that populate the streets of Baghdad in the Iraq War films. Standing in front of the flaming car, Pluto, Jason's pyromaniac doppelganger, is about to ignite a trail of gasoline that runs

FIGURE 5.02. *As in the streets of Baghdad, a flaming car; Pluto, Jason's pyromaniac doppelganger, stands in front.* Us *(2019).*

under the emergency vehicle containing the rest of the Wilson family, when Jason shouts, "It's a trap," realizing, just in time, that they have encountered what is, in effect, an IED.

I am not claiming that Peele has created an allegorical rendition of (or a 2019 postmortem on) the Iraq War, so much as that he is drawing on images that became media commonplaces as the war-without-a-mission dragged on. These images illustrate themes accruing to an American sense of privilege, projected onto an array of binary oppositions, domestic and foreign, economic and racial, cultural and political. In his analysis of the discursive construction of the War on Terror, Richard Jackson illustrates in extensive detail how an us/them binary constructed the parameters of a universal war and its manifestation in Iraq and Afghanistan:

The notion of the enemy as "foreign" or "alien" has always been a central element in the discursive construction of war; the enemy is characterized as belonging to an outside realm—they are not part of the "homeland" and thus are positioned outside the moral community in a place where civil rights have no relevance. The "war" against terrorism is no different. (70)

It is the reinforcement of the idea that there are two groups of people in the world: American citizens and foreigners/aliens. (72)

In that context, one lesson *Us* shares with the post–Mission Accomplished war films is that they make apparent the bogus distinction between "us" and "them" by exposing how much the untenability of that distinction correlates with the vehemence with which it is asserted. The references to the terrorists as fundamentally inhuman, and the insistence that they are motivated by intense hatred, are crucial to highlighting "the difference between 'them' and 'us': while we are loving and kind, the terrorist enemy is full of hate. As Bush expressed it, 'We understand they **hate** us because of what we **love**'" (Jackson, 63, boldface in the original). The discourse of Bush-Cheney-Rumsfeld and their numerous surrogates was replete with language representing the other as barbarous and evil:

> There is a sustained attempt by senior American officials, both in language and institutional practice, to construct the terrorist enemy as something alien to America. This is clearly part of the representational project—the attempt to maintain a sense of Americanness by maintaining boundaries between the inside and the outside—as well as an implicit means of dehumanizing the terrorists." (Jackson, 70)

Combined with language foregrounding the enemy's "foreignness" and lack of fidelity to his or her religion, the official discourse and media echo chamber created a sense of nation, in the way that the concept is understood by Benedict Anderson, as an imagined community. Hence, after 9/11, excluding the attackers or their (implicit) kindred from the community of human beings was an expression of cultural citizenship, as was relegating "them" to the unruly world of the subhuman (animals, savages) and the nonhuman realm of otherworldly evil.

Because Terror knows no limits, and Americans were at war with Terror, no national boundaries other than American borders matter. As *The 9/11 Report* explicitly stated, after 9/11, "terrorism against American interests 'over there' should be regarded just as we regard terrorism against America 'over here.' In this same sense, the American homeland is the planet" (517). Similarly, since Terror could not be held accountable under rules of war or grounds for war crimes, in this cultural narrative the rules ceased to exist, turning the invasion of Iraq from a military mission to a performative gesture: it would teach the "Arab World" a lesson. And that fact was grounded in the understanding that terrorism manifests otherworldly evil; the terrorist is, a priori, an agent of Terror. "Their essential nature," as Jackson points out, "is defined by their savagery, madness, hatred, and treachery" (61).

In this regard, the quintessential enemies in the War on Terror are identical to the Tethered, who claim the title "Americans." The Tethered too seem to be at war with pervasive evil, and with people so powerfully savage that they are justified in torturing them. The Tethered are thus the agents of Terror and/or the rebellion against it. They are the spirit of Abu Ghraib and/or the return of its repressed, the victims of "enhanced interrogation" and/or its perpetrators, "us" and/or the US.

Because of Terror's uncanny source and limitless range, this distinction is not only arbitrary and reversible but also timeless; it cannot claim a topography of objectives any more than the national narrative that identifies the United States as innocent can accommodate a reason for the 9/11 attack out of nowhere, an attack so unbelievable it had to have come from an imaginary elsewhere, in the same way as movie narratives do. "The pictures of airplanes flying into buildings," Bush said in his address to the nation, "fires burning, huge buildings collapsing, have filled us with disbelief."[11] In other words, despite the declaration of war that 9/11 seemed to demand, the cultural narratives that enveloped the attack exempted the nation from the normal logistics of warfare, which include a discernible mission, obtainable objectives, and recognizable temporal parameters. The point I am making is that preserving the myth of us/them is inextricably connected to the tenuous distinction between wartime and peacetime. Like *Green Zone*, therefore, *Us* focuses our attention on the difficulty of sustaining this vital component of a wartime imaginary in a war drained of its mission. Hence, as Peele explains, there is "this expanding idea of what the word 'us' means. The only thing consistent about the idea of 'us' is that when you have an 'us,' you have a 'them.'"[12]

This statement and Peele's elaboration upon it seems even more apt, given how "us" echoes "U.S.," so that when Peele says, "One of the central themes in *Us* is that we can do a good job of ignoring the ramification of privilege,"[13] he is identifying a central theme of the United States as well as of his film. "What we feel that we deserve," he explains, "comes at the expense of someone else's freedom and joy. The biggest disservice we can do as a faction with collective privilege, like the United States, is to presume that we deserve it, and that it isn't luck that has us born where we're born. For us to have our privilege, someone else suffers. Where the Tethered connection resonates the most is that those who suffer and those who prosper are two sides of the same coin."[14]

NOTHING TO STOP THEM, NOTHING TO STOP US

Redacted examines the same perspective through a series of increasingly negative prisms. Salazar, who filmed the rape break-in, runs out of the house to
avoid witnessing the rape (and, as it turned out, the massacre of the family).
When McCoy attempts to stop Rush, Flake puts a gun to his head, and when
McCoy refuses to participate in raping the girl, Flake threatens to kill him,
then throws him out of the house. After the rape, Rush in a very physical manner threatens, individually, McCoy, Salazar, and Blix, leaving each man terrified. Suffering from emotional turmoil, Salazar tells the camp therapist, "There
are things you shouldn't see. Just because you're watching doesn't mean you're
not part of it. That's what everyone does. They just watch and do nothing."

The official story is that the family was killed by insurgents who then set
fire to the house, a story strongly disputed by the family's father, who was not at
home during the incident. In an interview with an Arab television reporter, he
explains that the story is neither logical nor supported by the evidence. McCoy,
distraught about the event, Skypes with his father (Paul O'Brien), who cau-
tions him against reporting the incident because "We don't need another Abu
Ghraib. . . . If your brothers screwed up, that reflects on the whole corps." And
if McCoy were to bring charges, "the first thing that will come into question is
your sanity." His father feels, in other words, that bringing charges will undermine the US mission. By in effect asking, as Flake did, "Are you not supporting
the troops?" McCoy's father implicitly endorses Flake's claim that rape and
murder are acceptable aspects of their occupation.

In retaliation for the atrocities performed by the unit, Salazar is kidnapped
off the streets of Samarra by terrorists who torture him and, on a film distributed via the internet and the news media, subsequently behead him. This episode evokes several painful ironies: that Salazar was punished although he was
not a party to the rape, that he was apparently nonetheless correct in believing
he could be held responsible for doing nothing to stop it, that in this regard he
finds common ground with his abductors, that he correctly predicted he would
achieve his notoriety via homemade video documentation, and that doing so
would permanently prevent his admission to film school rather than facilitate it.

These ironies are neither consistent with one another, nor do they contra-
dict one another. Instead, like the stories generated in Washington or in the
Green Zone, they float on the surface of a quagmire, a sampling of the mediated detritus that, for over a decade, demonstrated little coherence, in the same
way that the specific narratives generated in the aftermath of *Redacted*'s rape
and murder do not cohere.

In this regard, *Green Zone* directly inverts the traditional assumptions of the war film essentialized in *Saving Private Ryan*, in which the soldiers put themselves at risk to help end the war so that they can go home. Here their mission—capturing the WMDs—started the war and continues after it is over, even though it cannot end the war it started. This situation turns their mission into the job of finding an excuse for a war that is over but cannot end. They are not sacrificing to achieve peace, but rather sustaining a war to find justification for the sacrifice the war has demanded. *Redacted*'s sociopathic Flake, in his interview with the officer investigating the rape and murder, provides one of the most accurate assessments of this situation:

> It really pisses me off when I think of everything we've done for them sand niggers . . . planted democracy, gave up our lives to protect them from their own insurgents. I'm not looking for a "Thank you," but I would like them to stop trying to kill us.

Asked "Did you find these weapons before or after you raped the girl?" Flake responds:

> Raped? I mean . . . that Haji bitch was all over me. What?—bombing and shooting them is OK, but fucking them isn't? I mean who said?—you said?—who said their pussies aren't part of their hearts and minds?
> . . .
> Soldiers like B. B. Rush and I—we're keeping the Arab scum off their doorstep. We shouldn't be in here answering this crap . . . We should be out doing our job, boots on the ground, finding bad guys, putting two in the heart, one in the head, keeping America safe, making sure the motherfucker's dead. You prosecute guys like us, you're saving the terrorists.

Flake is spewing sound bites, talking points, and jingoistic clichés that infused public discourse in the build-up to the war, extended into its first years, and multiplied as its anticipated outcomes dissolved. That almost every one of these policy fragments originates with a government spokesperson (except for the references to pussies and the rationalization of rape, which would have to await a subsequent presidential administration) is less interesting than that its assemblage requires (and hence reveals) consistently unstable definitions of "us" and "them." *They* are the people who have had democracy "planted" by *us*, but *they* are also the people who are trying to kill *us* and the people who are trying to kill one another, while *we* are the people protecting *them* from each other. (Therefore?) *they* are the people whom it is OK for *us* to rape, even though *they* are also the people who are not giving *us* a "thank you." *They* are the "Arab scum" and also *they* are the people who need *us* to keep the Arab scum off of their doorstep. *We* are the people whose job it is to find and execute the bad guys (the Arab scum? the insurgents? the terrorists?) so that *they* will not be on the doorstep of *them* (the Arab scum? the insurgents? the terrorists?) because our making sure they are dead will keep *us* (the American people) safe. Therefore, prosecuting *us* for rape will save *them*, the terrorists (the Arab scum? the Iraqis for whom we planted democracy? the raped fifteen-year-old Iraqi girl? her murdered family, whom *we* are protecting from *their* own insurgents, and off whose doorstep *we* are keeping the Arab scum?). Everything done to and for *them* (whomever) was done by *us* to protect *them* or to punish *them* for what *they* did to *us*. Given this sea of confusions, the mission that emerges is clear: to find the bad guys, even if we don't know who they are, or even if we do know but can't distinguish them from us.

Returned from service, McCoy, gathering with his wife (Bridget Barkan) and some friends at a bar, tells a war story: "When I first went there—to Afghanistan—I was, I was all amped up to kill for my country, was ready to kick some ass, you know, get some licks in for what they did at the towers, be a big fucking hero." McCoy's initial story, in other words, starts where Flake's concluded, with the assertion of the clear mission to avenge 9/11, but because, for McCoy, as it was for the American public, this story is unsustainable, he switches to a war story that derives its coherence from its focus on the absent mission:

> I get over to Iraq and man, it's just . . . it's just a totally different story. You grow up really, really fast over there, because everything you see, everywhere you look, is just death, and it's suffering, and the killing that I did do, it made me sick to my stomach, because of these smells and these sounds and these images. I have these snapshots in my brain that are burned in there forever, and I don't know what the fuck I'm going to do about them. And what was I doing there? What was I doing in a country that's done nothing to me? Just following orders? Bullshit! Bull! Shit! You better have a really good fucking reason for one of your buddies to die in your arms, be blown up right in front of you—a really good fucking reason. And I saw some shit there, man . . . I just don't know how I'm gonna live with it. I went on a raid in Samarra, and two men from my unit raped and killed a fifteen-year-old girl and burned her body. And I didn't do anything to stop it.

CHAPTER 6

COLLATERAL JOBS AND COLLATERAL DAMAGE

Immediately following McCoy's speech, *Redacted* concludes with the words "Collateral Damage" on screen, followed by photographs of civilian casualties, their identities hidden by black bars over the middle of their faces. The film that opened redacting words on the screen ends with the faces of Iraqi corpses under redaction. If "redaction" technically means to edit or obscure a text for legal or security reasons, the film concludes by illustrating in graphic detail that the term applies to lives as well as to words. In a war without a mission, where occupations replace an Occupation, redacting bodies and redacting reports that chronicle their fate become, the film's bookends suggest, complementary ways to serve the security state.

DRONE WORK

The fate of one young Kenyan girl (Aisha Takow), who sells bread for her mother at a street stand in Nairobi and plays gleefully with a hula hoop her father (Armaan Haggio) has fashioned for her, resides at the center of *Eye in the Sky*, where the crisis entails the conditions making it permissible for this girl to become collateral damage of the sort that concludes *Redacted*. *Eye in the Sky* follows one day in the lives of military figures running a British drone operation in collaboration with US Air Force personnel, along with people in Nairobi and US and British government officials, that turns the death of a Kenyan girl into an occupational hazard. The film makes this conversion possible by resituating the meaning of hazard. If removing the mission from the war makes the occupation of soldiering particularly dangerous, *Eye in the Sky* offers a remedy: In the War on Terror, the state can eliminate danger from soldiers on one side of the war by making *war* the occupation of experts who direct lethal drone attacks, and *terror* the hazard of those targeted by the drones. This is very much the point, Roger Stahl insightfully explains, of focalizing representations of drone warfare through the perspective of the pilot. It is "politically safe [because it] normalized the opacity of power [by obscuring] the two ends of the kill chain that [matter] most: the formation of policy on the one hand, and life under aerial occupation on the other" (78). In so doing, *Eye in the Sky* further dismantles the tenets of the traditional war film by killing terrorists with a drone attack planned, authorized, coordinated, and executed through the collaborative efforts of military officers, bureaucratic functionaries, skilled technicians, and high-level politicians in countries several thousand miles distant from the incumbent dangers of warfare.

After a scene introducing the Kenyan bicycle repairman and his daughter, followed by opening credits, a series of brief scenes show Colonel Powell (Helen Mirren) waking up in Surrey, England, at 4:15 a.m., walking her dog in the dark, and then turning on the computer in her home office. Next the aircraft commander, Lieutenant Steve Watts (Aaron Paul), wakes up at 8:45 p.m. PST, in Las Vegas, Nevada. Subsequent crosscutting shows them changed into their uniforms and entering their places of employment. Powell and Watts differ in age, gender, marital status, nationality, location, profession (Powell is an intelligence officer and Watts a [drone] pilot), and employer; Powell gets up before dawn while Watts wakes after sunset. Even though they literally exist in a different time and place, almost half a globe and half a day away from one another, the crosscutting—throughout the history of cinema a powerful technique for establishing parallels and creating contrasts—makes the commonalities clear: they both serve in the military while living at home, and when they arrive at work (Powell at Permanent Joint Headquarters, Northwood, London, and Watts at Creech Air Force Base in Nevada), they are both in the dark. That they both transition from home time to work time and back, on a daily basis, puts their lives in sharp contrast with the military service in the World War II combat films where obligations fall into the broad and poorly delimited categories of wartime and peacetime rather than quotidian units, with home inextricably connected to peace. In this regard, Powell and Watts more closely resemble the soldiers in the Iraq films we have examined, since those soldiers, similarly, will return home when their job contract specifies, regardless of the war's outcome, if they are not killed, which means the only meaningful mission they have is to stay alive, which makes their mission antithetical to engaging in combat.

Eye in the Sky's lack of reciprocity thus positions its soldiers and functionaries, unlike the troops in *The Hurt Locker*, *Redacted*, or *Green Zone*, as engaging

FIGURE 6.01. *Kenyan girl who will be collateral damage of a drone strike in* Eye in the Sky *(2015).*

in combat without being combatants. Snipers behind desks, they use computer screens to identify adversaries, evaluate strategies, and accomplish objectives isolated from any overriding mission: they no longer search for WMDs, and they will never defeat Terror; following and/or killing specific terrorists is what they do when they go to work and what they put aside (or try to) when they go home. Although they are highly trained, by making combat the job of conducting unilateral strikes, they have deprived war of the risk of confronting the enemy, the drawbacks of perpetual wartime, and the mission to restore peace. As in the cinema of war, "in the prosecution of actual war," Burgoyne explains, ordinary places

> are charged with significance, transformed into hostile or friendly zones, battlefields, perimeters, and no-man's-lands. Central to this spatial orientation is the idea of the battle zone as a space of exception,

where violence is the norm and weapons of war are as much a part of the mise-en-scene as the landscape itself. Demarcated from the battle zone, however, are areas that are ordinarily regarded as outside the purview of military action. . . . The vertical spaces of drone combat, however, necessarily redefine this fundamental genre code; the practices of drone warfare assume a borderless, deterritorialized battle space, not limited by older concepts of geography. (45)

As Stahl further points out in his overview of the drone program, "its technical development has fed into its legal and institutional development" (71). The professionals are less combatants than assassins or executioners. But that is only during their day job.

In some ways, therefore, the agents in *Eye in the Sky* resemble fishermen more than soldiers,[1] even the soldiers in *Green Zone* or *The Hurt Locker*, who also spend their days hunting for bombs or WMDs. The military in *Eye in the Sky* rise before dawn and work long days (or rise after sunset and work all night). And they spend most of their work fishing for terrorists, not knowing what they will find or whether they will land their catch. The job in *Eye in the Sky* is not defensive, like that of disarming bombs or searching for WMDs, nor is it keeping a checkpoint safe, as it allegedly is in *Redacted*. Rather, they are employed to maximize their catch by finding, tracking, and killing. Since their prey is Terror, however, they cannot be deluded into thinking that they can eliminate Terror any more than fishermen can eliminate fish.

Instead of presenting several typical workdays, as do *The Hurt Locker* and *Green Zone*, *Eye in the Sky* concentrates on one event lasting several hours, one workday that exemplifies the occupational collaboration of targeting enemies and executing strikes. During the course of the film, the team must decide whether or not to strike a house with prominent terrorists who are preparing suicide bombers to detonate themselves at an unknown site. The film's crisis arises, therefore, neither from a sense of military danger nor a fear of failure, much less of defeat, but from weighing the benefits of the strike against the cost of collateral damage to innocent civilians, like those dead Iraqis whose faces are redacted in *Redacted*'s coda.

Again, unlike *Saving Private Ryan*, this film provides no explicit or implicit chain of command connecting soldiers in harm's way to the authorities who put them there. Importantly, *Saving Private Ryan* presents this relationship at both the macro level (the Allied Command that organized the D-Day invasion connected by the senior officers on the beach to Captain Miller and the proliferation of captains and lieutenants directing hundreds of individual platoons) and at the micro level (Colonel Bryce and General Marshall, in the War Office, who order Lieutenant Colonel Anderson [Dennis Farina] to assign the mission of rescuing Ryan to Miller's unit). That chain of command connects war's dangers to specific men charged with achieving specific goals, thereby uniting the men in their opposition to forces who are equally united in opposition to the Allied agenda. The men's missions determine their risks and define their rewards. *Saving Private Ryan*, as I have noted, works out this equation mathematically, along the lines of traditional double-entry bookkeeping.

Eye in the Sky, too, is steeped in math, the arithmetic of probability projections and cost-benefit analyses. As Stephen Holden notes, the film "doesn't present an overtly critical view of drone warfare. The military officers take their work seriously and fret over every detail as they try to estimate the number of casualties for various scenarios." These calculations employ classifications that distribute space conceptually in ways that preclude warfare, if warfare defines a conflict between parties set on inflicting reciprocal damage, to the end of defeating the capacity of the other to sustain its attacks, as certified by the defeated side's submitting to the governance of the victors. In *Eye in the Sky*, however, we encounter warfare devoid of battles; in lieu of battlefields, we have fields of expertise, each discretely insulated from all sites of war and any prospect for peace. The military do not fight to return to peacetime because they have never left it, or, one could argue, because in a War on Terror, their battleground is ubiquitous and their conflict eternal, such that peacetime exists only as a concurrent supplement. That concurrence—sets of parallel tracks with occasionally intersecting spurs—mandates the spatialization of time, that is, of the narrative arcs of everyone in and outside the chain of command. And the calculus, as *Eye in the Sky* demonstrates, measures "probable" damage.

This is clear from the outset, when crosscutting among several sites around the globe—Kenya, London, Surrey, Las Vegas, Pearl Harbor—establishes an allied strike force that is everywhere and nowhere, one that, in the course of a few hours, converts a visual tracking mission into a drone kill. The mission is coordinated by a top-level British agency, operating out of "COBRA" (Cabinet Briefing Room A) in London. The group, composed of General Benson (Alan Rickman), the British attorney general (Richard McCabe), a member of Parliament (Jeremy Northam), and a political adviser (Monica Dolan), oversees the work of Colonel Powell, who has been tracking terrorists in Africa and is, on this day, working in conjunction with the Kenyan Special Forces in Parklands, Nairobi. By showing its Northern Hemisphere principals waking and going to work, the film represents them as living in secure domestic environments; so that, when they finish their day's work, they leave the workplace, shed their occupational costumes, and resume their peacetime lives. We see, for example, General Benson delayed in a London shop on his way to work because he does not know what doll his wife has instructed him to purchase and, a bit later, he is late for the high-level meeting overseeing the drone activity because he purchased the wrong doll.

While they are at work, however, each functionary concentrates on the demands of her or his job description. Their job this day is an authorized track-and-capture of a priority terrorist (number 4 on the "East Africa Kill List"), who is a British citizen, but when they discover that she and two other priority terrorists (numbers 2 and 5) have joined her in the act of initiating a large suicide bombing, Powell wants the authorization revised from "capture" to "kill." This puts her in conflict with the nonmilitary people at COBRA, one of whom asks, "Has there ever been a British-led drone attack on a city in a friendly country that is not at war?" The political objective is to return the British citizen to England to stand trial, because it will be good for the current government to show how effectively they are conducting the War on Terror. In addition, it will avoid the legal problems entailed in killing British citizens without due process and attacking a civilian in a foreign country. But Powell wants to kill the terrorist she has been tracking for six years. "This is as close as I've come," she shouts, imploring General Benson to get the kill authorized. The issue is complicated when a young girl sets up her bread stand outside the wall of the targeted house, which alters the Collateral Damage Estimate (CDE) required for the authorization.

From her perspective, Powell is executing her assignment instead of executing people. The girl selling bread has a mathematical *chance* of surviving and, equally, there is a mathematical *possibility* that the terrorists could kill many people. Therefore, instead of causing collateral damage, Powell sees herself as reducing (*the probability of*) it. Hence the film presents several recalculations of the odds, in which Powell pressures her subordinate, Sergeant Mushtaq (Babou Ceesay), whose job it is to calculate damage. She wants him to alter the variables (e.g., the exact point of impact, the probable effect of the explosives, the possible distance of the girl from the wall), until the probability that the girl survives is more than 50 percent, in which case, if the probability assessment is correct, in one hundred identical strikes, the girl would only die forty-nine times, give or take a few times within the margin of error. But no professional statistician would assert that a probability assessment can be "correct," in that probability calculations, by definition, indicate what is probable, not what is true.

The war in this portion of the film, therefore, is not between the East African terrorists and the Anglo-Americans at war with Terror, but between employees with conflicting fields of expertise, each attempting to meet her or his professional standards without jeopardizing their job prospects. Mushtaq is

FIGURE 6.02. *Aerial target with recalibrated "kill zone" including girl selling bread at a table in the lower left corner.* Eye in the Sky *(2015).*

obliged to apply appropriate mathematical formulas to appropriate data. Doing otherwise is professional malpractice, comparable to a corporate accountant's fudging the numbers in a corporation's annual report to the SEC; because Mushtaq is a soldier, it is also dereliction of duty. Similarly, Powell is obliged to track, capture, and/or kill terrorists. Allowing them to escape and complete an act of terrorism is professional malpractice; because she is a military officer, it is also dereliction of duty. The result is a negotiated settlement inside a corporate structure, wherein the outranked Mushtaq must compromise the most, by providing a CDE using the *minimum probability* of the girl's death, 45 percent, rather than the *probability range*, 45 percent to 65 percent.

This conflict between Powell and Mushtaq is a microcosm of the plot structure of a film replete with such conflicts, in which functionaries, each prioritizing his or her job, enlist the support of a higher-up in the table of organization. The military lawyer at Permanent Joint Headquarters (John Heffernan) twice requires Powell to "refer up" to the British attorney general for permission to go forward; the attorney general, stating that "There is a political as well as a legal call to be made here," passes the decision to the MP, who "refers up" to the foreign minister (Iain Glen), who is in Brazil, dealing with both an official event and a stomach virus. Since there is an American terrorist involved, the foreign minister demands authorization from the US secretary of state (Michael O'Keefe), but after that is secured, the girl arrives with her loaves of bread, which leads Watts to refuse to fire until he receives a revised CDE, which in turn leads to more referring up, all the way to the White House. When a White House representative (Laila Robins), explaining that American criteria are not the same as British, emphatically demands the strike, more debate ensues at COBRA that includes, via satellite, the foreign minister, who does not want to defend on talk shows the government's failure to prevent a suicide bombing in a shopping center. He also finds persuasive, however, the argument that "if Al Shabab kills 80 people, we win the propaganda war; if we kill one child, they do." So he too wants to refer up to the prime minister.

The division of tasks, in a hierarchical system, presents the job of warfare as one modeled upon (or perhaps as the ur model for) capitalism. The officers and officials in *Eye in the Sky* operate according to the industrial criteria established by Henry Ford and emulated by the Hollywood studio system: compartmentalization, distribution of responsibility, nomenclature, interchangeability, standardization.[2] This organizational model maximizes efficiency by isolating and limiting objectives. In studio-era Hollywood, the people hired to consider books for the purpose of optioning them used criteria discrete from those employed to decide whether to green-light an optioned work. The criteria they used were equally distinct from the those used, for example, for the musical scoring in postproduction.

These jobs also operated according to different timelines. Optioned works might lie on the shelf for years or never go into production; completed films might not be released. By the time a film was scored, the actors, art directors, and cinematographers were usually assigned to other projects. Similarly, some characters in *Eye in the Sky* view their job status, objectives, and trajectories very differently than do others, who are politicians and political appointees. The primary objective of the nonmilitary employees is sustaining their administration's longevity and their political party's control. Careerists such as Colonel Powell and General Benson operate on a much longer timeline than appointees in a current government, and they are not concerned with losing their jobs based on maintaining political power. Nor is their primary objective to sway public opinion. At the other end of the strike, Watts is piloting the drone not because he wants to kill terrorists but because he "racked up a lot of college debt; Air Force is guaranteed four years of work." As a result, the sundry agents conducting *Eye in the Sky*'s war do not pursue the same end temporally, any more than they do thematically, such that the fragmenting of occupational time frames effectively ruptures the relationship between wartime and warfare.

This Fordist organization of efforts that facilitates the rupture is only one symptom of the capitalistic foundation of the War on Terror. That war, as David Denny explains, "is interminable; and the only way to fight this war is with soldiers fully invested in the autistic, pulsating force of a drive that has no destination. The strange thing is that this brilliant insight fails to unsettle or provoke any anxiety. Why? Because this same autistic, pulsating force that has no destination is the real of capitalism itself. It is what is disavowed in order that the fruits of capital may be enjoyed" (14).

One of those fruits is the proprietary control of human flesh, as exemplified by the way the War on Terror's discrete organization of tasks and agendas makes capital punishment— something to which even the "enemy combatants" detained for decades at Guantanamo have not been subjected—a significant, and markedly unspoken, issue in *Eye in the Sky*.[3] If capital punishment is *Eye in the Sky*'s elephant (or drone) in the room, the film avoids acknowledging its presence in several ways. Because in the film many countries with discrete legal systems participate in one execution, the procedure sanctioning capital punishment is unclear, even though the entire film is about process.

Instead of calling attention to the central issue of capital punishment, the film's extensive compartmentalization calls attention to itself: Is this person or that person doing her job or his job properly? In performing their jobs, will they kill an innocent child or avoid doing so? Focus on the indisputable innocence of the child avoids the crucial issue in a capital trial—the innocence or guilt of the accused—in the same way that all the process involved in assessing the importance of the innocent child's life substitutes for the total absence of process in adjudicating the execution of those targeted by the strike. This would be the equivalent of having a judge and jury decide whether the wiring of the electric chair endangers the janitorial staff who clean the execution chamber of a prisoner sentenced to death without a trial.

The focus on process allows the little girl to be killed because Powell's personal mission was to kill someone whom she had been tracking for six years, so that her goal in the film is to find a procedural method for accomplishing that, while still claiming, from a procedural perspective, that "we did everything we could to save the little girl's life." For Powell, the procedure outweighs the life because, although her job is not threatened by politics or public opinion, she can get in trouble for ignoring procedure or disobeying orders. Her actions, therefore, have to be technically correct, even if "everything" they did to save the girl's life is only a technicality, in that what they did was everything to tweak the numbers to enhance the paper trail indicating the girl's slight probability of surviving. While the girl dies in a Nairobi hospital, her chances of survival on paper were better than 50/50, something Powell confirms before going home from work. As she leaves, she tells Mushtaq, "You will file your report at 45% CDE. Understood?" He repeats "45%" and she gives him a nod of approbation.

This is the ersatz theology of all the principals in *Eye in the Sky* who appeal to a higher power, that is, "refer up" in the corporate/military/governmental hierarchy, enabling them to identify with a greater good, meaning a "good" more in sync with rationales that justify their occupational interests. Hence the relationship of capital punishment to warfare more easily falls between the seams created by conflating higher values with higher rungs in the organizational hierarchy. Capital punishment—by definition, a nonreciprocal activity—thus becomes one more weapon in a unilateral war conceptually linked to the drone. Controlled by activities that are temporally and causally dissociated, the drone tends to purify death by making it the sole objective of the strike. Neither the "pilot" and "crew" in Nevada, nor the identification staff in Pearl Harbor, nor the commanding officers in Nevada and London, nor their superiors at COBRA, nor COBRA's superiors around the globe, are fighting to earn the right to go home, since their jobs never required them to leave home. Nor are they fighting to protect their comrades, because none are in direct danger. Nor are they involved in a narrative that advances their mission or that puts them in harm's way if they fail.

In this way, drone warfare typifies post–Mission Accomplished war by detaching death from the war narrative, while still retaining the exceptional conditions that, as Dudziak points out, characterize wartime, such as permitting capital punishment without due process. Thus, when Powell calls Benson after the kill (of the terrorists *and* the little girl) with the two-word message "Mission Accomplished!" she betrays no sense of irony in quoting the universally discredited statement made more than a decade earlier. General Benson seems equally impervious to the irony, or perhaps they both understand how more than a decade of War on Terror has divorced the concept of a mission from any larger context. Powell will be heading home, and Benson, as he leaves COBRA, is greeted by his aide-de-camp (Ed Suter) who had exchanged the wrong doll for the right one while the drone strike was planned and executed, so that when Benson gets home, he also can tell his wife, "Mission Accomplished."

As Watts and his co-pilot, Carrie (Phoebe Fox), exit their posts into the midmorning daylight, their commander, Lieutenant Colonel Walsh (Gavin Hood), stops them. "You did well, both of you," he says. Perhaps noticing that, despite acknowledging the compliment, they are visibly troubled by their first kill, Walsh tells them, "You should go home. Get some rest. I need both of you back here in twelve hours." In this way he reminds them that they were just doing a job, which they will resume the next day, while also making clear that, in between, they have the right to go home, a point underscored by the shot of them walking toward the parking lot, followed by the credits, shown over shots of the Kenyan girl playing with her hula hoop.

Although it is unclear what kind of mission this weaponization of capital punishment serves, in the War on Terror it seems to share the same narrative that weaponizes torture, once we eliminate the fallacious excuses for that practice. As the intelligence community widely acknowledges, torture is not an effective way to obtain useful information. People in agony tend to prioritize stopping their pain over telling the truth and, therefore, say what the torturers want to hear rather than what they need to know. In addition, the more pain a victim undergoes, the less that victim wants to assist the torturer, because misinforming is the only form of revenge that is left. Torture is also not expeditious, as evidenced by the many people in the War on Terror who were subjected to "enhanced interrogation" for months upon months.

But torture did suggest narratives apart from the mission of the Iraq War. It allowed the United States to bypass due process in punishing the people guilty of the 9/11 attacks. Since due process is the only way to determine guilt, however, bypassing the process means, by definition, that those punished were innocent (until proven otherwise). Like the Mission Accomplished narrative and many other narratives associated with the War on Terror, suspension of due process allowed the completion of a circular argument in which the fact that people were tortured (and in some cases confessed under torture) proves that they were guilty. Otherwise, what reason would there have been for torturing them? And if torture doesn't work, how is it that they eventually confessed?

The point I am making is that the absence of process in torture policy and the excess of process in the drone executions serve the same end of essentializing revenge rather than bracketing it out of a coherent narrative that makes the goal of wartime the return to peacetime. To the extent, therefore, that making drone death and torture standard operating procedures became the work of *us* to terrorize *them*, the mission of the war became to turn *us* into the terrorists and *them* into the victims of terror.

In this way, the characters in *Eye in the Sky* essentialize the experience of all the characters in the films we have examined. The Explosive Ordnance Disposal team in *The Hurt Locker* each day seeks out the most terrifying element of the war, a bomb primed to shed untargeted death. Its destruction is both vast and egalitarian; devoid of agent or target, it has no side, no "targeted" purpose other than generic destruction. For the team at the center of *The Hurt Locker*, terror is a condition of their employment. Whether or not they encounter a live bomb, were there not the possibility of a live bomb at every moment of their workday, they would have no job.[4] The same is true of the men at the checkpoint in *Redacted*, where every encounter is informed by its deadly potential, repeatedly disproved by the terrorized Iraqis, except when it is not: the sergeant is killed by an IED planted at night in an abandoned stuffed chair on the street; Salazar is kidnapped on the street, tortured, beheaded, and left in a lot. Every moment on the street is filled with incipient terror for Miller's squad seeking WMDs; the squad's failing to find them is failing at their job, especially so long as their superiors, all the way up to the White House, insist the WMDs exist. Thus, when the party line shifts from unearthing the weapons to "teaching the Arab world a lesson," the premise becomes that the absence of WMDs in Iraq correlates with their hypothetical presence elsewhere. Therefore, the terror inflicted on Iraq, because it was believed to have WMDs, will deter their use by other Arabs, such as those in Iran (even though Iranians are not Arabs); just as the massive fatalities from sectarian violence in the aftermath of the US invasion will turn Iraq into a "beacon of democracy" that will inspire the rest of the Arab nations to undergo similar violence in order to become the kind of democracy that would never use WMDs on the United States, if they have them, as the United States was certain *they* did in Iraq.

The fact that these narratives defy logic does not mean they weren't influential, with the degree of their influence directly proportional to a sustained faith in the existence of instruments of terror, a faith so abstract as to preclude formulating a governing mission. For this reason, *Eye in the Sky*, by isolating terrified actors in search of terrorist actors, consolidates an essential quality of post–Mission Accomplished war films.

SNIPER WORK: REFERRING TO A HIGHER POWER(ED) SOURCE

That capital punishment remains as ubiquitous as it is unacknowledged in *American Sniper* (2014) is less significant, I think, than the absence of the issue from almost all discussion of this biopic about Chris Kyle, a sniper who holds the record for the greatest number of verified kills (160) in American military history. In his case, a high-powered sniper rifle, instead of a drone, is the weapon of destruction. "In the context of the contemporary carceral security state," Elizabeth Steeby emphasizes,

> the sniper who "sees what others cannot" is integral to a scopophilic surveillance regime. The cult of the sniper derives pleasure and power

from being the unseen seer. That pleasure, so well-marketed by consumer culture, both mitigates and suffuses the violence wrought by the shooter. As gun-scope technology advances, through illuminated crosshairs (or reticule), snipers can fire at targets well over one mile away, adjusting for wind and elevation, while remaining invisible to those they target. (810)

Under most circumstances, therefore, victims of this high-tech weapon have no sense they are in the crosshairs because bullets traveling faster than the speed of sound arrive before the victims know they have been targeted. Like a bolt from the heavens, death arrives as an act of God.

In cinematic terminology, the "eye in the sky," that is, a shot looking down from on high, is sometimes called a "God's view shot," and in both *Eye in the Sky* and *American Sniper*, the strike hits its victims with divine intensity. At the same time, the cinematographic shot organized around the sniper's telescopic view, as Stahl explains, "grants the viewer the pleasure of contemplating mere mortals from an abstract distance before delivering the bolt of final judgment" (100). Although Stahl legitimately differentiates the sniper vision of *American Sniper* from the drone vision of *Eye in the Sky*, the two films do have in common the huge disparity between the effect of fateful mortality and the mechanisms of human instrumentality creating that effect. Whereas in *Eye in the Sky* the diffusion of a corporate-style structure separates individual actors from a coherent mission uniting their actions, in *American Sniper*, the isolation of a single decision maker's job divorces his actions from his sense of mission. Even though Kyle is in combat, comes under fire, and loses comrades, he still participates in, and engages the viewer in, nonreciprocal situations; so that, as Stahl says of drone vision, the "perspective obscured the two ends of the kill chain that mattered most: the formation of policy on the one hand, and life under aerial occupation on the other" (78).

Like the functionaries in *Eye in the Sky*, Kyle is just doing his job; his boss, however, is a lot higher up in the chain of command. In his outstanding reading of the film, Stahl provides the most extensive analysis of how the film's implicit ontology makes Kyle's actions as the angel of death akin to biblical destiny. The film, as Stahl puts it, "is [overcoded] with a particular religious mythology" (103) deriving from an incident in Kyle's childhood, revealed in a flashback to his childhood, separating the moment in the film when he first zeroes in on an Iraqi woman and her son from the moment when he decides to kill first the boy and subsequently the woman. This extended flashback places life and death in suspended animation for the first 20 percent of the film, with the tipping point determined by Kyle's life up until he aligned the boy in his sights. Inserting

Kyle's biography in that way, director Clint Eastwood makes clear that executing the boy and the woman involved none of the factors deliberated in *Eye in the Sky*. Only Kyle's personal experiences counted, which introduce, Stahl shows, "a powerful set of pastoral metaphors that structure the story of the War on Terror, the role of the military, and ultimately the ideal citizen" (103).

Crucially, about two minutes into the flashback, Kyle's father explains at dinner:

> There are three types of people in the world, sheep, wolves, and sheep dogs. Some people prefer to believe that evil doesn't exist in the world, and if it ever darkened their doorstep, they wouldn't know how to protect themselves. Those are the sheep. And then you've got the predators who use violence to prey on the weak. They're the wolves. Then there are those who've been blessed with the gift of aggression and the overpowering need to protect the flock. These humans are the rare breed that live to confront the wolves. They are the sheep dogs. Now we're not raising any sheep in this family. I will whoop your ass if you turn into a wolf.

Some may find it disconcerting that the film provides no resistance to his father's belief that aggression is what protects people, rather than what they need to be protected from, but that belief has long-standing precedent in American cultural narratives that represent the nation as simultaneously exceptionally powerful and precariously vulnerable. Consider the iconic image of a wagon train in a circle, under attack by hordes of Native Americans on horseback. Farmers, merchants, and craftsmen, women and children, vastly outnumbered by fearless, athletic warriors equipped with flaming arrows, try desperately to survive. In the classic representations, the situation for these outnumbered and underskilled settlers appears hopeless. But history reminds us that it was the other way around. The vast majority of these settlers got where they were going, took the land where these warriors had lived and their ancestors were buried, built homes and towns, acquired capital, and proliferated. Not so for the warriors and their kin, who were swindled, disenfranchised, and slaughtered.

Even though this outcome is well known, the image and significance of the besieged wagon train endures, a part of the American cultural lexicon. The fact that Anglo-Saxon settlers, many of them immigrants or first-generation Americans, established dominion from sea to shining sea does not dispel the cogency of narratives representing the nation as under constant threat. The same sensibility in the nineteenth century fomented the lynching of Catholics (or Papists, as they were called) and Freemasons on the grounds that the people in these groups were loyal to foreign powers; McCarthyism arose from similar fears, as did numerous expressions of anti-Semitism. In all cases, Anglo-Saxon aggression—in the case of Native Americans, genocide—was understood as self-protective.

Not surprisingly, numerous reviews and critical articles have associated *American Sniper* with the western, noting Eastwood's strong connection to the genre. David Buchanan convincingly delineates the film's strong debt to *A Fistful of Dollars*, especially regarding the indifference that the film's nameless hero evinces toward death. More generally, the film transfers from the western the assumption that the frontier is hostile, a place that needs to be "tamed" and "civilized." "The prevalence of the language of savagery," as Stahl notes, "also evokes the logic of the frontier" (109).[5] If a running motif of American exceptionalism is that the strategy for protecting Anglo-Saxons from savagery is to initiate aggression, the War on Terror can be seen as an episode in that ongoing war. Therefore, "the sniper today is an updated gunslinger, long a staple of American popular culture, integral to the white-colonial, settler-frontier fantasy, rugged (heteromasculine) individualism, and occupying an outlaw or sometimes reluctant desperado status" (Steeby, 806). In that regard, Agnieszka Soltysik Monnet points out that Kyle's portrayal as an idealized American is manifest "literally [as a] cowboy who discovers his talent for deploying righteous violence in an apolitical theater of combat where good American soldiers battle sadistic and evil Iraqis" (1378).

In the twenty-first century, moreover, many Americans felt, in the wake of 9/11, that aggression toward Muslims was self-protective. Not surprisingly, in *American Sniper*'s long flashback introducing us to Kyle, the bombing of US embassies in Kenya and Tanzania and then 9/11 underscore his acceptance of his father's tripartite version of humanity and his place in that trinity. 9/11 consolidated the lessons of all the vignettes leading up to the attack, which prepared him to protect his flock by employing the aggression of a ferocious sheep dog. We see snippets of brutal Navy SEAL training and his rifle range instruction intercut with his courtship of Taya. One of his first dates with Taya features his winning her a teddy bear at a boardwalk shooting gallery. The juxtaposition of these flashback scenes indicates the film's narrative structure, which systematically integrates his life as an aggressive sheep dog with his life among the flock that he is protecting. In the flashback, however, more time is given to his domestic life than to his training to be the blessed aggressor. Once Kyle squeezes the trigger on the Iraqi rooftop, however, his domestic life is heavily subordinated to his military life.

In consequence, the invaded country merges the frontier with the site where Kyle manifests his destiny as both the Lord's shepherd and angel of death. Serving in these roles simultaneously makes the invasion a defensive measure, an assault on evil savages. The mediating term "savagery," in the equation "Iraqis = savagery = evil QED," gives a biblical dimension to his assault on non-Western, non-Judeo-Christian Iraq, which is consistent with the film's allegorical representation of Kyle's upbringing and its "realistic" depiction of his experience in Iraq, a place where all the Iraqis are "evil" "savages." The film is informed by the hermeneutic circularity of biblical exegesis[6] that sanctifies his decisions to exterminate Iraqis as God's work. And he does so with workman-like efficiency.

As Monnet explains,

> Not interested in politics, the Iraqi people, or the meaning of his mission, he wants to "get the job done" and that job just happens to be killing as many "savages" as he can, either alone or with one spotter, exercising his unusual gift for accuracy when the target is "breathing." Moreover the large number of kills he can accumulate over his four tours gives him an air of professionalism, as does his calm and matter-of-fact demeanor while he is "working." This is not a warrior lost in an orgy of violence. This is a man methodically exterminating enemies for a living. The insidious genius of the film is to make this work look both serious and ultimately satisfying. (1832)

In other words, Kyle, like the soldiers in the other films we have examined, has converted his role in Iraq's Occupation into his occupation in Iraq: killing savages to protect his men. For that reason, when Kyle suffers from PTSD after his (four) tours of duty, he tells the VA therapist that the only thing haunting him "are all the guys I couldn't save." "Ultimately," Stahl points out, "his 'moral injury' is not attributed to having killed but to not having killed enough" (108).

If Kyle replaces the vacuum created by the absence of a mission with the objective of hitting a target, no single target can justify the divine role Kyle has assumed unless the film imbues his targets with fictionally inflated significance. In Kyle's actual military service, the initial kill of the young boy is fictitious (although the first Iraqi he killed was a woman), and the archvillains with whom he contends in the remainder of the film are also fictional. *American Sniper*, therefore, does to Kyle's targets exactly what Bush-Cheney-Rumsfeld did to Saddam prior to the invasion in order to justify the war, and to the Muslim Middle East after the administration's initial fictions were exposed. The film, in other words, fills the void created by fighting a war after its mission is debunked by substituting a personal motivation to kill individual Muslim Arabs, transformed into fictitious icons of evil. In this way, the film is consistent with the rhetorical cosmology of Bush-Cheney-Rumsfeld's wartime. "The enemy terrorists," Richard Jackson demonstrates in his rhetorical analysis of the War on Terror, "are constructed, among other designations, as evildoers, aliens and foreigners, and fundamentally inhuman" (61).

Eastwood singles out three (the Bad, the Worse, and the Ugly?) to focus Kyle's blessed aggression over the course of four tours of duty. One is Zarqawi, presented to the troops in the film as the biggest threat to US forces. While Zarqawi was an actual leader of Al Qaeda in Iraq, the film misrepresents his status when the commanding officer tells the men in Kyle's unit, "He is waging the biggest urban assault since Vietnam." It is hard to know what that description means, given that Vietnam was a war fought predominantly in the countryside and in small villages. Although there were some large urban battles, most of the largest urban assaults in that war were done by the United States, from the air. Zarqawi is said, moreover, to be commanding five thousand insurgents, a group the size of 1 percent of the US forces in Vietnam. The point I am making is that the film has to create a fictitious version of Vietnam in order to inflate the fictional villainy of a real person, one who was more involved in recruitment for Al Qaeda, organizing suicide bombings, and fomenting Shia-Sunni hostilities than in "urban assaults" and attacks on US forces.

The elevation of Zarqawi, however, mirrors his elevation by Bush-Cheney-Rumsfeld to better associate Iraq with 9/11. As the film presents it, 9/11 provides profound motivation for Kyle, and implicitly for Americans (he is the *American* sniper), to want to kill Iraqis. The focus on Zarqawi thus implies that Kyle is doing what he does to protect the flock injured in the 9/11 attack: kill members of Al Qaeda. But Chris Kyle had no contact with Zarqawi, who was actually killed *Eye-in-the-Sky*-style, when a US jet dropped a thousand pounds of bombs on his safe house. In Zarqawi's place, therefore, the film invents a completely fictional second archvillain, a target within the range of Kyle's scope, "The Butcher," Zarqawi's invented chief henchman, a person so purely evil that he uses a power drill to kill other Iraqis (even children).

The invented threat posed by Zarqawi's large "urban assault" requires, furthermore, that the troops "root these guys out" by going "door to door, house to house, until we find them or we find someone who will give us their whereabouts, so you need to clear ten structures an hour." "In these street-level encounters," Burgoyne points out, "Kyle finds himself breaking into street-level family homes, intimidating children, women, and older men, and essentially violating the domestic worlds of families who are not unlike the one he and Taya hope to establish in the States" (104–105). His rationale, like the home assaults in other Iraq War films, exemplifies Jordan Peele's central premise that we have to create a "them" in order to have an "us." In this instance, the only

FIGURE 6.03. *The (fictional) "Butcher," who uses a drill to kill people, even children.* American Sniper *(2014).*

way the US can stop *them* from their urban assault is to enact aggressive urban assaults against *them*, just as the Tethered do to the Wilsons in *Us*. When Kyle and company break down doors and pour into Iraqi homes (in scenes that, as I noted in chapter 5, have become an Iraq War film convention), if the inhabitants ask, "Who are you?" the accurate response would be the same one given to the terrified Wilsons in *Us*: "Americans."

American Sniper's third archvillain, Mustafa, is a pseudonym for a fictional composite that includes some reference to a marksman who may have represented Syria in the Olympics. In a narrative thread that seems to be derived from the Batman franchise, he and Kyle stalk one another for years, by which time Kyle has achieved the same superhero status as Mustafa, as evidenced by a wanted poster with Kyle's face on it, widely circulated in *American Sniper*'s Iraq, albeit not in the real Iraq. In their climactic "shoot-out" only one shot is fired, Kyle killing Mustafa from a mile away, before Mustafa can line up a shot on him.

This is one more way in which *American Sniper* substitutes a personal rivalry for a (national) mission. Hence, the individual decision of a neoliberal subject replaces the tortuous chain of command in *Eye in the Sky* deployed in a network of global economies, thereby allowing the sniper rifle to purify the drone operation by substituting the myth of individual initiative for a global network of political economies. In this way, neoliberalism becomes the mask of global capitalism inscribed on the psyche of the subject. That subject, however, is a Sergeant York stripped of his moral compass. Whereas York, the World War I marksman who singlehandedly captured 132 German soldiers, overcame his devout reservation about killing in order to serve his country, he never made killing his objective. As represented in the award-winning 1941 film, York never abandoned his religious values. Eastwood, however, internalizes Kyle's faith—to the extent that he has deep convictions—in such a way that it replaces the Lord's will, in the same way that Bush-Cheney-Rumsfeld replaced Osama bin Laden with Saddam Hussein, and 9/11 with WMDs. As a result, the Bush-Cheney-Rumsfeld fictional world created the conditions under which power over life and death emanates not from the Lord's powerful will but from the executioner's will to power.

PUBLIC RELATIONS WORK—BILLY LYNN'S HALFWAY WALK OUT

Billy Lynn's Long Halftime Walk (2016), made two years after *American Sniper*, is the story of a fictional hero that raises questions about the meaning of heroism in a missionless war, initially conceived and subsequently marketed in cinematic terms. Lynn (Joe Alwyn), a soldier just out of high school who enlisted to avoid a prison sentence, becomes a national hero when a video goes viral that shows him under fire, single-handedly fighting off Iraqi attackers in a vain effort to save his wounded sergeant's life. His overnight notoriety earned him and his unit (eight men in all) a celebrity visit back to America to bolster support for the war, culminating in a halftime appearance on Thanksgiving Day in the Dallas stadium of an unnamed professional football team. During this event—set immediately before the unit's scheduled return to Iraq—Billy wrestles, at his sister's urging, with his desire to be discharged or redeployed stateside, instead of returning to a war where he suspects that he may die without knowing what he's fighting for.

Although Billy's heroism is nationally celebrated, he has nothing like Chris Kyle's accomplishments. Kyle accumulated 160 kills of Iraqis dozens or hundreds of yards away from him, over the course of four tours of duty, whereas Billy's fame is based on two kills in his first combat encounter. While attempting to rescue Sergeant Bream (Vin Diesel), he shoots one Iraqi with a pistol at relatively close range and then, in intimately close combat, slits the throat of another insurgent whose face, as he dies, is only inches from Billy's. Yet in *Billy Lynn's Long Halftime Walk*, Billy quickly acquires a national profile much larger than Kyle's (until the release of Kyle's memoir, *American Sniper*, and the subsequent film). The point, stated explicitly and repeatedly in *Billy Lynn*, is that the basis for heroism in the twenty-first century is not heroic deeds but media imagery.

The entire film focuses on the Thanksgiving Day NFL game when he and the other seven men in his Bravo Company participate in the halftime show. The unnamed home team is the thinly disguised Dallas Cowboys, complete with an unflattering parody of Cowboys owner Jerry Jones, a jingoistic bombast called, in the film, Norm Oglesby (Steve Martin). The soldiers, in their last hours before redeployment, are being lavishly hosted by the football team, with Josh (Ben Platt), the team rep, in charge of guiding them from the moment they are picked up the morning of the game by a stretch limo until the limo takes them from the stadium to the airport for their return to Iraq. In between, they meet members of the team, attend a press conference, and are hosted at an extravagant lunch buffet attended by the wealthy owners of luxury suites at the stadium. At game time, they are escorted to good, sideline seats, and shortly before halftime are gathered by a media person to prepare for the halftime show in which they appear in a nationally broadcast tribute featuring Destiny's Child and concluding with a spectacular fireworks display in and atop the stadium. Accompanying them through all of this is Albert (Chris Tucker), a film agent constantly on the phone, trying to put together a Hollywood deal for Bravo Company's story, the prospects for which fall through by the time they leave the stadium.

Interspersed with these events, flashbacks show Billy's recollections of the preceding day with his family, and of his experiences in Iraq culminating with the death of Sergeant Bream. Some of these flashback scenes resemble those of Kyle's SEAL training, although Kyle's physical training demonstrates that he has the "right stuff" to become a superman, while Billy's is punishment for, as Sergeant Dime (Garrett Hedlund) shouts at him, his "long glorious history of being a shitbag." Responding to Dime's demands, Billy shouts responses as he goes through punitive drills. At first, he echoes Kyle's "aggressive sheep dog" motivation for joining the service. "I wanted to defend my homeland, Sergeant," Billy yells, to which Sergeants Bream and Dime immediately respond "Bullshit!" When Billy substitutes different official bullshit, "Hunt them terrorists," Dime is even more sarcastic: "Well, let us know when you find them." While mocking the emptiness of Billy's clichés, Dime is also acknowledging that the reason Billy will not find the terrorists is because they are looking in the wrong place; the only terrorists US troops will find in Iraq are those created by the invasion. Dime's comment thus makes Billy's obvious insincerity exemplify Bush-Cheney-Rumsfeld cant, rather than betray deficient patriotism.

Billy's real reason for enlisting, he subsequently explains, is that when his sister, Kathryn (Kristen Stewart), had a horrific car accident during her sophomore year in college, requiring multiple operations and leaving her with numerous scars on her face and body, her fiancé dumped her while she was still in the hospital. In retaliation, Billy, then a high school student, "fucked up [her fiancé's] car" and then "chased after him with a tire iron [just] to see him run." The fiancé agreed not to press charges in exchange for Billy's enlisting the next day. While Billy's motivations appear antithetical to Kyle's, they are not completely dissimilar. Billy, too, has been what Kyle's father would call "blessed with the gift of aggression [to] confront the wolves." And both Billy and Kyle end up, according to Bush-Cheney-Rumsfeld dogma, fighting in Iraq to protect the people at home, even though their "aggressive sheep dog" service is not in fact doing that.

The disparity between the troops' ostensive missions and their actual jobs is a motif uniting all of *Billy Lynn*'s episodes, both on Thanksgiving Day and in the flashbacks. In one, showing his family dinner the day before Thanksgiving, his sister-in-law asks how the war is going. "It's weird," Billy says, trying to explain the difficulty of assessing progress in the absence of a mission: "I mean we got rid of their dictator and now they're fighting each other as well as us. We're getting sewer systems and building schools. They don't even have textbooks." His answer ends up explaining not how close they are to fulfilling their mission but how difficult it is for them to perform their occupation: "We're soldiers. What we know about stuff like that?"

Billy's mother, unintentionally missing the point or intentionally attempting to ignore it, says, "I'm sure you all are doing the best you can." But Kathryn takes her mother's reassurance to the place her mother was clearly trying to avoid, by pointing out that the context for the "best you can" is in "an illegal war that we should have never started in the first place." As the dinner-table debate escalates, Billy's sister-in-law and father take strong issue with Kathryn; so that when she refuses to heed her mother's admonishment to stop criticizing the war, her mother slams the table, making a noise modulated on the soundtrack to resemble a gunshot, such that it triggers a violent twitch in Billy's body.

The tension between the sound of the table slam and of the gunshot it resembles thus has the same effect on Billy as the discussion that led up to it, contrasting the official reasons he was in Iraq with his actual job there. Billy's facial expressions and body language suggest the table slam had triggered a traumatic response, differentiating the use of flashbacks in *Billy Lynn* from their use in *American Sniper*. In that film, they show Kyle's backstory with a coherence that makes his service in Iraq thematically consistent with his upbringing and personality. In *Billy Lynn*, however, the episodes often represent PTSD flashbacks that can suddenly trigger a repressed memory.

For example, when the limo drives through the bustling stadium parking lot filled with tailgaters dressed in a panoply of team regalia, and, a few minutes later, when Bravo Company, in their uniforms, walks the long corridor of stadium food concessions full of fans, concessionaires, and stadium employees, Billy finds himself in an Iraq marketplace. There, lively people mingle freely, while he, armed and in battle fatigues, moves cautiously. The scene resembles a more crowded version of street scenes in *The Hurt Locker*, a film about another Bravo Company, so that drawing on tropes from that film enables us to share Billy's nervous apprehension when a man reaches inside his jacket, only to retrieve a cigarette lighter, not a phone that could detonate an IED. A few seconds later, Billy sees two figures appear at the ledge of a rooftop, like many Iraqis who in other films are initiating an ambush; but these two are just boys tossing pigeons into the air. Other abrupt sounds cause similar alarm for Billy, as well as for viewers familiar with Iraq War films, but here they are all normal and harmless. The flashback ends with a close-up of Sergeant Bream looking back at Billy, saying "life during wartime," implicitly contrasting the normal daily life of Iraqis with the normal hypervigilance of their American invaders that comprises the Iraq War's strange coexistence of wartime and peacetime. By interweaving the abnormalities of life in an Iraqi market and those of a Texas family dinner, *Billy Lynn*'s PTSD flashbacks foreground the traumatic consequences of being unable to conceive of a mission that could disentangle wartime from peacetime.

Some PTSD flashbacks can be so strong that those experiencing them cannot distinguish the place where they are living from an event they are reliving, which is exactly what happens to Billy on the stage during the halftime show, when rockets, flares, and fireworks explode all around him. These pyrotechnics return Billy to the combat that made him a "hero" and cost Sergeant Bream his life. This uninterrupted flashback, which runs almost five minutes, ends when one of the other soldiers in the halftime show breaks Billy's trance. The show had ended, and the stage was being broken down to prepare for the game's second half.

Billy had had a similar flashback earlier, at the buffet luncheon, while Oglesby introduced the men of Bravo to his affluent guests. "This Thanksgiving, I want to honor my special guests, the group of soldiers called Bravo. Their presence here serves as a reminder that we must not only give thanks for our bounty, but we must also defend it. And in times of great threat . . ." Oglesby's voice starts to trail off, as though fading into a receding echo chamber, while Billy, looking at the elegant food display and then at a stuffed buffalo head on the wall, finds himself back in Iraq. The members of Bravo are interrogating a terrorized Iraqi family whose home they have invaded.

FIGURE 6.04. *Halftime show pyrotechnics that trigger Billy's PTSD combat flashback.* Billy Lynn's Long Halftime Walk *(2016).*

A version of this scene, as we have noted, appears in every film we have examined (with the exception of *Eye in the Sky*, where the privacy of the home is first penetrated by small flying devices that resemble a bird or an insect, and then by two successive drone missiles that reduce the home to rubble). Although this Bravo Company is a little less brutal than US intruders in the other films, the result is the same: the family cries, screams, and protests in Arabic, most of them, especially the women and children, cowering on the floor. The two adult males, the apparent heads of this packed household, are allowed to speak to the sergeant through an Army interpreter, avoiding some but not all the panic seen in other films. Nevertheless, because the man possesses a handgun (which is not illegal), an ID showing he had been an officer in the Iraqi Army, and, finally, because he has a book with a picture of Saddam in it, they determine that they must take him away. Sergeant Bream assures the family that all they want to do is "verify his identity" and then they will return him, but the hood placed over his head makes his family, and possibly Billy, doubt this promise.

This cinematic representation of Billy's PTSD flashback ends with a close-up of a small boy sitting on the floor. He has dark brown skin and hair, and large brown eyes that lock with Billy's, as Oglesby's voice slowly reimposes itself on Billy's consciousness: "Let's give them a big as all Hell Texas welcome." Perhaps the large brown eyes of the stuffed buffalo head took Billy back to the

FIGURE 6.05. *Oglesby introduces Bravo Company to affluent guests at the lavish luncheon buffet.* Billy Lynn's Long Halftime Walk *(2016).*

boy looking at him while they hauled his father away, but now Billy is back in the Texas stadium, in Oglesby's suite, and it is Thanksgiving Day. But Oglesby's intro and the numerous interactions Bravo have with the team's wealthy guests, with the stadium field crew, with the players, with the fans in the seats, and with the cheerleaders all underscore how the war has alienated Bravo as much from the country they have the job of protecting as from the Iraqis, from whom they are protecting America, from whom they are protecting themselves, and from whom they are protecting the Iraqis.

Like the other films, *Billy Lynn* treats military service as doing a job rather than fulfilling a mission, but this film makes clear that a wide range of American civilians also see them as doing a job, although they insist on defining that job in terms of their own needs and desires. When some football players ask Billy what it felt like to kill someone, he attempts to explain that "it doesn't feel like anything, not while it's happening," but because the players indicate this description is unsatisfactory, he revises his response to meet their needs:

"What's it feel like," he asks them, "when you hit somebody . . . like really connect?" to which they nod in satisfaction, having been assured that war is like a football game.

Because they are professional athletes, moreover, it makes killing a professional game, allowing these pro athletes, when they do their job well, to see themselves as heroic killers. They appreciate Billy, in other words, not because he keeps America safe or because he avenges 9/11, but because he validates their fantasies. When they "really connect" on a hit, they can now imagine that they really connect with Billy when he kills someone. We don't know the names of these fictitious players, but they are played by two major NFL stars and sports celebrities, Richard Sherman and J. J. Watt. Whether director Ang Lee chose defensive players intentionally is hard to know, but the fact that they both play *defense* helps make the scene consistent with the Bush Doctrine that defending America requires preemptive strikes. This turns the invasion of Iraq from an act of aggression to a defensive strategy and Bush-Cheney-Rumsfeld into Kyle's father's sheep dogs, blessed with the aggression to protect the sheep, who don't know what to do when evil darkens their doorstep.

While Bravo Company is eating lunch, an oilman named Fister (Tim Blake Nelson) approaches their table. Like the football players, he is intent on connecting his own job with Bravo's. If striking a powerful blow on a quarterback makes a defensive end or a cornerback feel as though they are killing Iraqis, which in turn makes them feel as though they are striking a blow for freedom, Fister wants the same connections to apply to operating an oil shale business. "Some of my friend's kids are serving over there with you," he explains,

> so it's a personal thing with me: lessening our dependence on foreign oil. I figure the better I can do my job, the quicker we can bring you youngsters home.

Fister's broad self-satisfied smile indicates he has no idea how the connection he's forging with Bravo contradicts the official reasons these "youngsters" are killing people and risking their own lives. After Bravo's abashed silence, Sergeant Dime finally says, in a pro forma way, "Thank you sir. We certainly do appreciate your efforts," but the implications in Dime's tone go over Fister's head.

"From your own perspective," Fister asks, "how do you think we're doing over there?" The question is doubly unanswerable. They cannot tell how close they are to achieving a mission that doesn't exist, and Fister, in any case, only wants answers that will stroke his ego. In this way, Fister is one more person representative of an American population watching the war on television, through the prism of its most current rationale. With absolute deadpan, Dime assures Fister that the men are committed to brute force, and concludes,

> You see these men. I don't know how they were before the Army got them, but you give them a weapon system and a couple of Red Bulls, and they'll blast the hell out of anything that moves. Ain't that right, Bravo? ["Yes, Sergeant" they shout in unison.] See what I mean, sir. They're killers. They're having the time of their lives, so if your company wants to frack the living shit out of the Barnett Shale, that's fine. That's your prerogative, but don't go doin' it on our account. You got your business, sir, and we got ours. You just keep on drilling, and we'll keep on killing.

Later, Mango, a Latino member of Bravo, introduces Billy to his friend Hector, who works at the stadium. While the three of them are getting stoned, Hector tells Billy and Mango that he is thinking of enlisting.

"I've got a kid and her mom, but the way it is now, it just isn't working out. Once I'm in the Army, won't have to worry about insurance, plus they're offering an enlistment bonus— $6,000."

"One of the days I was over there," Mango tells Hector, "I just kept thinking I am so done with this shit. And then, I'm like, OK, so when my time's up, what the hell's waiting for me here going to be any better? Like working at Burger King, you know? Fuck that. That's when I remember why I signed up in the first place."

"Exactly," Hector responds. "What I got out here sucks, so I might as well join."

The meaning of Billy's job is further compounded by the degree to which it depends on cinematic representation. Although *Redacted* underscores the layers of mediation that representations of the war undergo, *Billy Lynn* is the first of the films we have been examining that foregrounds how the war is also the *product* of cinematic representation. The Iraq War, I have been arguing, was conceived, sold to the public, and (to the extent that Rumsfeld's approach allowed planning) planned according to cinematic conventions rather than military strategies. It makes sense, therefore, that the war's reality in the public imaginary depends on how well it conforms to cinematic expectations. Billy is reminded repeatedly that the reason he is a national hero is because his actions were recorded and televised. As Oglesby says when introducing Bravo at a press conference, "I have never been prouder to be an American than when I saw that footage of Bravo in action."

It is also the reason that Bravo has Albert, the agent working on a movie deal. When he is present in the film, he is usually talking nonstop, either on the phone to people in Hollywood or to the men of Bravo about how much money they each may receive for the rights to their story (his estimate gets as high as $100,000 each), or about who may be interested in the project; at one point, he says Hilary Swank might want to play Billy. By the end of the day, however, all they have is Oglesby's offer of $5,500 each—less than the enlistment bonus Hector expects. Oglesby meets with Billy and Dime, who turn him down because they feel it demeans Bravo's job. Dime, furious, walks out, but Oglesby asks Billy to stay behind, thinking he can convince him to accept the deal.

"Now what you did that day . . . was caught on camera, Billy. And for many folks that is when the war became real."

"But for us it was always real. We never needed cameras to tell us that."

Acknowledging that Billy is right, Oglesby says Billy knows things the rest of them will never know: "That kind of friendship, taste of death in the back of your throat, the enemy going limp with the final twist of the knife . . ." Oglesby is doing the same thing that everyone is intent on doing, from the cheerleader, with whom Billy has four very brief encounters before deciding that he may be in love, to President Bush: turning the war into a movie and employing their own genre conventions and advertising clichés to garner acclaim for it. When Oglesby introduced Bravo Company to the press conference, he expressed his "personal feeling that the War on Terror may be just about as pure a fight between good and evil as we're likely to ever see." One can easily visualize these phrases in print ads for the movie they are negotiating or splashed across the screen in Technicolor coming attractions:

WAR ON TERROR!

A PURE FIGHT BETWEEN GOOD AND EVIL

Oglesby goes on by imitating a folksy pundit, à la the late Rush Limbaugh, who wants his listeners to imagine Iraqis as typical citizens in a Frank Capra movie: "I bet a Mr. and Mrs. Mohammed Q. Public in Baghdad would have a thing or two to tell our nay-sayers about that." The Iraqis are a bunch of decent folks who were simply waiting to applaud the Americans who freed them of their evil leader, so that they could go back to their normal life. Oglesby is so enraptured by his own sound bites that he fails to acknowledge that Saddam has already been toppled and that, in Saddam's absence, the *pure* fight between good and evil has emerged. Richard Jackson has written a book (before *American Sniper*'s release) attempting to explain, in part through statistical analysis, the reason that Iraq War films have been toxic at the box office. Perhaps one reason is hinted at by Oglesby's confused and confusing sound bites. In advertising, success requires clear, consistent messaging. In war, the mission is both the message and the measure of success. In the absence of both, the messengers have as tough and endless a job as does Bravo Company and all the troops looking for WMDs that don't exist, while avoiding IEDs that do, while trying to support the Iraqis' efforts at sovereignty without being able to tell the evil Iraqis from the good ones.

In the classical Hollywood style, plots required clear objectives and, with the help of the Production Code Administration, an unambiguous consensus about what was good and who was evil, without which it was impossible to provide satisfactory resolutions with no loose ends. But by 2006, three years after "Mission Accomplished," the plot-ends were shredded, as was the government that was supposed to make Iraq a beacon of freedom, as was the country the Bush-Cheney-Rumsfeld war liberated by creating mass destruction in the interest of preventing it. If the war were a movie, it would have ended when Bush landed on an aircraft carrier, hoisted a banner, and heard resounding cheers. But the movie war that it was supposed to end, more like a television series, kept accumulating discrete episodes in search of a Hollywood plot, while its backers, finding they had too much invested in the venture to scrap it, instead scrambled and flailed, trying to devise one ad campaign after another to sell the war.

Oglesby, as a big Bush supporter ("Now I was visiting with the President recently, and he assured me we are winning this war. Make no mistake. As long as we keep our eye on the ball, we shall prevail"), wants to finance the film glorifying what Billy has called the worst day in his life, out of a belief that he has finally found the movie they were looking for, the movie that will make the war real for the American audience.

"Your story," he tells Billy, "It no longer belongs to you. It's America's story now [in the same way that Dallas Cowboys owner Jerry Jones unilaterally anointed the Cowboys "America's Team"]. That's what this country's built on. You take this great state of Texas. Cattle, land, oil—that's the stuff that made us rich, but what made us Texas is the story of some local boys that made a valiant stand at the Alamo. And so it is, with this war, Billy. It's all about ideas. Your battle foreshadows America's triumph over the forces of terror. Bravo is us, and that's why I gotta get you boys to accept my offer."

Because *Billy Lynn's Long Halftime Walk* comes down to making a film about a filmed battle in Iraq, in an attempt to support a war that was based on the cinematic reality, *Billy Lynn* creates a mise en abyme that serves as a metaphor for the entire war. That is the reason that Albert, the frenetic agent, figures importantly in the film. Like everyone else, he just seems to be doing his job, however unsuccessfully, and his hype seems no different from the hype that relentlessly comes at Bravo from all directions. Yet after Billy turns down Oglesby's offer, he also tells him he is wrong—something Oglesby is clearly not used to hearing—and that they would not let him make the film, even if he were not "such a tightwad," because "you got no clue what it means . . . you want to turn it into something it's not."

Immediately after leaving Oglesby, Billy runs into Albert in the men's room. The film has prepared us to expect Albert will make one last pitch or perhaps suggest a compromise plan that can allow the Frank Capra ending, but instead Albert tells Billy, "The way that you stood up to that arrogant prick in there, now that . . . that's what we call in my world a real movie moment." While not abandoning his assumption that reality is a movie—hence the faith he shows in the power of movie moments—Albert tells Billy, "You got to do what you think is right, and that sure wasn't right."

Albert is shot in close-up, looking directly into the camera, a shot usually avoided by Hollywood-style filmmakers because it creates the impression that the character is speaking directly to the audience. By breaking the fourth wall, the shot undermines the viewer's experience of limited omniscience and the voyeuristic enjoyment of seeing without being seen, which is part of the pleasure of watching a Hollywood movie. In speaking directly to Billy while also speaking directly to us, Albert acquires a degree of authority when he says, "It's real hard for us over here to get it, but we need to get it, and the country needs to get it." "I know how hard you worked for us," Billy responds, apologizing for ruining Albert's deal. But Albert says, "No. Getting an offer is bad enough. The hard part is making a decision. And that's on you."

Because Albert is still looking directly into the camera, we can assume he is still also addressing the audience, that is, the American public, paraphrasing the same message that concluded *Green Zone*. "We got to get this done," Albert says, "and get it done right." Like Miller in that film, Albert is admitting he is wrong, the only person in this film, other than Billy, to do so. In other words, he is telling us that Bush-Cheney-Rumsfeld have been trying to make the wrong movie, and that it is our responsibility to correct them.

The film ends with Billy trying to decide whether he should get into the limo to start his return to Iraq, or get in his sister's car so that she can take him to a VA psychiatrist who will certify, correctly, that Billy is suffering from PTSD and can be discharged or at least transferred stateside. In the end, Billy makes the same decision as Private Ryan who, similarly, is offered a ticket home, but turns it down in solidarity with his unit. Ryan does so for the same reason Miller's men join them: they recognize that they all have an important mission to accomplish. Billy, on the other hand, knows he has no mission, only his job, but that job, he has come to realize, is the same one that Chris Kyle thought was most important, protecting his men. Instead of participating in the façade of an Occupation, he leaves having decided to make protecting his unit his occupation.

WORKING AS A CONTRACTOR—*13 HOURS*

All of the post–Mission Accomplished films discussed to this point have been films featuring military for whom war is defined as an occupation rather than a mission. In that situation, wartime and peacetime become more concurrent than conterminous, while the personal time frame for those in the military is divorced from their specific job accomplishments. They will return home when their enlistment is over, regardless of how they performed, unless they reenlist. As the time stamps in *The Hurt Locker* indicating the number of days left in the tour of duty show, the number of bombs the men dismantle, the location of the bombs, or the consequences of not dismantling them (so long as they are not killed or injured) will neither expedite nor retard the termination of their service.[7]

13 Hours (2016), a film about the 2012 assault on the US diplomatic outpost and CIA station in Benghazi, Libya, in which four Americans, including Ambassador Chris Stevens, were killed, extends this situation to its logical limit. The film, although not set in Iraq or Afghanistan, deals with anti-American radicals in the Muslim Middle East during the time of the Iraq War, and it presents many of the same problems that the United States encounters in Iraq, but without the specter of Al Qaeda, Saddam Hussein, WMDs, Iraqi insurgents, or, most significantly, US troops. The men here are all private employees. Most work for the CIA, and some for the State Department, but none are soldiers, although the six principals are contractors who defended the CIA station from attack until a rescue convoy arrived to evacuate them and twenty-six CIA personnel. All the contractors were trained by the US military; four had been Marines and two Navy SEALS.

We have been considering a war fought by an "all-volunteer" military in a "privatized" Department of Defense, in which the war's "mission accomplished" was proclaimed before the adversaries surrendered. We have seen in numerous ways that these conditions tend to diminish the role of combat in making wartime discrete from peacetime. *13 Hours* in effect removes the scare quotes from "all-volunteer" and "privatized" by isolating their literal essentials. The film recounts the true story of private contractors battling unspecified assailants in a failed state, where the outcome has no consequence for anything other than the body count. Because they are mercenaries, the contractors are not torn between their occupation and their service to their country. Because they have not pledged to defend the United States and are not subject to the military chain of command, their employer has more authority over their jobs than does the commander-in-chief, in the same way that the president cannot give orders to employees of Microsoft or Walmart. These companies, like all private businesses, may fall under the purview of pertinent governmental regulations, but those regulations strictly limit the realm of governmental authority. While the contractors working in Iraq could have assignments connected with the war, they have no obligation to affect the war's outcome. If such contractors were assigned to rescue Private Ryan, they would have never stopped to help troops in the first town (where Caparzo was killed), never attacked the machine-gun nest (where Wade was killed), and never stayed to fight the Nazis at Ramelle (where Miller, Jackson, Horvath, and Melish were killed). In fact, when Ryan insisted on staying with his company at Ramelle, the contractors would have taken him by force, even if they had to bind his hands and put a hood over his head. They were paid to retrieve Ryan, not defeat Hitler, and, as Milo Minderbinder demonstrated in *Catch-22*, the marketplace is more important than the nation, and free enterprise always trumps patriotism.

The film begins interspersing newsreel footage from 2011 and 2012 with titles on a black screen explaining conditions in Libya in 2012:

The Libyan people violently deposed dictator Muammar Gaddafi after 42 years of tyrannical rule.
Warring militia gangs raided Gaddafi's massive armories.
Massive turf wars broke out.
Benghazi became one of the most dangerous places on earth.

The phrasing of these messages echoes the tone of the opening crawl of *The Empire Strikes Back* (1980)[8] and *Star Wars* (1977) (two years after the US evacuation of Saigon), and just as those movies elide the recent past by transporting war to an ahistorical context ("a long time ago in a galaxy far, far away"), these messages essentialize the violence in the Middle East by setting it adrift in the timelessness of a terror that predates history. Even though the wars in Iraq and Afghanistan continue, and Benghazi is only fourteen hundred miles from Baghdad, Libya is designated as a place where time has stopped; the forty-two years of evil rule has been replaced by nothing. Like the rebel outposts in the pockets of the *Star Wars* universe, a US diplomatic site and a US CIA base remain the last, isolated vestiges of freedom amid a sea of warring gangs, devoid of affiliation or allegiance, not fighting for nation or ideology, but for turf. In the same way that these militia gangs represent purified evil, the contractors represent the pure (Jedi?) force of the neo-liberal, nonmilitary military, composed of employees whom the marketplace has chosen to reward for their training and expertise, which they sell, voluntarily, for $150,000 a year ($193,000 in 2024 dollars), plus room, board, and per diem allowances. For that remuneration, they have responsibilities concurrent with, but independent of, the war. Thus, in Iraq, contractors hired to protect specific officials (not necessarily US officials) or to provide specific services had jobs connected to the war, but discrete from it.

The same is true of these contractors protecting the CIA outpost in Benghazi, who are restricted to the specific tasks determined by their employer, within the terms of their contract. In the case of Benghazi, however, the contractors cannot be drawn into the war because there is no war, only warring gangs—generic violence, devoid of political import. Rone (James Badge Dale) is the contractor in charge of the group, five in all, who live at the CIA base they have been hired to protect. The film starts when Rone picks up Jack (John Krasinski), a newly hired sixth contractor, at the Benghazi airport. On their way to the CIA station, they are stopped and nearly killed by one of the militia gangs controlling a section of the city.

They don't know the gang's identity and it doesn't matter. The film has "not a single minute devoted to the Libyans," one review points out; "their motives and personal lives are utterly disregarded. When they are shown, they are often seen at a distance, or in groups, shot in wide frames which further emphasize their lack of singular identity."[9] But this willful ignorance of the Libyans accurately reflects the events from the perspective of the contractors, who are repeatedly told not to associate with the Libyans or attempt to differentiate between factions. As Rone says to Jack when they arrive at the station: "Not only is it hot as balls . . . you can't tell the good guys from the bad guys." And when Rone tries to tell the intelligence people about the roadblock returning from the airport, saying, "It's not just tribal groups and freedom fighters anymore," Bob, the CIA base chief, cuts him off. "If you have useful info, Tyrone, put it in the memo. You guys bunk here, but you're not CIA. You're hired help. Act the part."

Because the job of this CIA station is to watch for "lethal weapons before they spread to the global black market," it behaves with relative indifference regarding which faction holds what turf. The CIA staff seems only to be focused on what weapons the Libyans cumulatively have, how they are selling them, and to whom. These may not be weapons of mass destruction, but they are lethal, and they are not limited to a specific country but are, potentially, items in the global marketplace.

The situation in Libya, therefore, removes the question of sides, goals, and missions that perplexed Billy Lynn and the troops in *Green Zone*, *The Hurt Locker*, *Redacted*, and *American Sniper*. Even the global network of military and governmental employees who authorize strikes in *Eye in the Sky* identify their enemies based on allegiances. The work in Benghazi does not put the mission to defeat terrorist groups at odds with tasks that occupy the servicemen. No one is enlisted in the cause of restoring peace or keeping America safe. The people in *13 Hours* are just doing their jobs, pure and simple, of their own volition, which is by mutual agreement with the CIA and the State Department. As Bob explains to Jack, "We have the brightest minds, from the farm, educated at Harvard and Yale, doing the important work. Best thing for you to do is stay out of their way."

The central problem in the film is that an attack on the anniversary of 9/11 destroys the US diplomatic outpost and costs two lives, followed by an assault on the CIA base that causes two more deaths and, were it not for the expertise of the six contractors, would have resulted in 100 percent fatalities. The crisis is facilitated by the disparity between the practical concerns of the contractors and the ideological position of the State Department, which is replicating the mistake it made in Iraq. Without making any plans for stabilizing the country and restoring conditions for civil society, the administration expected toppling Saddam would be sufficient to ingratiate the United States to the Iraqi nation. Despite ten years of evidence to the contrary, US policymakers persisted in believing the approach that had proved disastrous in Iraq would succeed in Libya. Because US (along with British and French) air strikes helped topple Gaddafi, the United States assumed it had made Libya an ally. Therefore, even after most countries had, because of the country's deteriorating situation, evacuated their Libyan diplomatic corps, the United States maintained an embassy post in Tripoli and a diplomatic outpost in Benghazi. Bob even thinks Rone's presence is unnecessary at the CIA base. "The Company thinks he should be here," he informs Jack. "I don't. The truth is there is no real threat here. We won the revolution for these people."

Thus, the US diplomatic outpost in Benghazi has an elegant nine-acre facility, a mini-version of the US embassy in Baghdad's 280-acre Green Zone, minus the extensive fortifications. When the contractors visit the diplomatic outpost to assess its security prior to the scheduled visit to Libya by US Ambassador Stevens, they find the facility extremely vulnerable and severely lacking personnel with skills comparable to those of the contractors at the CIA base.

The ambassador, they are told, is "staying at the special mission compound at his own insistence" because "the Ambassador isn't some dilettante political appointee. He's the real deal, a true believer. He's there to win hearts and minds. Now you can't very well do that operating out of a classified facility that doesn't officially exist."

"Our biggest mistake," the ambassador explains when he arrives, "would be to not view this moment as an opportunity. Relationships between governments are important, yes, but relationships between people are the real foundations of diplomacy, and I believe that it is our mission as Americans to help Benghazians to form a free, democratic, and prosperous Libya."

Following up on this, he meets with the mayor the next day and assures the huge assembly from the Libyan media that "America is here for you." His warm welcome and the celebratory quality of this event confirms the State Department's belief that Libya is friendly to America. But this is the same mistake that Poundstone, the agent of the Department of Defense in *Green Zone*, made in assuming the officials in Baghdad represented the people of Iraq, which meant that the country was not going to be as free, democratic, and prosperous as Ambassador Stevens hoped Libya would be. Instead, a huge, coordinated Libyan assault on the diplomatic outpost results in two deaths, including the ambassador's, before the contractors from the CIA based a mile away can rescue the remaining people at the outpost. After burning the outpost down, the Libyans launch a series of attacks through the night on the CIA station, much more ably defended by the contractors, who are besieged by well-armed assailants.

GETTING THE RIGHT TO GO HOME

Late at night, sitting on the roof of one of the CIA base's four buildings, Jack and Rone, in a lull, knowing that another attack is imminent, reflect not on their job but on their profession. "I'm thinking about my girls, man," Jack tells Rone.

Thinking: what would they say about me? He died in a place he didn't need to be, in a battle over something he doesn't understand, in a country that meant nothing to him. Every time I go home to Becky and those girls, I think, this is it, I'm going to stay. Then something happens, and I end up back here. Why is that? Why can't I go *home*? Why can't I go home and just stay there?

In his last phone conversation with his wife, she told him she is expecting their third child, which further intensifies issues that have become particularly acute for Jack not only because the next onslaught may bring—in fact does bring—more casualties, but also, he says, because "That can't be the last [phone] call. That can't be the last call because . . . and I'm sitting up here and I'm thinking about some other guy raising these girls."

Jack apologizes for unloading on Rone in this way, but Rone says, "No. I get it. I know what it's like to be in a place like this—letting another man raise your children. When I was young, I was giving myself to something bigger, but Jack, that 'something bigger' is gone now."

Rone is clearly referring to his service as a Navy SEAL, when, like Chris Kyle, he was motivated by ideals, by some conception, we can infer, of patriotism or the desire to protect freedom. It was, in other words, his sense of a mission, but he and Jack, also a former Navy SEAL, have exchanged an ideal for an occupation. What differentiates *13 Hours* from the other films, therefore, is that it is beyond grappling with the opaqueness, if not complete absence, of a mission. Because the mission does not exist, they have no concerns about accomplishing it. The question now is about changing their current occupation to one that allows them to be home.

The film concludes with the surviving contractors at the airport waiting to board the plane that will evacuate them. They are still struck by the fact that most of them have survived and are extremely proud of how well they did their jobs. "Listen," Tanto (Pablo Schreiber) says, "Any other six guys, I don't think we make it. I think we were meant to be together last night."

"How do you think the [CIA] Chief's eval is going to go?" Boon (David Denman) asks, implicitly contrasting how well they did their jobs with how poorly the chief did his.

"He's gonna get a medal. You'll see," Tig (Dominic Fumusa) correctly predicts, as will the rescue team.

"All of them," Tanto says.

"What about us?" Tig asks. "The odds were 1,000 to 1, easy. What do we get?"

"We get to go home," Jack answers, definitively. If these combat survivors end up in the same place as the survivors in *Saving Private Ryan*, they do so having taken a very different route. The reason they get to go home is that they did their jobs so well that they saved their own lives rather than sacrifice them for "something bigger." As Rone pointed out, that "something bigger" no longer exists for them. To have a normal home life, their efforts do not have to bring an end to wartime. They just have to get them to other jobs.

CHAPTER 7

THE ONLY MISSION IS TO GET OUT

As we have seen in chapter 5, even though Jordan Peele's *Us* was not about the Iraq War, it explored an us/them cultural narrative important to our understanding of films dealing with the war and the American culture that informed them. In the decade after "Mission Accomplished," a genre of war film emerged exposing cultural narratives that problematized the effects on the job of soldiering in a war without a mission. As the Iraq War, to the extent it could be called a war, or the Iraq Occupation, to the extent that government policy allowed it to be called an Occupation, persevered into its second decade, discussions about objectives seemed to dissolve into debates about an exit strategy. Victory had long ago been declared but never achieved, and the ostensible objectives of the US military engagement had been tacitly ignored. For some, those stated goals were too embarrassing to utter, and for others they were simply old news. The basic question in the war's second decade was whether it was safe to abandon Iraq or was too dangerous to stay there. Troop levels increased or decreased; ISIS emerged, replacing sectarian militia conflicts as the greatest threat to Iraq, or at least to the idea of Iraq that the United States wished to imagine, in the way we imagine, at the end of *The Wizard of Oz*, that Dorothy's having killed the Wicked Witch in her dream will kill Miss Gulch's court order to have Toto put down the next day. Somehow, the concurrent invasions of Iraq and Afghanistan turned into separate wars, with different timelines, but the same objectives: to stabilize the chaos the US invasions created at least enough to exit with the appearance of cinematic closure. Doomed to failure, that mission, like those that had preceded it, was unaccomplished in every way, except that the United States eventually got out.

Us reflected the narrative of the fatal confusion between the invaded and the liberated, the terrorists and the terrorized, a narrative that acquired increasing media cogency with the prolonged presence of US forces enforcing US rule

175

in the name of "freedom." In the same way, Jordan Peele's 2017 film, *Get Out*, foregrounds another cultural narrative informing more recent films related to the dilemma posed by decades of sustaining wars that have no mission. To be clear, I am not saying that *Get Out* is an Iraq/Afghanistan war allegory or any form of war film. It has been rightfully lauded for drawing deftly on several genres—horror, social satire, sci-fi (*Guess Who's Coming to Dinner* meets David Cronenberg)—in order to debunk the transparent comfort of white privilege.

The film recounts a visit by Chris Washington (Daniel Kaluuya), a young Black photographer, and his white live-in girlfriend, Rose Armitage (Allison Williams), to her affluent parents, somewhere in upstate New York, during which time Chris discovers he is one of several Black men and women who had been lured to this estate so that their bodies, through a process involving hypnotism, drugging, and neurosurgery, could be inhabited by aging or dis-abled white people seeking to avoid the physical afflictions that time imposes. These affluent white liberals bid for the Black people in a coded slave auc-tion disguised as an annual bingo game. The targets of the film's satire, how-ever, are not white supremacists or Klansmen, but liberals, especially wealthy, Hollywood-type liberals who promote genre films that exploit fetishistic inter-est in African Americans for the dual purposes of ego gratification and financial profit. One way to read the phrase "get out," therefore, is as a plea, directed at the audience as well as at Hollywood, to escape the complacency of the genres they produce and the stereotypes and clichés upon which those genres depend.

Early in the film, Rose's father, Dean (Bradley Whitford), who "would have voted for Obama a third time, if he could have," Rose assures Chris, is showing Chris the house. Noting a mounted deer head, Dean indicates that he doesn't like deer because "they're taking over." "Every time I see a dead deer on the road," he tells Chris, "I say 'It's a start.'" He also brags to Chris about his travels: "I keep bringing souvenirs back—such a privilege to experience another per-son's culture."

What at one time would have been called the "black humor" of these com-ments is that, in juxtaposition, they invert our understanding of figurative and literal. The cliché that "they are taking over" suggests that the deer represent Black people (or more recently, immigrants from the Global South), often sub-ject to that white-backlash charge. It is the cultural narrative at the core of the attacks on affirmative action: policies and programs are allowing "aliens" to usurp roles that would legitimately go to white Anglo-Saxons; the same cul-tural narrative was iterated in the "English only" movement that peaked in the late twentieth century, and more currently informs the myth that noncitizens are being "imported" to "take Black jobs," cast illegitimate ballots, proliferate crime, and create a housing crisis. All these cultural narratives are derivatives of the wagon-train-under-attack narrative discussed in the last chapter, which sees white settlers, who a priori have a "natural" claim, besieged by nonwhites who would deny them their rightful place in the "natural" order. The solution, as indicated by "it's a start"—the punchline to a genocide joke—is extermination of the species.

At the same time, when Dean describes the basically colonialist enterprise of souvenir collecting as "the privilege of experiencing another person's culture," he is alluding to the ability to *experience*, through his mad science, another person, and thus "privilege" refers not figuratively to an honor, but literally to his privileged position as the exploiter of natural (human) resources. The same inversion of figurative and literal pertains when he says about the cellar, "black mold down there"; the cellar, as we learn, is the site of the medical procedures that allow privileged whites to fill the molds of Black bodies.

In this guest-host relationship, the inversion of figurative and literal reveals a perversion that makes the Armitage estate a site of menace, enveloped by a rhetoric of exploitation that invests its users with self-serving magnanimity, akin to the previous century's "white man's burden."[1] Under that mantle, white Christians undertook the management of nonwhite, non-Christians so as to liberate them from heathen ignorance. It was applied most broadly by the British in justifying their control of large portions of Africa and of the Asian subcontinent. Analogous rhetoric was used a century earlier in the United States to support the "peculiar institution" of slavery and the practice of segregation: if left to their own devices, the argument went, African Americans, who were naturally simplistic, would not have the ability to survive in the complex societies of the industrialized Western world. The pillaging of the Middle East has been conducted under similar rhetorical premises, with a history of expropriation that spans from centuries of stocking the British Museum to the rampant looting this century in US-liberated Iraq.

Get Out, in other words, does not have to focus on the Iraq War to expose the same cultural narratives underpinning the conflation of terrorist and terrorized, liberation and exploitation, protection and aggression, invasion and captivity that characterized American attitudes toward Muslim countries. These attitudes were crucial in underwriting a mission to eliminate weapons of mass destruction along with those who would use them on a white (Judeo-) Christian country that enjoys the lifestyle the Muslim Middle East resents.[2] Because Chris is entrapped by a body of notions, assumptions, and rhetorical conventions as much as by physical restraints, *Get Out* cannot achieve a Hollywood ending that corrects the Armitage household or finds legal recourse outside of it. A "good cop" will not figure it out in the nick of time; the arms of the law will not arrest the Armitages or restore normalcy to their community. Chris is betrayed by everyone, including Rose, whose professions of love were a trick employed to execute her family's pathological hi-tech slave trade.

To get out, Chris massacres three generations of Armitages, those inhabiting white liberal bodies and those (Rose's grandparents) inhabiting the previously captured Black bodies they acquired to forestall their own mortality. When, at the end of the massacre, a car with lights flashing arrives, the fear is that Chris will face the same fate as Ben (Duane Jones), the Black hero of *Night of the Living Dead* (1968). Having survived the night, Ben is shot in the morning by a member of an armed posse who assumes he is one of the ghouls whom he had spent the night fighting. Instead, Chris's friend, Rod (Lil Rel Howery), in a TSA car, drives him away before the authorities can discover the dead white bodies. Because, in the world this film presents, rectifying the historically specific conditions that have created the Armitage enterprise is impossible, no conceivable narrative can credibly represent legitimate US authorities as providing safety or enforcing justice. As with Iraq and Afghanistan, the only answer is to get out, not only of the place but of the historical conditions that created the untenable circumstances, exactly the same conclusion at which the contractors arrive at the end of *13 Hours*.

WAR IS A TOXIC WORKPLACE

If *Get Out* were a one-off, it would still be noteworthy in its call to get out of the genre of warfare that makes war an endless occupation and the genre of the traditional war film that informs the endless occupation of Iraq. But more importantly, the film consolidates another new genre, distinct not only from the World War II combat films that found their apotheosis in *Saving Private Ryan*, but also from the war-as-occupation films discussed in this book. In the middle of the second decade of the twenty-first century, some war films appear in which we do not see soldiers persevering at a dangerous occupation. Instead, in these films they succeed in escaping it. Rejecting war as a mission *and* as an occupation, these films—*13 Hours, Dunkirk, Hacksaw Ridge*—celebrate the triumph of people who manage to escape the battle with their lives.

As I noted at the outset, cultural narratives are not defined by specific topics but rather by a set of causal relations that acquire cogency for a culture or subculture by virtue of their explicit and implicit iteration. Copious examples of these cultural narratives, I noted, can be found in Roland Barthes's *Mythologies*, a collection of essays that connect aspects of postwar French culture to narratives about such topics as class, gender, and national values, made all the more cogent by virtue of their ostensible transparency, that is, as Barthes explains, their appearing to be natural, rather than ideological. By virtue of their dispersed iteration, they achieve an ostensible ubiquity to the point of becoming—at least for a critical mass—commonplaces: "what everyone knows." People, for example, who in this decade believe the 2020 presidential election was corrupt commonly say, "*Everyone knows* the election was stolen."

One indication, therefore, that *Get Out* reflects an emerging cultural narrative is the degree to which, after ten years of missionless warfare, we start to see films not only about war but also about an array of dangerous occupations, all of which require trained workers to be away from home for long periods of time, in potentially hazardous situations. These new get-out films, moreover, are based on true events that, in a moment of crisis, radically redefine the immediate and long-term priorities of the principals, forcing them to abandon their normal duties and devote all their energies solely to escaping.

In this way, the films resemble the disaster film genre that was particularly popular in the 1970s, including *Airport* (1970) and its three sequels (1974, 1977, 1979), *The Poseidon Adventure* (1972), and *The Towering Inferno* (1974). Those films, however, featured a large cross section of people, only some of whom were involved for occupational reasons. The fictional events in those films, moreover, were intentionally sensational and heavily contrived. In the twenty-first-century get-out films, all the hazards are job-related, and, far from being escapist entertainment, they demand we accept the reality of the circumstances, just as most of the Iraq War films we have examined do. Even *Get Out*, despite its sci-fi elements, repeatedly calls its audience uncomfortably back to realities of race relations in America, including the danger for a Black man walking in a white residential neighborhood after dark or being stopped for no reason by a white policeman while driving with a white woman in an upscale area. Being targeted for seduction, abduction, and auction, moreover, was an occupational hazard for Chris because he is a photographer whom a blind white photographer wanted to appropriate because of his astute eyesight and aesthetic way of seeing.

This get-out genre is anticipated by *Billy Lynn's Long Halftime Walk*, which, by tracing one day in which Billy is barraged by fraudulent reasons for his "heroic" service, considers the possibility that getting out could be the only sane way to deal with his lethal occupation. The halftime show, with its militaristic display of fireworks, triggers flashbacks and trauma, intensifying his guilt about being celebrated for the worst day in his life. Although the film, like *The Hurt Locker* or *Jarhead*, repeatedly treats military service as a job, not as a heroic or patriotic cause, *Billy Lynn* treats it as a pointless job, which Billy wants to quit. If, after vacillating, he decides to return to Iraq, he does so not because he comprehends the war's mission, but because, like Chris Kyle, he wants to protect his fellow soldiers. For Lynn, this takes him from Texas back to Iraq, while for Kyle, it extends from Iraq back to Texas, where his attempt to help another soldier proves just as fatal as may Lynn's attempts to do so in Iraq. Both films, therefore, emphasize the importance of getting out alive and, equally, the difficulty of doing so. Whether in Iraq or Texas, after more than a decade in a post–Mission Accomplished war, surviving appears to be the only mission worth accomplishing, and escaping is the only way to accomplish it.

This is exactly what the contractors in Benghazi concluded. *13 Hours* starts by consolidating all the crucial elements of the war-as-occupation narrative and ends by replacing it with a get-out narrative. As Jack tells his wife on the phone at the end of the film, "We had a problem here, and whatever you hear on the news, it's over. I'm coming home. For good."

At the outset, the six contractors, beneficiaries of Rumsfeld's outsourcing policy, have turned their military service into a lucrative occupation that embraces no political or philosophical loyalty. Unlike the soldiers in *Saving Private Ryan*, the contractors' jobs do not facilitate their return home, and scenes of their speaking to their families in the United States via Skype or FaceTime show they do not think their work makes their families safe or keeps their country free. *13 Hours* pinpoints the moment when these contractors, who thought they had good occupations, decide they must quit their jobs to save their lives. Jack articulates the problem—by implication a problem common to all the post–Mission Accomplished war films—when he expresses the fear that his girls will think that he "died in a place he didn't need to be, in a battle over something he didn't understand, in a country that meant nothing to him."

Like Jack, the rest of the contractors decide to get out, as we are told in short postscripts, accompanied by photos of the actual contractors. Each has resigned from the CIA and is now living with his family. If these contractors were responding to the job conditions after Bush-Cheney-Rumsfeld converted the Occupation to an occupation that entailed the hazards of war without the promise of peace, they represented several hundred thousand American troops stationed in Iraq and Afghanistan over the last twenty years. Many did multiple tours; for some, the stop-loss policy extended those tours beyond the scheduled end of their tour of duty. Whether contractors or GIs, the men have been damaged, psychologically or physically, or they have simply been deprived of the pleasure of living at home in peace.

Many recent war films iterate this theme. Survival is the sole mission in *Dunkirk* (2017), which begins with several tracking shots of a soldier (Fionn Whitehead) running away from combat. His escape—around which the film's two other plot threads are organized—is not a combat strategy and has no relationship to restoring peace or returning to normal. In fact, at the end of the film, *nothing* promises to be normal for any of the characters, all of whom represent those trying to escape from combat. The film intercuts three narrative strains, one focusing on soldiers gathered by the thousands on the beach, desperately attempting to evacuate, while the German soldiers advance and several of the vessels evacuating the men are attacked by German aircraft. Another narrative strain follows a British civilian, one of thousands who crossed the Channel in private vessels to rescue more than three hundred thousand stranded troops. The third strain involves three Spitfire pilots who battle the Luftwaffe over Dunkirk to give cover to soldiers awaiting evacuation. Although the film has several episodes, there is no unifying plot, just repeated attempts to get out, some successful, others not.

Hacksaw Ridge (2016) is the true story of medic Desmond Doss (Andrew Garfield), a conscientious objector so adamant about his convictions that he will not even touch a gun. This contrasts him directly with his outfit, making him such a pariah that he is brutally tormented in basic training and, at one point, seriously beaten by the men in his unit. Although the objective the men share is taking Iwo Jima, the scope of that mission never overpowers Doss's personal convictions. The ending's prolonged and bloody combat sequence, therefore, concentrates not on conquering Iwo Jima but on evacuating seventy-five wounded men from combat. In the face of heavy fire, Doss saves these men by extricating their wounded bodies from a steep ridge, belaying them down by rope, one at a time, and returning to the battlefield, unarmed, to retrieve more men. The story of Doss's upbringing and the ordeals of his training are aimed at the film's defining action, helping men get out.

Significantly, since both *Hacksaw Ridge* and *Dunkirk* are set in World War II, they substitute the get-out narrative for the narrative arc traditionally associated with the good war, specifically reversing the direction of the energy in *Saving Private Ryan*, where the men drive from the water inland, in pursuit of the enemy. In these films, instead, they struggle to escape from the land to the water, in flight from the enemy.

Deepwater Horizon (2016) is another true story in which a hazardous occupation isolates workers in the Gulf (in this case, the Gulf of Mexico), so far from land they must take a helicopter to get to work. The film resembles *13 Hours* in that it too focuses on skilled professionals working for a private contractor, Transocean, operating an oil drilling rig for BP. Like the contractors in *13 Hours*, these skilled employees have good-paying jobs that take them away from their families for long periods of time. Working on what is tantamount to a floating city, through which runs, at extremely high pressure, a virtually infinite river of highly combustible liquid, they live and work in an environment as precarious, at least potentially, as Iraq outside of the Green Zone, or Benghazi after the fall of Gaddafi. Their occupational hazards are greatly heightened because their work conditions are controlled by self-interested bureaucrats, like the State Department and CIA officials in the Green Zone and in Benghazi, who place their occupational interests over the welfare of the professionals placed at risk by their cavalier attitudes.

In this case, the Transocean bureaucrats ignore warnings that an underwater pipeline is not properly sealed; a safety test shows "a disparity between the drill line and the kill line." As in the other films, the occupational difficulties of distance and danger threaten the contractors' domestic lives. The threat is realized violently when an explosion sets aflame the man-made island on which they work, creating an emergency in which eleven workers die and seventeen others are injured.

The second half of the film, resembling the majority of *Dunkirk*, therefore, concentrates on the efforts of the men to save themselves and their coworkers. Tellingly, when water is crashing in, amidst fires and explosions, the palette and imagery of *Deepwater Horizon* is almost identical to portions of *Dunkirk*, including underwater shots of men trying to avoid drowning or swimming away from oil burning on the surface of the sea. In both films, men covered with oil are hard to distinguish from one another. The same is true of men running through or away from fire in *Dunkirk* and *13 Hours*.

In *13 Hours*, as in *Deepwater Horizon*, one of the central characters continues to function as a leader despite being covered with bloody cuts, wounds, and bruises. Similar shots characterize the night evacuation of the people on the Deepwater Horizon and the seventy-five soldiers in *Hacksaw Ridge*. As a group, these films present imagery so similar that, at moments, shots from the films appear almost indistinguishable. Like *Dunkirk*, and to some degree *Hacksaw Ridge*, which culminates in an attack on an island launched from the sea, all these films link the change of occupation to the exchange of environs and elements.

The end of *Deepwater Horizon*, like the end of *13 Hours*, shows photos of the real people who lost their lives. *Hacksaw Ridge* ends with footage of Doss receiving the Medal of Honor and footage of him, late in his life, talking about his war experiences. *Sully* concludes in an airplane hangar, where Sully poses for a group photo with the passengers and crew he saved. *Captain Phillips* ends with briefer statements on the screen telling us that Phillips is home with his family and Muse is serving a long term in a federal prison. All of these get-out films, in other words, seem deeply invested in differentiating these movies about escape from escapist movies. These are films, they remind us, where the people have real lives that can only be saved by heeding the urgency of leaving their workplace and occupation.

FIGURES 7.01A *and* **7.01B.** *Men attempting to evacuate in* Dunkirk *(2017, top) and* Deepwater Horizon *(2016, bottom).*

THE HANKS EFFECT

In this emergence of a cultural narrative that substitutes getting out for accomplishing a mission, Tom Hanks's star persona plays an interesting role. As Captain Miller in *Saving Private Ryan*, Hanks epitomized the hero of the World War II combat film. That role contributed to the cultural work of reviving the traditional war film narrative, wherein men fighting to achieve peace were furthering the long-term goal of preserving the American way of life. Thus,

Hanks's reemergence, fifteen years after *Saving Private Ryan*, as a central actor in two get-out films foregrounds the dramatic shift in cultural narratives. In *Captain Phillips* (2013), made at the inception of this genre, and *Sully* (2016), made at its peak, Hanks again plays captains, both real captains, Phillips and Sullenberger, who, like Miller, are responsible for the lives of others. Each captain finds his normal occupation violently disrupted by circumstances that require abandoning that occupation's tasks for the sole purpose of escaping.

In *Captain Phillips*, an American cargo ship is hijacked by Somali pirates, requiring that Phillips devise and execute plans that will prevent the crew members from dying. Significantly, the film starts with Phillips at home, driving to the airport with his wife, to fly to Oman, where he will take command of a container vessel headed for Kenya. While they are talking about their children, we can see that, without saying anything to that effect, his wife (Catherine Keener) is anxious about his assignment. This could easily have been a scene from *American Sniper*, as Chris Kyle begins a new tour in Iraq, or something akin to the moment, we can imagine, when Hanks, as Captain Miller, leaves home for what would turn out to be Normandy and then Ramelle. All of these narratives require a site of domestic normality against which to contrast the hazardous job, and, as it turns out, Captain Phillips too is going into combat with parties of undefined allegiance.

As in several of the films we have examined, the distinction between hostile and friendly does not sort out as it does in traditional war films. In Iraq, "insurgent" is a generic term lumping together numerous groups hostile to the United States and to one another. In Benghazi, even the CIA office could not agree on which factions were operative, and which of those were friendly or antagonistic to the United States. The pirates here also indicate that they answer to bosses, just as Phillips does, and the parallels at the outset of the film between Phillips, arriving for work at the container vessel in Oman, and the head of the pirate attack group, Abduwali Muse (Barkhad Abdi), assembling his crew in Kenya, show that they both have dangerous jobs. As the story develops, the pirates and the vessel's crew both engage in forms of guerrilla warfare, first the pirates in their attempts to board the vessel, and then the crew by hiding, booby-trapping, and sabotaging the pirates after they have taken charge of the ship. Finally, the pirates, who have taken Phillips hostage, are killed by Navy SEAL snipers (one of whom, Glen Doherty, became one of the four casualties in Benghazi three years later).

Similarly, in *Sully*, Hanks, as Chesley Sullenberger, the captain of a passenger aircraft (an Airbus A320), encounters a freakish influx of birds when lifting off from LaGuardia Airport. These birds jam his jet engines, rendering the plane unflyable and necessitating that he crash-land on the Hudson

FIGURE 7.02A. *Tom Hanks as Captain Miller (*Saving Private Ryan, *1998).*

FIGURE 7.02B. *Tom Hanks as Captain Phillips (*Captain Phillips, *2013).*

FIGURE 7.02C. *Tom Hanks as Captain Sullenberger (*Sully, *2016).*

River, saving the lives of all 155 people on board. The film revolves around the subsequent investigation, in which Sully enjoys media celebrity while he is being investigated for negligence, when flight simulations indicate he could have safely landed the plane at one of two nearby airports. In the end, however, he is exonerated and allowed to go home.

Both films invoke the sensibility of Hanks's Captain Miller, who, despite the immense pressures that hazardous work entails, and despite any personal doubts, is able to prioritize the safety of his men (or crew or passengers) and demonstrate extraordinarily good judgment. In *Saving Private Ryan*, however, that captain's good judgment subordinates the safety of the men to the mission that grounds the good war's narrative arc; therefore, instead of removing Ryan from action, Miller convinces his unit to join him in staving off the Nazis.

In *Captain Phillips* and *Sully*, although the sensibilities of Hanks's characters have not changed, their circumstances have. In both films, our glimpses of the normal domestic lives led by Phillips and Sully show that their occupations take them away from—and potentially threaten—normal domesticity. Instead of seeing the goal of their occupations as earning the right to go home, they have to balance their home life against their missions.

Hanks's screen persona over several decades has seemed to internalize that sense of domestic normality. (No wonder he played Mr. Rogers.) Whether he enjoys domestic peacetime, or tries to create it, or longs to restore it, Hanks always seems to embody it. When Captain Miller reveals to his men his peacetime persona—high school English teacher—and says back home people say, "that figures," he is trying to tell the men how much the war has changed him, but at the same time he is revealing to the audience that he remains the figurative representation of normal life, the vestige of peacetime carried into war. His presence conveys the same thing whether a castaway on a Pacific island or an astronaut approaching the moon aboard Apollo 13. His separation from domestic stability adds poignancy to the road to perdition, and his attempts to achieve that stability distinguishes him from his dysfunctional family in *You've Got Mail*. In *Sully* and *Captain Phillips*, therefore, when Hanks prioritizes getting out, he implicitly essentializes why Americans need to.

Paul Greengrass, who made *Captain Phillips* immediately after he made *Green Zone*, appears to be explicitly referencing *Saving Private Ryan* when he gives *Green Zone* star Matt Damon the same name that Hanks had in *Saving Private Ryan*, when Damon played Ryan, saved by Hanks, who played Miller. Whether or not Greengrass was intentionally alluding to the Iraq War's inversion of the conventions and values of the traditional war film, the names nevertheless illicit the contrast. In his confrontation with Al Rawi near the end of

Green Zone, Miller attempts to prevent Al Rawi from being killed by a military unit that wants him dead, because Al Rawi can prove the information about WMDs was fabricated to fuel the support for the invasion. But because Al Rawi is convinced that the Americans are his enemy, he captures Miller and is about to have him killed. At this point, the action of the film, concluding with a thrilling chase and shootout, is devoted to saving Miller.

Both films, in other words, save Matt Damon, whose character in *Green Zone* has the same name as Hanks in *Saving Private Ryan*. Damon's rank in *Green Zone,* "Chief Warrant Officer," is an interesting military category that has the authority of an officer (and must be saluted) without the requirement of a college degree, and hence is a hybrid of enlisted man and officer, like a combination of Damon's Private Ryan and Hanks's Captain Miller. In *Saving Private Ryan*, however, as Mike tells Miller (Hanks), saving Ryan might earn them the right to go home, a charge Miller passes on to Ryan with his dying command: "Earn it." If *Green Zone*'s allusions to *Saving Private Ryan* have any resonance, then the charge has come full circle, where Miller (Damon) ventriloquizes Miller (Hanks) by indicating that there is no way he can earn the right to go home because it is not in his job description. In this context, we can say that World War II Miller's charge to Private Ryan is revised by Iraq War Miller's concluding words in *Green Zone*, written as an email message to *Wall Street Journal* reporter Dayne: "Let's get the story right, next time."

CODA

In 1980, Iraq commenced a war with Iran, in part out of Saddam's fears that Iran, a Shiite Muslim country, would instigate the Shia majority in Iraq to overthrow his Sunni regime. Although the war, after eight years, ended in stalemate, it did impede a Shia rebellion in Iraq. Fifteen years after the Iran-Iraq War ended, however, the United States achieved the result Saddam feared and Iran desired. At this moment, more than twenty years after the US invaded Iraq, all the efforts, all the wasted money and sacrificed lives—American and Iraqi—have resulted in converting Iraq into a pro-Iranian haven for Hezbollah terrorists.

Just as the Libyans in 2012, freed from Gaddafi's rule, used their freedom to throw the United States out, the Iraqis, freed from Saddam's oppression, are now (as I write this) asking, at Iran's behest, that the US withdraw its remaining twenty-four hundred troops. Was installing a regime allied with Iran, a leading source of state-sponsored, anti-American terrorism, the mission US troops in Iraq were fighting to accomplish? When the last US troop exits Iraq, will a "Mission Accomplished" banner, thanks to US assistance, be raised in Tehran?

And so long as US political leaders subordinate national security to personal loyalties and political interests, so long as they find no fault with monetizing state secrets and/or selling influence to international bidders, so long as it is acceptable to disdain the sacrifices made by those who fought to preserve national values, so long as these leaders find more value in undermining public consensus than in building it, what are the chances of getting the story right next time?

NOTES

Introduction. A Banner Day for a War that Oughta' Be in Pictures

1. Douglas Kellner, in *Cinema Wars*, refers to the Bush administration as "Bush-Cheney." Numerous facts legitimate referring to the administration as one in which the decision-making was shared between President Bush and Vice President Cheney. As the head of Bush's VP vetting team, Cheney selected himself as Bush's running mate (see Corley); Cheney was contacted on 9/11 before Bush and was making crucial decisions early in the crisis (see Goldstein; Mann); Bush insisted Cheney be present when he answered questions from the 9/11 Commission (see King and Loughlin); Cheney played a very instrumental role in the buildup to the invasion of Iraq (see Goldstein, 119–121; Feldmann); Cheney assumed the power to exert "Executive Privilege" (see Page). Perhaps most telling was Cheney's involvement in the outing of CIA undercover agent Valerie Plame, in connection with which Cheney's chief aide, Scooter Libby, went to prison (see Seidman; York). Kellner also refers to the era as the "Bush-Cheney-Rove" era, another appropriate choice, in light of the degree to which Bush's strategic thinking was attributed to his adviser, Karl Rove (see, for example, Moore and Slater). When focusing on the conduct of the Iraq War, however, because Bush-Cheney ceded so much strategic and operational authority to Rumsfeld, the term "Bush-Cheney-Rumsfeld" seems a more apt shorthand.

2. The central disputes concern how to go about defeating that enemy, who should be in charge, and whether defeating the enemy is worth it.

3. These included prohibitions on any suggestion of homosexuality, or valorization of miscegenation, promiscuity, adultery, premarital sex, successful criminal acts, or left-wing politics; it prohibited any deprecation (serious or humorous) of religious figures or of capitalism. While the code remained unchanged, its interpretation and enforcement became increasingly less rigid from the mid-1950s to the late 1960s, when it was replaced by a rating system, which replaced all proscriptions on content with disputes over the appropriate rating classification warranted by specific representations. This link contains the entire Production Code: https://digitalcollections.oscars.org/digital /collection/p15759coll11/id/10888/rec/1.

4. My book *Television in Black-and-White America* details how the structure and regulatory agencies of the television medium in its first decade allowed for a very narrow spectrum of diversity, and were particularly instrumental in sustaining the validity of the cultural narrative that America is a white nation and that Black bodies in (white) public space constituted a public threat.

5. See White's *Metahistory* (1973), *The Tropics of Discourse* (1978), and *The Content of Form* (1987).

Chapter 1. Narrative, Culture, and Cinema

1. See Redfield; Jackson, *Writing the War on Terrorism*.
2. See Rothschild.

3. This is why, as Gramsci explains, hegemonic power depends on structures of invisible compliance.

4. Jerry Falwell and Pat Robertson blamed 9/11 on the ACLU for "throwing God out of the schools," along with other groups, including the abortionists, the pagans, the feminists, the gays, and the lesbians, because "God will not be mocked." September 19, 2001. https://www.youtube.com/watch?v=kMkBgA9_oQ4.

5. See Michelle Garcia, "It's All Our Fault! The Ten Disasters the Gays Supposedly Caused." https://www.advocate.com/politics/2012/10/31/10-disasters-gays-were-blamed-causing.

6. See Horsman.

7. What I mean by this is that "time" has a long history of philosophical and cultural constructions, some figurative, some theoretical, some mathematical projections. The question is not what time "really" is, but what meanings are ascribed to its historically specific cultural constructions. These constructions, not some objective natural phenomenon, are the referent for any given usage. A "light year," for example, organizes time and distance throughout the entire universe in relation to the rotation of a tiny planet around a very small star in a minor galaxy in the corner of that universe. See Frazer; Hawkins; Kern.

8. This topic has been explored extensively regarding specific figures and events and regarding the way formal qualities of Hollywood time and space privilege specific ways of knowing. I started exploring this aspect of American culture in *Flatlining on the Field of Dreams*, and I touch on it in regard to television in *Television in Black-and-White America*; some germane articles include "Second Nature, Cinematic Narrative, the Historical Subject, and *Russian Ark*" (2005), "From the Industrial Unconscious to the Cinematic to the Televisual to the Networked" (2019), and "Mapping the Other: *The English Patient*, Colonial Rhetoric, and Cinematic Representation" (2004); see also Feeny; Gabler; Rogin.

9. Johnson recorded phone call, 1964. callhttps://www.cnn.com/2022/02/16/politics/lyndon-b-johnson-secret-audio-origseriesfilms/index.html.

10. See Kennan; Gaddis.

11. The Gulf of Tonkin Resolution, used as the legal basis for the escalation of US forces into a major war, passed in August of 1964 with no fanfare and miniscule dissent. https://www.archives.gov/milestone-documents/tonkin-gulf-resolution.

12. The most successful war film during the Vietnam War was *The Green Berets* (1968). After the war, *The Deer Hunter* (1978), the majority of which is not a war film, was very successful; so was *Coming Home* (1978), which was an anti-war film that takes place in California.

Chapter 2. Private Ryan and the Last Good War (Narrative)

1. Michel de Certeau elaborates extensively on the theoretical significance of the practices of everyday life.

2. This was one of the most infamous symptoms of the strong pro-Nazi sentiments among a segment of the American population. Steven Ross has documented an extensive array of plots during the 1930s, organized against Hollywood and America by undercover Nazi subversives, and thwarted by undercover Jews. See also Hart; Churchwell; Maddow.

3. As Thomas Doherty extensively documented, fascist infiltration of Hollywood was strong and, in the mid-1930s, more insidious than the anti-fascist output by the major studios. "The Hayes office," Doherty explains, "had always discouraged the production of politically sensitive motion pictures, not needing the [Production] Code to act on what it considered 'the good of the industry as a whole'" (*Hollywood and Hitler*, 209).

4. I am indebted to my colleague Jordan Brower for pointing out that, in the context of World War II, the film's ending also affirms the importance of entertainment, and especially MGM entertainment, to American life, and of continuity across a disruption.

5. Film critic Amy Taubin (*Village Voice*) was repulsed by it.

6. Usually included in this group are Ron Howard, George Lucas, Francis Ford Coppola, and, in a more ironic, if not arch, way, Quentin Tarantino; Clint Eastwood, Martin Scorsese, Brian De Palma, and Peter Bogdanovich have also been identified as having a strong reverence for that tradition.

7. Basinger herself devotes several pages (258–262) to outlining how the film conforms to the conventions of World War II combat films established in the 1940s.

8. Although questions have also been raised about the veracity of this policy, a number of actual cases support the credibility of this fictional one. Landon: "Ryan bears some resemblance to Fritz Niland, a member of the 101st Airborne who was taken out of combat after three of his brothers had been reported killed [but Spielberg explained] the Ryan/Niland connection only provided 'the kernel of truth around which [his] morality play has been fictionalized.'" See also Kodat.

9. This letter has, for several reasons, been called into doubt. Catherine Kodat well summarizes the crucial issues surrounding its veracity.

10. "Nearly every commentator criticized this prologue and epilogue. Janet Maslin conceded that these scenes are among the film's 'few false notes.'" Others derided this opening and closing as "maudlin," "completely unnecessary," and "a burst of schmaltzy ritual."

11. I am grateful to Jordan Brower for pointing out that this scene anticipates elements of the "terror" that will become the universal enemy of the United States after 9/11; in this film, however, Miller is able to locate and defeat it. There is room, I think, to develop the connection between this and the war trauma—signified by his hand tremors—that he struggles to overcome throughout the film.

12. Elisabeth Bronfen insightfully points out that the cinematic realization of Miller, his men, and the Nazi machine gunners they are about to take out is achieved not through montage but by using the mirror as inset in the shot, creating "a mise en abyme of the cinematic image itself . . . with a miniature image of the enemy, unnaturally framed by the darkened sides of the mirror, appearing like a freeze-frame, on top of a second image in the background, depicting those about to destroy them" (137).

13. Bronfen notes that the shot of the stenciled name on the back of a dead man, lying face-down in the sand, replicates the shot of John Wayne as Sergeant Stryker at the end of *Sands of Iwo Jima*, another detail that underscores Spielberg's conscious effort to construct the classic World War II combat film.

14. Auster also notes that the imagery in this segment alludes to Wyeth paintings, but also claims, incorrectly I believe, that it is also drawn from Grant Wood, whose style, palette, imagery, and school of painting all differ significantly from Wyeth's.

Chapter 3. *Lost* in Iraq and the Collapse of Wartime

1. Although, in terms of its mission, the Persian Gulf War resembled the Korean War in that its purpose was to restore a violated border, the truncated trajectory of that war made it closer to a "police action," the misnomer technically defining the action in Korea, which lasted three years, most of it fighting over issues other than the border dispute that initiated it.

2. See Bordwell, Staiger, and Thompson.

3. See Fourth Geneva Convention, https://ihl-databases.icrc.org/en/ihl-treaties /gciv-1949.

4. See Poniewozik.

5. From the song "Bali Ha'i," in the musical show *South Pacific*, lyrics by Oscar Hammerstein II.

6. From the song "Bali Ha'i."

7. In chapters of this sort, it is customary upon a character's first introduction to describe briefly his or her situation, but in the case of *Lost*, the number of characters and the abundance of their situations would easily double the length of this chapter. Thus, unless it is absolutely necessary for the thread of my discussion, I have chosen whenever possible to suffice with minimal information. A detailed summary of each character can be found, among other places, on <lostpedia.wikia.com/wiki/Lost>, a wiki that contains 7,292 pages, with more than nine thousand words devoted, for example, to the story of the character Jack.

8. The show's brief mini-obituaries echoed those in the *Times*, which ranged between 125 and 200 words. These excerpts indicate the similarity in tone and detail:

> Craig Gibson had a number of keen interests, starting with soccer (he played for a Manhattan team called Barnestonworth, but rooted for Liverpool) and continuing with the movies. (He had to be the first to see a new release, and there had to be plenty of popcorn on hand.) And he loved his wife, Dannielle, with whom he immigrated from Australia last December.
> ***
> On the Monday night before the terrorist attack, Joanna Vidal, a 26-year-old event coordinator for Risk Waters, the London-based financial publishing house, was ecstatic. The first day of the company's conference at Windows on the World, an event she had helped create, had been a brilliant success. And at dinner with her father, Enrique, and her mother, Lesbia, in their Yonkers home, "she was so hurried, making her preparations, that she was eating standing up," Mr. Vidal recalled.
> ***
> He enjoyed fast trips in his motorboat on Lake Hopatcong, N.J., near where he lived, and friends labeled him the "Fun Guy," because of his adventuresome streak and his abiding passion for jokes. He belonged to a joke circuit of sorts on the Internet, and e-mailed friends fresh jokes every day. His wife got them too. "There were a lot of blonde jokes," she said.

9. Like the Freudian fetish narrative, the island conflates projected fears with imagined retribution. Fetishism, according to Freud, originates in the castration posited by the male child when he first sees his mother's vagina. Because what was lost was never

there, the child's narrative merges the violence of the imagined castration with the denial of that violence, which is a double denial: of the belief that the mother lost her penis, and of the fact that she did not have a penis to lose. For Freud, this violence (the revelation of a violent narrative and the revelation that it is impossible) consolidates around substitute objects that reify both the violence and its denial. Like the mother's "lost" penis, in other words, the act that removed it is also lost, both replaced by an object that substitutes for the lost violence and for that which was violently lost: "What happened, therefore, was that the boy refused to take cognizance of the fact of his having perceived that a woman does not possess a penis. No, that could not be true: for if a woman had been castrated, then his own possession of a penis was in danger" (Freud, 155).

10. See Anon., "Bush's Iraq WMD Joke Backfires" and Anon., "Bush Takes Heat for WMD Jokes."

11. See Scahill.

12. See Smith; Noah.

13. See Taylor.

14. Friedman's *Free to Choose* has become the layman's Bible of neoliberal economic philosophy. With arguments based on cherry-picked examples and the methodologically flawed assumption that correlation proves causality, it connects democratic freedom with free markets and free markets with the proliferation of prosperity.

15. Packer, 123.

16. So obsessed is Trump with the idea of ownership that he seems to have forgotten (or perhaps never learned) that oil is a liquid, making his remark the equivalent of saying, "When we left Utah, we should have taken the Salt Lake."

17. *The Ultimate* Lost *and Philosophy: Think Together, Die Alone*, a collection of essays that attempts to elucidate the philosophical foundations of the series, in fact does a very poor job of doing so. An essay devoted to the character John Locke, for example, starts out asserting that he has "a close relation to his philosophical namesake" (301), but in fact devotes only one very general sentence to supporting this assertion, relating to "Locke's emphasis on observing nature and testing experience" (302). The rest of the essay explains the character's very non-Lockean adherence to Eastern philosophies, most notably Taoism, as well as aspects of Hinduism and Buddhism.

18. At the same time, the Iraqis "complained that the Americans didn't know how to be occupiers. . . . Americans were both too soft and too hard. . . . Love me or I'll kill you. They had allowed the lootings, the Iraqis said, and they were allowing criminals and extremists to have the run of the country. At the same time, they turned friends into enemies with impulsive, violent reactions" (Packer, 238).

Chapter 4. It's Not an Occupation, It's War, and War Is a Shit Occupation

1. "Five Years since 'Mission Accomplished' Speech," Associated Press, https://www.youtube.com/watch?v=vH-r3OdMVR4.

2. Anon., "Military Pay Chart 2004."

3. See O'Brien and Bender.

4. Anon., "The Enlistment/Reenlistment Contract," 2020, Section 9b.

5. The "money shot" names the moments of filmed ejaculation that are the highlights of porn films.

6. The quote is from Chris Hedges, whose book *War Is a Force that Gives Us Mean-*

ing is a cautionary attempt to balance the unique thrill of war with both the residual damage of that sensation on those who experience it and the dangers of those who are able to exploit it; Hedges is particularly condemnatory of those who evoke it for political gain.

7. See Baker, "Democracy in Iraq Not a Priority in US Budget."

8. As I noted in the preface, the estimates of the direct and indirect civilian deaths resulting from the Iraq War vary greatly. According to the Watson Institute for International and Public Affairs at Brown University, as of 2024, taking the broadest possible view, "The U.S. post-9/11 wars in Iraq, Afghanistan, Pakistan, Syria, Yemen, and Somalia have taken a tremendous human toll. The total death toll in these war zones, including direct and indirect deaths, is at least 4.5–4.7 million and counting. Of these, an estimated 408,000 civilians died directly from war violence." https://watson.brown .edu/costsofwar/costs/human/civilians.

Chapter 5. Us, Them, and the Spoils of War

1. In *The One Percent Doctrine*, Ron Suskind documents how this doctrine undermined fact-based intelligence gathering.

2. See Noah. Poundstone has also been seen as an allusion to Paul Bremer, who headed the Coalition Provisional Authority (CPA) in 2003.

3. Dayne bears a strong resemblance to Judith Miller, the *New York Times* reporter who published false information regarding WMDs and refused to reveal her sources.

4. There is no accurate tally of Iraqi civilians who met violent deaths between 2003 and 2020. Numerous sources (Iraq war logs, Iraqi Health Ministry, the Associated Press, Iraq Body Count Project, Iraq Family Health Survey, Opinion Research Business poll, Lancet studies, PLOS Medicine Study, Costs of War Project) calculate using different data, spanning different periods of time, using different criteria (e.g., deaths from direct violence, deaths attributable to destroyed infrastructure or limited treatment facilities, etc.). It seems safe to assume that the US invasion resulted in a minimum loss of 100,000 and a maximum loss of 600,000 Iraqi lives.

5. Stuart Murray convincingly marks Freddy's confrontation of Miller at this moment, coupled with the revelation of his prosthetic leg, as the crucial moment when Miller "turns from a cog in the military machine to an idealist searcher for the truth in confronting his superiors with the details of their cover up" (446), but Freddy is clearly addressing Miller as a representative of the United States and an avatar of its "mission" in Iraq. In this context, we can see Greengrass as illustrating that to the extent Freddy causes Miller to reassess that mission, he also isolates Miller from US objectives.

6. Anon., American Attitudes toward the Iraq War, 2006.

7. Anon., Public Attitudes toward the War in Iraq, 2003–2008.

8. Scott, "Rage, Fear and Revulsion." John Trafton also explores the variety of media representations.

9. The quote is from supplemental material on the *Us* DVD.

10. Supplemental material on *Us* DVD.

11. Bush 9/11 address to joint session of Congress.

12. Supplemental material on *Us* DVD.

13. Supplemental material on *Us* DVD.

14. Supplemental material on *Us* DVD.

Chapter 6. Collateral Jobs and Collateral Damage

1. Burgoyne refers to them as hunters (47–48).

2. See Bordwell, Staiger, and Thompson.

3. From a slightly different perspective, Stahl discusses this topic at length in chapter 4 of *Through the Crosshairs*, "Drone Vision," 67–93.

4. I don't mean that they would be unemployed, but rather that they would be assigned to a different job.

5. See also Scott ("A Sniper Does His Deeds"); Lutrick; Buchanan; Soberon; Friedman, "God/Country/Family."

6. The concept of the hermeneutic circle originates from the circular reasoning entailed in the fact that finding a secret/sacred message in a text proves that one existed, but that proof requires first assuming the presence of such a message, that is, assuming the validity of the premise one is trying to validate.

7. The "stop-loss" exception also allows for the military to unilaterally extend a soldier's term of service after his tour of duty has expired.

8. "It is a dark time for the Rebellion. Although the Death Star has been destroyed, Imperial troops have driven the Rebel forces from their hidden base and pursued them across the galaxy."

9. See Shannon.

Chapter 7. The Only Mission Is to Get Out

1. Coined by Rudyard Kipling in his poem "The White Man's Burden." See Rudyard Kipling Society, https://www.kiplingsociety.co.uk/poem/poems_burden.htm.

2. See the introduction to *The 9/11 Report*.

FILMOGRAPHY

Films Discussed

13 Hours. Dir. Michael Bay, 2016.

American Sniper. Dir. Clint Eastwood, 2014.

Billy Lynn's Long Halftime Walk. Dir. Ang Lee, 2016.

Captain Phillips. Dir. Paul Greengrass, 2013.

Deepwater Horizon. Dir. Peter Berg, 2016.

Dunkirk. Dir. Christopher Nolan, 2017.

Eye in the Sky. Dir. Gavin Hood, 2015.

Get Out. Dir. Jordan Peele, 2017.

Green Zone. Dir. Paul Greengrass, 2010.

Hacksaw Ridge. Dir. Mel Gibson, 2016.

The Hurt Locker. Dir. Kathryn Bigelow, 2008.

Jarhead. Dir. Sam Mendes, 2005.

LOST: The Complete First Season. Creators: J. J. Abrams, Jeffrey Lieber, Damon Lindelof, Buena Vista Home Entertainment, 2004.

Meet Me in St. Louis. Dir. Vincente Minnelli, 1944.

Mrs. Miniver. Dir. William Wyler, 1942.

Redacted. Dir. Brian De Palma, 2007.

Saving Private Ryan. Dir. Steven Spielberg, 1998.

Since You Went Away. Dir. John Cromwell, 1944.

Sully. Dir. Clint Eastwood, 2016.

Tender Comrade. Dir. Edward Dmytryk, 1943.

Us. Dir. Jordan Peele, 2019.

Films Mentioned

Air Force. Dir. Howard Hawks, 1943.

Airport. Dir. George Seaton, Henry Hathaway, 1970.

Airport 1975. Dir. Jack Smight, 1974.

Airport '77. Dir. Jerry Jameson, 1977.

All the President's Men. Dir. Alan J. Pakula, 1976.

Apocalypse Now. Dir. Francis Ford Coppola, 1979.

Bataan. Dir. Tay Garnett, 1942.

The Bourne Identity. Dir. Doug Liman, 2002.

The Bourne Supremacy. Dir. Paul Greengrass, 2004.

The Bourne Ultimatum. Dir. Paul Greengrass, 2007.

Coming Home. Dir. Hal Ashby, 1978.

The Concorde . . . Airport '79. Dir. David Lowell Rich, 1979.

Dark Waters. Dir. Todd Haynes, 2019.

The Deer Hunter. Dir. Michael Cimino, 1978.

Destination Tokyo. Dir. Delmer Daves, 1943.

The Empire Strikes Back. Dir. Irvin Kershner, 1980.
The Exorcist. Dir. William Friedkin, 1973.
Field of Dreams. Dir. Phil Alden Robinson, 1989.
A Fistful of Dollars. Dir. Sergio Leone, 1964.
Full Metal Jacket. Dir. Stanley Kubrick, 1987.
The Green Berets. Dir. Ray Kellogg, John Wayne, 1968.
Guadalcanal Diary. Dir. Lewis Seiler, 1943.
Guess Who's Coming to Dinner. Dir. Stanley Kramer, 1967.
Homeland. Creators: Alex Gansa, Howard Gordon, 2011–2020.
The Insider. Dir. Michael Mann, 1999.
Lawrence of Arabia. Dir. David Lean, 1962.
Mr. Smith Goes to Washington. Dir. Frank Capra, 1939.
Night of the Living Dead. Dir. George Romero, 1968.
Platoon. Dir. Oliver Stone, 1986.
The Poseidon Adventure. Dir. Ronald Neame, 1972.
Sahara. Dir. Zoltán Korda, 1943.
Sands of Iwo Jima. Dir. Allan Dwan, 1949.
Sergeant York. Dir. Howard Hawks, 1941.
The Silence of the Lambs. Dir. Jonathan Demme, 1991.
Spotlight. Dir. Tom McCarthy, 2015.
Star Wars. Dir. George Lucas, 1977.
The Towering Inferno. Dir. John Guillermin, 1974.
The Wizard of Oz. Dir. Victor Fleming, 1939.

WORKS CITED

Anon. *The 9/11 Report: The National Commission on Terrorist Attacks upon the United States, with reporting and analysis by the* New York Times. St. Martin's Paperbacks, 2004.

Anon. American Attitudes toward the Iraq War, 2006. Pew Research Center. https:// www.google.com/search?q=American+attitudes+to+the+Iraw+War+in+2006&rlz =1C5CHFA_enUS942US943&oq=American+attitudes+to+the+Iraw+War+in +2006&gs_lcrp=EgZjaHJvbWUyBggAEEUYOTIKCAEQABiiBBiJBTIKCAI- QABiiBBiJBTIKCAMQABiABBiiBNIBCTE2NTgxajBqN6gCALACAA&- sourceid=chrome&ie=UTF-8.

Anon. "Bush & Cheney Meet 9/11 Panel." CBS News, April 29, 2004. https://www .cbsnews.com/news/bush-cheney-meet-9-11-panel/.

Anon. "Bush's Iraq WMD Joke Backfires." BBC News, March 26, 2004. http://news .bbc.co.uk/2/hi/americas/3570845.stm.

Anon. "Bush Takes Heat for WMD Jokes." CNN, March 27, 2004. https://www .militaryforums.co.uk/forums/viewtopic.php?t=7272.

Anon. "The Enlistment/Reenlistment Contract." 2020, Section 9b. https://www.esd .whs.mil/portals/54/documents/dd/forms/dd/dd0004.pdf.

Anon. Fourth Geneva Convention. https://ihl-databases.icrc.org/en/ihl-treaties/gciv -1949.

Anon. Johnson phone recording, 1964. callhttps://www.cnn.com/2022/02/16/politics /lyndon-b-johnson-secret-audio-origseriesfilms/index.html.

Anon. "Military Pay Chart 2004." https://www.navycs.com/charts/2004-military-pay- chart.html.

Anon. Public Attitudes toward the War in Iraq: 2003–2008. https://www.pewresearch .org/2008/03/19/public-attitudes-toward-the-war-in-iraq-20032008/.

Anon. Tonkin Gulf Resolution (1964). https://www.archives.gov/milestone-documents /tonkin-gulf-resolution.

Anderson, Benedict. *Imagined Communities: Reflections on the Origins and Spread of Nationalism.* Rev. ed. Verso, 1983.

Andrejevic, Mark. *Reality TV: The Work of Being Watched.* Rowman & Littlefield, 2003.

Aristotle. *Poetics.* Translated by Malcolm Heath. Penguin Classics, 1997.

Auster, Albert. "*Saving Private Ryan* and American Triumphalism." In *The War Film,* edited by Robert Eberwein. Rutgers University Press, 2006.

Bailey, Beth. *America's Army: Making the All-Volunteer Force.* Belknap-Harvard, 2009.

Baker, Martin. *A Toxic Genre: The Iraq War Films.* Pluto, 2011.

Baker, Peter. "Democracy in Iraq Not a Priority in US Budget." *Washington Post,* April 4, 2006. https://www.washingtonpost.com/archive/politics/2006/04/05/democracy -in-iraq-not-a-priority-in-us-budget/ad87ebfb-03a9–4fdf-9ddc-2c12a2e060be/.

Barthes, Roland. *Mythologies.* Translated by Richard Howard and Annette Lavers. Hill & Wang, 1957 and 2012.

Basinger, Jeanine. *The World War II Combat Film: Anatomy of a Genre*. Wesleyan University Press, 2003.

Bersani, Leo, and Ulysse Dutoit. *The Forms of Violence: Narrative in Assyrian Art and Modern Culture*. Schocken, 1985.

Biguenet, John. "The Profound Contradiction of *Saving Private Ryan*." *Atlantic*, June 5, 2014. https://www.theatlantic.com/entertainment/archive/2014/06/the-false -patriotism-of-saving-private-ryan/371539/.

Binns, Daniel. *The Hollywood War Film: Critical Observations from World War I to Iraq*. Intellect, 2017.

Bodnar, John. "AHR Forum: *Saving Private Ryan* and Postwar Memory in America." *American Historical Review* 106.3 (June 2001): 805–817.

Bordwell, David, Janet Staiger, and Kristin Thompson. *The Classical Hollywood Cinema: Film Style and Mode of Production to 1960*. Columbia University Press, 1985.

Boysha, Judy. White House spokesperson. https://www.youtube.com/watch?v=vH -r3OdMVR4.

Bremer, Paul. *My Year in Iraq*. Threshold, 2006.

Bronfen, Elisabeth. *Specters of War: Hollywood's Engagement with Military Conflict*. Rutgers University Press, 2012.

Buchanan, David. "Another Fistful: The American Sniper Franchise and Clint Eastwood's Post-9/11 American War Film as Neo-Western." In *The Films of Clint Eastwood: Critical Perspectives*, edited by Matt Wanat and Leonard Engel, 169–186. University of New Mexico Press, 2018.

Burgoyne, Robert. *The New American War Film*. University of Minnesota Press, 2023.

Burnetts, Charles. "Of Basterds and the Greatest Generation: The Limits of Sentimentalism and the Post-Classical War Film." *Journal of Film and Video* 68.2 (Summer 2016): 3–13.

Bush, George. "Address to Joint Session of Congress." CNN, September 21, 2001.

Bush, George. "Bush on Airline Safety Measures." *Washington Post*, September 27, 2001.

Bush, George. "President Bush on Homeland Security." *Washington Post*, November 8, 2001.

Chandrasekaran, Rajiv. *Imperial Life in the Emerald City: Inside Iraq's Green Zone*. Vintage Books, 2007.

Chandrasekaran, Rajiv. "Ties to GOP Trumped Know-How among Staff Sent to Rebuild Iraq. *Washington Post*, September 17, 2006.

Churchwell, Sarah. *Behold, America: The Entangled History of "America First" and "The American Dream."* Basic Books, 2018.

Corley, Matt. "As Bush's VP Vetter in 2000, Cheney 'Sidestepped the Scrutiny He Imposed on Others.'" *ThinkProgress*, September 18, 2008. https://archive .thinkprogress.org/as-bushs-vp-vetter-in-2000-cheney-sidestepped-the-scrutiny -he-imposed-on-others-4e6dc4fe1965/.

de Certeau, Michel. *The Practice of Everyday Life*. Translated by Steven Rendall. University of California Press, 1988.

Denny, David. "On the Politics of Enjoyment: A Reading of *The Hurt Locker*." *Theory and Event* 14.1 (2011).

Doherty, Thomas. *Hollywood and Hitler, 1933–1939*. Columbia University Press, 2013.

Doherty, Thomas. *Projections of War: Hollywood, American Culture, and World War II*. Columbia University Press, 1993.

Dudziak, Mary. *War-Time: An Idea, Its History, Its Consequences*. Oxford University Press, 2012.

Eiji, Takemae. *The Allied Occupation of Japan*. Continuum International Publications Group, 2003.

Fallows, James. *Blind into Baghdad: America's War in Iraq*. Vintage, 2006.

Feeny, Mark. *Nixon at the Movies: A Book about Belief*. University of Chicago Press, 2004.

Feldmann, Linda. "Dick Cheney: No Change of Role Visible." *Christian Science Monitor*, November 3, 2005, 1.

Frazer, J. T., ed. *The Voices of Time: A Cooperative Survey of Man's Views of Time as Expressed by the Sciences and the Humanities*. George Braziller, 1966.

Freud, Sigmund. "Fetishism." In *The Complete Psychological Works of Sigmund Freud*, translated by James Strachey, vol. 21, 152–157. Hogarth, 1953.

Friedman, Lester. "'God/Country/Family': The Military Movies." In *Tough Ain't Enough: New Perspectives on the Films of Clint Eastwood*, edited by Lester D. Friedman and David Desser. Rutgers University Press, 2018.

Friedman, Milton, and Rose Friedman. *Free to Choose: A Personal Statement*. Harcourt, 1990.

Furlough, Ellen. "Packaging Pleasures: Club Méditerranée and French Consumer Culture, 1950–1968." *French Historical Studies* 18.1 (1993): 65–81.

Gabler, Neal. *Life: The Movie: How Entertainment Conquered Reality*. Knopf, 2000.

Gaddis, John Lewis. *Strategies of Containment: A Critical Appraisal of American National Security Policy during the Cold War*. Oxford University Press, 2005.

Garcia, Michelle. "It's All Our Fault! The Ten Disasters the Gays Supposedly Caused." *Advocate*, October 31, 2012. https://www.advocate.com/politics/2012/10/31/10 -disasters-gays-were-blamed-causing.

Gleiberman, Owen. "Saving Private Ryan" (review). *Entertainment Weekly*, July 24, 1998.

Goldstein, Joel K. "The Contemporary Presidency: Cheney, Vice Presidential Power, and the War on Terror." *Presidential Studies Quarterly* 40.1 (2010): 102–139.

Gramsci, Antonio. *Selections from the Prison Notebooks of Antonio Gramsci*. Edited and translated by Quintin Hoare and Geoffrey Nowell Smith. International Publishers, 1971.

Hart, Bradley W. *Hitler's American Friends: The Third Reich's Supporters in the United States*. St. Martin's, 2018.

Hawkins, Stephen. *A Brief History of Time*. Random House, 1998.

Hedges, Chris. *War Is a Force that Gives Us Meaning*. Public Affairs, 2002.

Heller, Joseph. *Catch-22: A Critical Edition*. Edited by Robert M. Scotto. Dell, 1973.

Hoberman, J. "Mission Fatally Accomplished" (review of *Green Zone*). *Village Voice*, March 10–16, 2010, 43.

Holden, Stephen. "Drone Precision vs. Human Failings." *New York Times*, March 11, 2016, C1.

Hoopes, James. *Hail to the CEO: The Failure of George W. Bush and the Cult of Moral Leadership*. Praeger, 2008.

Horsman, Reginald. *Race and Manifest Destiny: The Origins of American Racial Anglo-Saxonism*. Harvard University Press, 1981.

Jackson, Richard. *Writing the War on Terrorism: Language, Politics, and Counter-Terrorism*. Manchester University Press, 2005.

Jeffords, Susan. *The Remasculinization of America: Gender and the Vietnam War.* Indiana University Press, 1989.

Kaye, Sharon, ed. *The Ultimate* Lost *and Philosophy: Think Together, Die Alone.* Wiley, 2010.

Kellner, Douglas. *Cinema Wars: Hollywood Film and Politics in the Bush-Cheney Era.* Wiley-Blackwell, 2010.

Kennan, George. "Sources of Soviet Conduct." *Foreign Affairs* 25 (1947): 566–582.

Kern, Stephen. *The Culture of Time and Space, 1880–1918.* 2nd ed. Harvard University Press, 2003.

King, John, and Sean Loughlin. "Bush, Cheney Meet with 9/11 Panel." CNN, April 30, 2004. https://www.cnn.com/2004/ALLPOLITICS/04/29/bush.911.commission/.

Kipling, Rudyard. "The White Man's Burden." Kipling Society. https://www.kiplingsociety.co.uk/poem/poems_burden.htm.

Klein, Naomi. "Baghdad Year Zero: Pillaging Iraq in Pursuit of a Neo-Con Utopia." *Harper's,* September 2004.

Kodat, Catherine. "Saving Private Property: Steven Spielberg's American Dream Works." *Representations* 71 (Summer 2000): 77–105.

Koppes, Clayton R., and Gregory D. Black. *Hollywood Goes to War: How Politics, Profits, and Propaganda Shaped World War II Movies.* University of California Press, 1990.

Landon, Phil. "Realism, Genre, and 'Saving Private Ryan.'" *Film and History* 28.3 (January 1, 1998): 58–62.

LaRocca, David, ed. *The Philosophy of War Films.* University Press of Kentucky, 2014.

Lostpedia: The Lost Encyclopedia. https://lostpedia.fandom.com/wiki/Main_Page.

Lutrick, Landon. "The Legend: Situating American Sniper in Clint Eastwood's Canon." In *The Films of Clint Eastwood: Critical Perspectives,* edited by Matt Wanat and Leonard Engel, 187–198. University of New Mexico Press, 2018.

Lyotard, Jean-Francois. *The Differend: Phrases in Dispute.* University of Minnesota Press, 1989.

Maddow, Rachel. *Prequel: An American Fight against Fascism.* Crown, 2023.

Mann, James. "The World Dick Cheney Built." *Atlantic,* January 2, 2020. https://www.theatlantic.com/ideas/archive/2020/01/dick-cheney-charted-americas-future-september-11/603313/.

Marx, Karl. *Capital: A Critique of Political Economy, Volume I.* Cosimo, 2007.

Maslin, Janet. "Panoramic and Personal Visions of War's Anguish" (review). *New York Times,* July 24, 1998.

Monnet, Agnieszka Soltysik. "American War Adventure and the Generic Pleasures of Military Violence: Clint Eastwood's *American Sniper.*" *Journal of Popular Culture* 51.6 (2018): 1376–1397.

Moore, James, and Wayne Slater. *Bush's Brain: How Karl Rove Made George W. Bush Presidential.* John Wiley & Son, 2004.

Motion Picture Production Code. https://historymatters.gmu.edu/d/5099/.

Murray, Stuart. "Disability and Memory in Posthuman(ist) Narrative: Reading Prosthesis and Amnesia in Hollywood's Re-membering of the 'War on Terror.'" *Parallax* 23.4 (2017): 439–452.

Nadel, Alan. *Flatlining on the Field of Dreams: Cultural Narratives in the Films of President Reagan's America.* Rutgers University Press, 1997.

Nadel, Alan. "From the Industrial Unconscious to the Cinematic to the Televisual to the Networked." *Arizona Quarterly* 75.2 (Summer 2019): 23–36.

Nadel, Alan. "Mapping the Other: *The English Patient*, Colonial Rhetoric, and Cinematic Representation." In *The Terministic Screen: Rhetorical Perspectives on Film*, edited by David Blakesley, 21–36. Southern Illinois University Press, 2004.

Nadel, Alan. "Second Nature, Cinematic Narrative, the Historical Subject, and *Russian Ark*." In *A Companion to Narrative Theory*, edited by James Phelan and Peter Rabinowitz, 427–440. Blackwell Publishing, 2005.

Nadel, Alan. *Television in Black-and-White America: Race and National Identity*. University Press of Kansas, 2006.

Noah, Timothy. "Doug Feith Flim Flam Man." *Slate*, March 9, 2007. https://slate.com/news-and-politics/2007/03/doug-feith-flimflam-man.html.

O'Brien, Keith, and Bryan Bender. "Chronology of Errors: How a Disaster Spread." *Boston Globe*, September 11, 2005, A1.

Packer, George. *Assassin's Gate: America in Iraq*. Farrar, 2005.

Page, Clarence. "Nation Ill-Served by Dick Cheney's Secret-Keeping." *The Sun*, February 17, 2006, 15A.

Pellegrini, Frank. "The Bush Speech: How to Rally a Nation." *Time*, September 21, 2001.

Poniewozik, James. "Lyst: Cuse and Lindelof on Lost and Videogames." *Time*, March 19, 2007.

Provencher, Ken. "*Redacted*'s Double Vision." *Film Quarterly* 62.1 (Fall 2008): 32–38.

Rasor, Dina, and Robert Bauman. *Betraying Our Troops: The Destructive Results of Privatizing War*. Palgrave MacMillan, 2007.

Redfield, Marc. *The Rhetoric of Terror: Reflections on 9/11 and the War on Terror*. Fordham University Press, 2009.

Ricks, Thomas. *Fiasco: The American Military Adventure in Iraq, 2003 to 2005*. Penguin, 2006.

Rodgers, Richard, and Oscar Hammerstein II. "Bali Ha'i." *South Pacific*, 1949.

Rogin, Michael. *Ronald Reagan, the Movie, and Other Episodes in Political Demonology*. University of California Press, 1987.

Ross, Steven. *Hitler in Los Angeles: How Jews Foiled Nazi Plots against Hollywood and America*. Bloomsbury, 2017.

Rothschild, Matthew. "A Tribute to Molly Ivins." *Texas Observer*, October 25, 2012. https://www.texasobserver.org/2438-a-tribute-to-molly-ivins/.

Rumsfeld, Donald. *Known and Unknown: A Memoir*. Penguin, 2011.

Scahill, Jeremy. "Blackwater Founder Implicated in Murder." *The Nation*, August 4, 2009.

Scott, A. O. "Rage, Fear and Revulsion: At War with the War" (review of *Redacted*). *New York Times*, November 16, 2007, E1.

Scott, A. O. "A Search for That Casualty, Truth" (review of *Green Zone*). *New York Times*, March 12, 2010, C1.

Scott, A. O. "A Sniper Does His Deeds, but the Battle Never Ends." *New York Times*, December 25, 2014, C12.

Seidman, Joel. "Armitage Added to CIA Leak Civil Suit." NBC News, September 12, 2006. https://www.nbcnews.com/id/wbna14805910.

Shannon, Gary. "Michael Bay's '13 Hours': Truth or Fiction?" *Young Folks*, January 31, 2018. https://www.theyoungfolks.com/film/71944/michael-bay-13-hours-truth-or-fiction/.

Sklar, Robert. "*The Hurt Locker* by Kathryn Bigelow, Mark Boal, Nicolas Chartier, Greg Shapiro" (review). *Cinéaste* 35.1 (Winter 2009): 55–56.

Smith, R. Jeffrey. "Hussein's Prewar Ties to Al-Qaeda Discounted." *Washington Post*, April 6, 2007. http://www.washingtonpost.com/wp-dyn/content/article/2007/04/05/AR2007040502263.html.

Soberon, Lennart. "'The Old Wild West in the New Middle East': *American Sniper* (2014) and the Global Frontiers of the Western Genre." *European Journal of American Studies* 12.2 (2017): 1–18.

Stahl, Roger. *Through the Crosshairs: War, Visual Culture, and the Weaponized Gaze*. Rutgers University Press, 2018.

Steeby, Elizabeth. "The Cult of the American Sniper in the Age of the Imperial Security State." *Interventions* 21.6 (2019): 803–820.

Suskind, Ron. *The One Percent Doctrine: Deep Inside America's Pursuit of Its Enemies Since 9/11*. Simon & Schuster, 2006.

Taubin, Amy. "War Torn." *Village Voice*, July 28, 1998.

Taylor, Christian. "Al-Qaeda Is Stronger Today than It Was on 9/11." *The World*, July 2, 2019.

Trafton, John. "The 'Anti-War Film' and the 'Anti-War-Film': A Reading of Brian De Palma's *Redacted* (2007) and *Casualties of War* (1989)." *Journal of War and Culture Studies* 4.1 (2011): 113–126.

Travers, Peter. "'Saving Private Ryan': Spielberg Goes to War." *Rolling Stone*, August 6, 1998.

Turan, Kenneth. "Even Matt Damon Can't Find WMD's: *Green Zone* Is a Thriller that Deals Candidly with the Invasion of Iraq." *Los Angeles Times*, March 12, 2010, D1.

Turan, Kenneth. "Soldiers of Misfortune: 'Saving Private Ryan' Is a Raw and Powerful Work from Steven Spielberg that Overcomes a Conventional Script." *Los Angeles Times*, July 24, 1998.

Virilio, Paul. *War and Cinema: The Logistics of Perception*. Translated by Patrick Camiller. Verso, 1989.

White, Hayden. *The Content of Form: Narrative Discourse and Historical Representation*. Johns Hopkins University Press, 1987.

White, Hayden. *Metahistory: The Historical Imagination in Nineteenth-Century Europe*. Johns Hopkins University Press, 1973.

White, Hayden. *The Tropics of Discourse: Essays in Cultural Criticism*. Johns Hopkins University Press, 1978.

Williams, Linda. *Hard Core: Power, Pleasure, and Frenzy of the Visible*. University of California Press, 1989.

York, Byron. "Scooter Who? In Closing Arguments, Fitzgerald Points the Finger at Dick Cheney." *National Review*, February 21, 2007. https://www.nationalreview.com/2007/02/scooter-who-closing-arguments-fitzgerald-points-finger-dick-cheney-byron-york/.

INDEX

Note: Page numbers in italics indicate an illustration. Page numbers followed by n refer to endnotes that add information to the text. The numbers following n indicate the numbers of the notes.